THE NEW RANK AND FILE

Rank and File: Personal Histories by Working-Class Organizers

Living Inside Our Hope: A Steadfast Radical's Thoughts on Rebuilding the Movement

Homeland: Oral Histories of Palestine and Palestinians, with Sam Bahour

Nonviolence in America: A Documentary History

" 'We Are All We've Got': Building a Retiree Movement in Youngstown, Ohio," in *Law Stories*, ed. Gary Bellow and Martha Minow

THE NEW RANK AND FILE

EDITED BY

Staughton Lynd

and

Alice Lynd

ILR Press

an imprint of

Cornell University Press

Ithaca and London

Copyright © 2000 by Cornell University

All rights reserved. Except for brief quotations in a review, this book, or parts thereof, must not be reproduced in any form without permission in writing from the publisher. For information, address Cornell University Press, Sage House, 512 East State Street, Ithaca, New York 14850.

First published 2000 by Cornell University Press
First printing, Cornell Paperbacks, 2000

Printed in the United States of America

LIBRARY OF CONGRESS CATALOGING-IN-PUBLICATION DATA
The new rank and file / edited by Staughton Lynd and Alice Lynd.
      p. cm.
    ISBN 0-8014-3806-3 (cloth : alk. paper) — ISBN 0-8014-8676-9 (pbk. : alk. paper)
    1. Labor unions—Organizing—United States—History.   2. Working class—United States—History.   I. Lynd, Staughton.   II. Lynd, Alice.
    HD6490.O72 U654 2000
    331.88'0973—dc21   00-009146

Cornell University Press strives to use environmentally responsible suppliers and materials to the fullest extent possible in the publishing of its books. Such materials include vegetable-based, low-VOC inks and acid-free papers that are recycled, chlorine-free, or partly composed of nonwood fibers. Books that bear the logo of the FSC (Forest Stewardship Council) use paper taken from forests that have been inspected and certified as meeting the highest standards for environmental and social responsibility. For further information, visit our website at www.cornellpress.cornell.edu.

Cloth printing   10 9 8 7 6 5 4 3 2 1

Paperback printing   10 9 8 7 6 5 4 3 2 1

**Dedicated to the memory of
Edward S. Mann (1928–1992)**

When the Union's inspiration
Through the worker's blood shall run,
There can be no power greater
Anywhere beneath the sun;
Yet what force on earth is weaker
Than the feeble strength of one?
But the Union makes us strong

Chorus:
Solidarity forever, solidarity forever,
Solidarity forever, for the Union makes us strong

In our hands is placed a power
Greater than their hoarded gold;
Greater than the might of armies,
Magnified a thousand-fold.
We can bring to birth a new world
From the ashes of the old,
For the Union makes us strong

Chorus

CONTENTS

ACKNOWLEDGMENTS

Cal Winslow and Steve Early suggested that we do a sequel to the first *Rank and File*. We thank them and hasten to add that they are in no way responsible for how we did it!

The contributors to these two dozen accounts—between thirty and forty persons, because several of the narratives are group interviews—deserve special thanks. There was always some inconvenience involved for the persons being interviewed. Moreover, without exception they proceeded in trust that the other contributors whom we interviewed would be folks with whom they would be happy to be associated and that our Introduction would not cause them to be ostracized, defunded, or fired.

The translators of the interviews outside the United States were, if anything, more heroic. Martha Lynd translated her friend Manuela's interview into English, then translated the English written account back into Spanish so that Manuela could review it. Our conversation with the Hebron trade unionists took place as we pursued with Sam Bahour a book of oral histories of Palestinians that the three of us subsequently edited. Father Joe Mulligan, S. J., did not translate our original interviews with Mauricio Vallejos and Virginia Roman, but managed to find them in Managua, Nicaragua, more than ten years later so that they could read and approve what we proposed to publish. Claudia Fabiola Cabrera Vasquez translated the FAT interview in the back seat of a moving bus. We thank all who were involved in these interviews with rank-and-file workers abroad, perhaps the most distinctive aspect of the present book.

Others should be mentioned because they helped to identify or find a contributor. Dick Flacks knew how to locate Marshall Ganz. Stan Weir put us in touch with Andrea Carney. Pam Chude Allen, a friend from our days in the South in the early 1960s, directed us to the Coalition of University Employees (CUE). Jeannette Gabriel introduced us to the Chinese Staff and Workers' Association. We thank them all.

Jim Jordan works for a company that manufactures metal barrels in Masury, Ohio. He is a poet and a fellow member of the editorial board of *Impact: The Rank & File Newsletter*, P.O. Box 2125, Youngstown, Ohio 44504, where a few of these accounts previously appeared. When our prospective publisher asked us to cut the manuscript as originally submitted by a third, we asked Jim to help us decide what to delete. Instead, he returned the manuscript with passages marked, "Leave this in!" His comments were enormously helpful and we are very grateful.

We want to thank Frances Goldin, friend, sometime tenant organizer, and latter–day literary agent, whose diligence led us to Cornell University Press when we were seeking a publisher for Staughton's essays. We are delighted to publish *The New Rank and File* with Cornell University Press, as well. We appreciate the way in which the Press, and editor in chief, Fran Benson, stood by us and gave us the opportunity to make the manuscript we originally submitted into a better book. Above all, we appreciate the willingness of the Press, which handles more work about unions than any other publisher in the United States, to extend its hospitality to a work in which many criticisms of mainstream unionism are expressed. By so doing, the Press recognizes the contributors to *The New Rank and File* (ourselves included) as legitimate participants in the great and exciting dialogue currently underway as to the future of the labor movement.

S. L. and A. L.

Niles, Ohio
Thanksgiving 1999

THE NEW RANK AND FILE

INTRODUCTION

The New Rank and File is a sequel to our *Rank and File: Personal Histories by Working-Class Organizers,* a book which was first published in 1973.[1] This new collection of personal histories concerns labor organizing in the 1970s, 1980s, and 1990s. The book is directed especially to two groups of readers: rank-and-file workers, and young people who are seeking long-term service in the labor movement.

Those who tell their stories in this book are for the most part workers on the job. A few were or are full-time union officers. A smaller number were or are full-time organizers for unions. What they all share is a tradition of working-class self-organization. They are men and women who, rather than waiting for someone else to solve their problems for them, took whatever individual or collective action they considered necessary. Their activity was directed primarily against intolerable employers, but on occasion they opposed unresponsive unions as well.

The Union Movement and the Labor Movement

The purpose of labor unions is to help workers sell their labor power as advantageously as they can. Unions will always be needed for this purpose. But while unions are necessary, they are not sufficient.

---

1. *Rank and File: Personal Histories by Working-Class Organizers,* 1st ed. (Boston: Beacon Press, 1973); 2d ed. (Princeton, N.J.: Princeton University Press, 1981); 3d ed. (New York: Monthly Review Press, 1988). Since the third edition is still in print as of the publication of this book, page references to *Rank and File* are to the third edition.

In the early 1970s, the real wages of working people in the United States began to decline. The disastrous air traffic controllers' strike in 1981 signaled, on the one hand, the federal government's readiness to use scabs to break a strike, and, on the other hand, the unwillingness of even the most progressive unions to risk their treasuries in all-out support of other workers. Employers pushed "jointness," the "team concept," "quality circles," and other forms of labor-management cooperation, to co-opt workers and to weaken the union as an exclusive mechanism for problem-solving in the workplace. Collective bargaining agreements tended to become "living agreements," subject to perpetual modification by small groups of company and union negotiators. Even for companies not in financial difficulty, concession bargaining became the norm. Ten- and twelve-hour shifts became commonplace as management sought to operate expensive equipment continuously. So did two- and three-tier wage schemes, whereby the wages and benefits of senior employees were protected in exchange for evisceration of the compensation package for new hires.

During the last thirty years of the twentieth century, a number of reformers sought election to top union offices. They thereby brought about modest improvements in several labor organizations. But at century's end, the trade union movement had not yet reversed the decline of "union density" in the United States.[2] Successes in organizing, when they have occurred, have been largely in service occupations where the workplace cannot easily be closed and moved, such as the public sector, clerical work, food services, hospitals, home health care, trucking, and airline transportation.

Nor have union reformers been willing to challenge the fundamentals of capitalism, such as management's supposed right to shut down factories unilaterally. These leaders are committed to what labor historians call "business unionism": the goal of signing collective bargaining agreements complete with management prerogative and no-strike clauses; the dues checkoff as the means of funding union bureaucracies; the protection of jobs in one's own nation at whatever cost to workers in other countries; and the capitalist system as the desired context of all of the above. Therefore, the *labor movement* must find ways to be more visionary, more in-

2. Shortly after World War II, when union membership was at its height, 35.3 percent of working men and women belonged to unions. At the end of 1997, 14.1 percent of employed Americans belonged to unions, the lowest proportion since 1936. Andrew Hacker, "Who's Sticking to the Union?," *New York Review of Books,* Feb. 18, 1999. In 1998 union membership grew by 100,000 but "union density" (the percentage of workers in unions) declined from 14.1 percent to 13.9 percent. Union membership in the public sector climbed to 37.5 percent from 37.2 percent, while membership in the private sector declined to 9.5 percent from 9.7 percent, pulled down by the 126,000 drop in the number of unionized workers in manufacturing. *New York Times,* Jan. 26, 1999. During 1999, the percentage of union members in the work force held steady at 13.9 percent. *New York Times,* Jan. 20, 2000.

clusive, more democratic, and more willing to take risks than the *union movement* can be expected to be.

Union organizing today is typically top-down "blitz organizing." The objective of blitz organizing is to increase the number of workers who belong to unions and the amount of dues they pay. Far from consulting workers, devising strategy with them, or otherwise empowering those who are sought to be organized, the blitz organizer induces workers whom he or she hardly knows to vote for a union the worker has barely met. As vividly described in Gary Stevenson's account, typically the blitz organizer is recruited from a college campus and trained at some central think tank. He or she is likely to be "parachuted" into an unknown setting and to check out of the motel the day after the National Labor Relations Board (NLRB) election, win or lose.

The contributors to this book offer a different, more bottom-up model, in which worker and organizer relate as equals. When worker encounters organizer, as described by Margaret Keith and Jim Brophy, there are "two experts" in the room. The worker is an expert on his or her own experience, on the way the contract is actually applied, on the culture of his or her fellow workers and the values and objectives they seek to achieve. Instead of the organizer seeking to guide the behavior of the worker, both collaborate on an equal footing, to achieve common goals.

Organization of the Book

The accounts in *The New Rank and File* are presented in four parts with titles taken from the song "Solidarity Forever."

The first part, "The Union's Inspiration," contains stories of union organizing. *The New Rank and File* begins with Vicky Starr (known to readers of the first *Rank and File* and viewers of the movie *Union Maids* as Stella Nowicki, an organizer of meatpackers in the 1930s) who was one of the early organizers of office clericals. She and Hugo Hernandez describe the gains that can be won by determined direct action even before an NLRB election or a first contract.[3] Marshall Ganz and Gary Stevenson describe unions that sought recognition—in one case by necessity, in the other by choice—by strike action against the employer rather than through the NLRB.

"The Ashes of the Old," the second part of the book, is about capital

---

3. Compare John Sargent's description in the first *Rank and File* of the gains won by steelworkers at Little Steel between 1937 and the beginning of World War II. "Without a contract, without any agreement with the company, without any regulations concerning hours of work, conditions of work, or wages, a tremendous surge took place. . . . Without a contract we secured for ourselves agreements on working conditions and wages that we do not have today, and that were better by far than what we do have today in the mill." *Rank and File,* 3d ed., p. 99.

flight and disinvestment. The single biggest change in the environment of the labor movement in the last quarter of the twentieth century was the massive economic reorganization variously referred to as disinvestment or globalization. Managers of capital may now consider the entire planet when choosing a site for a new plant. Prisoners in China and children in Bangladesh make products for sale in North American shopping malls. The accounts in the second part of *The New Rank and File* chronicle the devastating impact of plant shutdowns, on rank-and-file efforts generally and, more specifically, on the struggle of minorities for equal treatment in the workplace. The narratives in this part also describe efforts to stop the flight of manufacturing capital, both when capital closes whole plants and departments (as in steel) and when management pursues a strategy of letting jobs erode through retirement and other forms of job attrition.

Part three of *The New Rank and File*, "Anywhere beneath the Sun," is drawn from workers outside the United States. The labor movement, if it is to stand up to multinational corporations, must find ways to practice solidarity across borders. This book includes narratives by organizers in Guatemala, Palestine, Nicaragua, Mexico, and Canada. We do not pretend to measure the relative worth of the struggles they recount against similar, possibly more significant, activity in South Africa, South Korea, Brazil, or elsewhere. Those who speak in these accounts are persons the editors encountered during foreign travels between 1985 and 1997. What we hope to encourage by sharing their stories is a recognition that for all working-class organizers, in all countries, there are certain common values: above all the demand for respect and human dignity.

Finally, part four, "In Our Hands Is Placed a Power," is a group of accounts by rank-and-file organizers who exemplify what has been termed "solidarity unionism." Solidarity unionism is the idea that in the absence of effective national organizations from which they can seek help, rank and filers turn to each other and create horizontal networks for mutual support.[4] The labor movement is in crisis. No one has all the answers as to how we can address the effects of globalization and new technology. Workers will need qualitatively different kinds of organization and qualitatively new forms of struggle. The final section of *The New Rank and File* offers a sampling of such possibilities.

Selection of Contributors and Other Questions of Method

The contributors to this book are not unique. We feel sure they would wish us to say that many others like themselves can be found in shops and offices across the United States and throughout the world.

4. See the examples of solidarity unionism collected in *"We Are All Leaders": The Alternative Unionism of the Early 1930s*, ed. Staughton Lynd (Urbana: University of Illinois Press, 1996).

We interviewed people whom we knew and were able to observe in action over a period of time, or who were recommended to us by persons we trust. Because we wanted to be sure that the individuals we interviewed actually did "walk their talk," a disproportionate number of the accounts come from the Youngstown area where we have lived since 1976. It was less important to us that every occupation, nationality, or part of the United States involved in the labor force should be represented in the book. We acknowledge gaps in this regard, especially in the South, and hope that others will step forward to fill them.

In compiling this new collection, we have tried not to duplicate stories already well-told elsewhere. For this reason we do not offer accounts of dramatic strikes in the 1980s at southwestern copper mines, or against the Hormel meatpacking corporation, the International Paper Company, and Pittston Coal. Nor do we draw from the innovative organizing by clerical workers at Yale or steel industry retirees in Youngstown. All these experiences are accessible in other books.[5]

In the first *Rank and File*, there were only three women among the twenty persons who told their stories, though it was these three women whose stories came to be told in the documentary movie *Union Maids*.[6] In *The New Rank and File* almost half the narrators are female, reflecting demographic changes in the labor force itself.

Many of the contributors come from working-class backgrounds. In some of those accounts, we have included the narrator's description of how he or she grew up and became radicalized. There are also among both older and younger contributors a number of "colonizers." These are individuals from middle-class backgrounds who decided that change had to come, or was most likely to come, from the working class. They deliberately sought employment in a union of farm workers (Ganz) or an industrial plant (Leary, Feldman, Glaberman) or a hospital (Eisenhower) in order to do political organizing. We believe that all participants in *The New Rank and File*—whether or not they initially sought out the workplace be-

5. See Jonathan D. Rosenblum, *Copper Crucible: How the Arizona Miners' Strike of 1983 Recast Labor-Management Relations in America*, 2d ed. (Ithaca: Cornell University Press, 1998), and Barbara Kingsolver, *Holding the Line: Women in the Great Arizona Mine Strike of 1983*, 2d ed. (Ithaca: Cornell University Press, 1996); Peter Rachleff, *Hard-Pressed in the Heartland: The Hormel Strike and the Future of the Labor Movement* (Boston: South End Press, 1993); Julius Getman, *The Betrayal of Local 14* (Ithaca: Cornell University Press, 1998); Jim Sessions and Fran Ansley, "Singing Across Dark Spaces: The Union/Community Takeover of the Pittston Coal Company's Moss 3 Coal Preparation Plant," in *Fighting Back in Appalachia: Traditions of Resistance and Change*, ed. Stephen Fisher (Philadelphia: Temple University Press, 1993), pp. 195–222; Toni Gilpin, Gary Isaac, Dan Letwin, and Jack McKivigan, *On Strike for Respect: The Yale Strike of 1984–1985* (Chicago: Charles H. Kerr, 1988); Alice and Staughton Lynd, " 'We Are All We've Got': Building a Retiree Movement in Youngstown, Ohio," in *Law Stories*, ed. Gary Bellow and Martha Minow (Ann Arbor: University of Michigan Press, 1996), pp. 77–99.

6. *Union Maids*, a 48-minute film, is available in video for rent or purchase from New Day Films, 22D Hollywood Avenue, Hohokus, NJ 07423.

cause of radical ideology—are persons who have been willing to learn from their experience and whose ideas changed over the years.

Belonging to a group, perhaps reading or studying, definitely talking and listening, taking collective action and then reflecting together on what happened, sustains many organizers. In several group accounts (such as CUE and Chinese Staff), but not only in the group accounts, we see workers reaching out to help others, and asking for help from a wider community than their own workplace.

We began most of the interviews by saying, "start at the beginning: where were you born, what did your parents do, how did you get to be the person you are?" In the edited transcripts, our questions were left out, and fragmentary sentences were combined into sentences that are readable and convey the meaning that we thought was intended. We asked each contributor to read and correct the transcript, to be sure it contained what he or she wanted to be there. Some of the contributors provided us with written materials created at or near the time of the events. We used these materials, the testimony of other eye witnesses to the same events and, when we were ourselves participants, our own experiences and documents we collected, to corroborate the oral accounts.

About the Editors

The reader may find it helpful to know something about the editors. While gathering the accounts for the first *Rank and File,* we met workers who needed legal assistance. Often the union was part of the problem, and the worker could not find a lawyer who knew labor law but was not already working for either management or organized labor. Later, as coordinators of a team of health professionals and local union activists who worked on occupational health and safety, we could not find lawyers who knew environmental law and industrial hygiene, or, if they did, would give the time needed to educate or represent rank-and-file workers. So we decided to go to law school ourselves, Staughton Lynd in the 1970s, Alice Lynd in the 1980s.

As a lawyer, Staughton represented individual discharged workers, many of whom were not protected by a collective bargaining contract or represented by a union. For a number of years he also devoted much time and energy to fighting plant closings and trying to develop worker/community ownership of abandoned steel mills.[7] When companies went bank-

---

7. Staughton Lynd, *The Fight Against Shutdowns: Youngstown's Steel Mill Closings* (San Pedro: Singlejack Books, 1982); "The Genesis of the Idea of a Community Right to Industrial Property in Youngstown and Pittsburgh, 1977–1987," in *Living Inside Our Hope: A Steadfast Radical's Thoughts on Rebuilding the Movement* (Ithaca: Cornell University Press, 1997), pp. 159–188.

rupt and reneged on their commitments to retirees, retirees sought legal assistance concerning their pensions and health insurance benefits. Alice made that one of her fields of concentration, along with employment discrimination.

As lawyers we jointly assisted a group of visiting nurses to form their own union, and successfully represented African American operating engineers who were not being fairly referred to work by union dispatchers. Together we helped to create the Workers Solidarity Club, an organization of retirees known as Solidarity USA, and Workers Against Toxic Chemical Hazards (WATCH).

We retired from employment as Legal Services attorneys in 1996. For three years, until the election of James Hoffa, Jr. as president of the International Brotherhood of Teamsters in 1998, Staughton served as Local Education Coordinator for Teamsters Local 377. Meantime Alice pursued a concern to assist prisoners in the prisons that Youngstown has substituted for steel mills as its economic base.

Moving Forward

In the Introduction to the first *Rank and File*, the editors said they would be pleased if that book could play the part of a friend in the life of its readers. We have the same hope for this, its successor.

One of the first readers of the manuscript that became *The New Rank and File* remarked that there seemed to be a great deal about the 1960s in it. If that is so, there are good reasons. Like the editors, many contributors to *The New Rank and File* took part in the Movement of the 1960s before devoting their lives to labor. In the civil rights, anti-war, and university reform movements, scattered individuals sought each other out, came to know one another across racial and class divides, talked about their underlying values, hashed out their various tactical and strategic differences, made decisions by consensus, and took personal risks together. They experienced no need for, and in fact resisted, top–down leadership.

Many such people became, as Kay Eisenhower says about herself, permanent rank and filers. The CUE organizers comment on those campuses in the University of California system where, before experiencing a typical top–down union bureaucracy, union members spent a few years building from the bottom up a union with no exclusive bargaining status, no dues checkoff, and no full-time staff. They drew on that experience later in rebelling against staff-driven unionism. In the same way, many folks who experienced participatory democracy in the movements of the 1960s have not been willing to accept the guided democracy of most mainstream unions. A society characterized by participatory democracy, they believe, cannot be built by organizations that are centralized and hierarchical. There is scholarly support for this perspective.[8]

Some readers will be lucky enough to have found work in labor unions—typically, we suspect, in local unions—by means of which they can express the long-term values of the labor movement, and take steps toward what the late Ed Mann called a "better way." We wish them well in that activity.

Our book is also intended for readers not so fortunate. Many workers in the Youngstown, Ohio, area might be termed broken-hearted lovers. They are persons who poured their lives into building unions, only to see those unions fail to fight for them when the mills closed and the companies tried to chisel on paying retiree benefits. We want to reach out to such folks and say, "Don't give up. Don't become cynical. There may be new things you can try, either within or outside traditional unions."

The accounts in this book describe efforts to take hold of global problems at a local level. The tactics and viewpoints described will not be acceptable to everyone. They are here to stimulate the imagination, to suggest that alternatives are possible, so that, rather than waiting for external forces to mold the future, those most affected by corporate decision-making can seize the initiative themselves.

None of us can make the journey alone to the new world where we all wish to arrive. We need one another's help to keep going. In the words of Manuela Aju Tamriz, we must be stubborn to keep moving forward ("necio para seguir adelante").

8. Nelson Lichtenstein writes that the tens of thousands of new organizers needed by the union movement "cannot be recruited in the absence of a democratic, participatory union culture.... [Without that] democratization, the union movement will remain a shell." "Workers' Rights are Civil Rights," *Working USA* (Mar./Apr. 1999), p. 65. Howard Zinn asks us to imagine a future society in which "decisions would be made by small groups of people in their workplaces, their neighborhoods—a . . . 'neighborly socialism.' " *A People's History of the United States, 1492–Present* (New York: HarperCollins, 1999), p. 653.

I
THE UNION'S
INSPIRATION

Vicky Starr and granddaughter Robin

Hugo Hernandez

Vicky Starr

"Thank you, thank you, thank you"

Using the fictitious name "Stella Nowicki," Vicky Starr told of her years as an orga-
nizer of packinghouse workers in the book Rank and File *and the movie* Union
Maids. *Here she describes a second career as a rank-and-file organizer, this time of*
clerical workers at the University of Chicago. The National Labor Relations Board
(NLRB) election of November 1978 in which over 1800 clerical employees chose to
be represented by Teamsters Local 743 "was the largest . . . involving white-collar
workers in the academic field" as of that time (Chicago Tribune, *Nov. 20, 1978).*

Two kinds of organizing are evident in this account. There was a traditional
top-down style, represented by Teamsters Local 743. The local union president
made over $200,000 a year (too much, Vicky Starr told him). The Teamsters "sent
a lot of organizers" and there "was leafleting all over the place."

Underneath that top-down process, however, something very different devel-
oped. Acting stewards were elected before the NLRB election, almost all of them
women. Complaints were pursued and resolved in an improvised manner even be-
fore the election.

During the interview with Vicky Starr in October 1997, her former co-worker
Charlotte Podolner dropped by and joined the conversation. Vicky Starr's papers,
on which we have drawn for footnotes corroborating her account, may be con-
sulted at the Chicago Historical Society.

VICKY: My granddaughter Robin asked me to speak to her second
grade class about my experiences in the stockyards. I asked her, "If you
want me to speak to the children in your class, what do you think would

interest them?" And she said, "Tell them why you had to change your name!" When I worked in the stockyards and we were organizing, if you announced in any way that you were interested in a union you were put on a blacklist. You couldn't get a job. So you tried to get a job under another name. Again and again and again this happened.

After the stockyards, I married and we had four children. As soon as I could I looked for work outside the home.

I had learned typing in high school, and bookkeeping when I was Secretary-Treasurer of my local in the stockyards. I needed a job where I could sit.

When my son Steve was about two and a half years old, I got a job working in an office. It was horrible. The people I worked with were anti-Semitic, they were anti-black, they were anti-everything that I stood for. This was around 1950.

I took another job where I worked four days a week and had Thursdays off, so I could go to my PTA group. This was after the twins were born. By the time I got through paying for child care for the twins, gasoline for driving to work and minimum maintenance, I came out with zero dollars.

I went to a vocational service and was tested as to the kind of work I could do. The social worker said, "You should work at a place where you will be involved with other people. An educational institution would be fine." So I went to the University of Chicago and filled out a job application. I used my real name, Vicky Starr. I left "Stella Nowicki" and "Vicky Kramer" in the stockyards. But I lied about my age by about ten years. They told me I could have any of three openings.

I thought I would like to have a job at the School of Social Work. I was offered the job of clinic coordinator, but that would have meant working Saturdays. I took a job as a secretary.

Union

There were different attempts at organizing the clerical workers. One that came to my attention was by a professor named Curtis McDougal. This was the United Office and Professional Workers of America (UOPWA). In that union part-time workers were paid *more* than full-time workers, because they did not get benefits. Then later on, District 65 of the Distributive Workers of America sent in people to organize.[1] I was involved in that. We got out a bulletin.

CHARLOTTE: Then the Teamsters came in, and unlike any of the other groups, they had the money and the clout to do a big job. We were not so happy with the Teamsters because we didn't like their reputation. They as-

1. Newsletters in Vicky Starr's papers indicate that District 65's effort took place in 1972–1975.

sured us that Local 743 was different from the national union, that they were good people. It took two years. This was 1977, 1978, 1979.

VICKY: The clerical workers in the hospital had a union, with which they were dissatisfied. Some of them had friends who were connected with the Teamsters. So these employees approached the Teamsters about coming to the University. And the NLRB decided that the bargaining unit should include not only clerical workers at the hospital, but also clerical workers throughout the whole University.[2] There were more than 1800 people in the bargaining unit.

I was very hesitant about becoming involved with the Teamsters. Before I signed up, I called Jessie Prosten from the Packinghouse Workers Union. I asked him about Don Peters who was the president of Local 743. He said, "They're tainted, that's true. But in Chicago, if you want a good union negotiator, the best is Don Peters."

I talked with Peters. His salary had been in the newspaper. I said, "You're head of a union, and you earn over $200,000? Come on!" He said, "Why, you think that's too much?" I said, "Sure is!" He said, "How much do you think I should get?" I said, "At most $40,000 or $50,000." He said, "I put in a lot of time." I said, "So do a lot of other people." He said, "I was at a meeting in San Francisco and they decided this is what I should have." I looked at him and said, "That's hard to believe."

The Campaign

By that time I was in the Department of Education. It was one of more than eighteen buildings that had to be organized.

The Teamsters sent a lot of organizers. There was leafleting all over the place. There were meetings on the lawn. There were free lunches at the Center for Continuing Education. The Teamsters had a script, they invited people there, and they talked union.

Acting stewards were chosen before the NLRB election, on company time, by secret ballot. Of the twenty-one stewards, I was the oldest one in years, and I had the most years working at the University. Eighteen were women.[3]

---

2. The NLRB ruling in November 1977 was sought by the University. While it represented a temporary setback for organizing clerical workers at the University hospital, the ruling paved the way for "unionization of clericals in the entire campus." *Union Report*, v. 8, no. 1 (Sept. 27, 1978), a publication of the Faculty Association of the University of Chicago Laboratory Schools.

3. A memorandum from Edward C. Coleman, University Director of Personnel, July 5, 1979, lists Charlotte Podolner as steward for the Center for Continuing Education and Industrial Relations, and Vicky Starr as steward for Rockefeller Chapel, the Divinity School, and Social Sciences. The memo indicates that there were twenty-three "acting stewards" as of that time.

A lot of the women felt that they should not belong to a union. They were not union people. They were beholden to the professors for whom they worked. It took a lot of convincing and personal attention to break down these negative attitudes.

We broke down these attitudes by pursuing grievances, and taking actions, even before the election. In the library they started to organize before anywhere else. One of the women was fired. The reason given was that she was overweight. The woman who headed the activity in the library pointed out that there was a supervisor who was much fatter than the woman who'd been discharged. She argued that this was discrimination. The employee was rehired with back pay. This was *before* we got our contract.

There was a rumor in my department that there was going to be a layoff, because the department had not received certain grants. People were demoralized. I got together with an employee at the Lab School and a social worker who had been involved in the UOPWA organizing. We decided there should be a bag lunch meeting. We invited all the secretaries.

At the meeting, we said that we should take a position about what was going on, and why. We should know if there was going to be a layoff. If there was to be a layoff, how many? And people affected should have a chance to go to the University employment office and check out job postings.

We circulated a petition. We walked into the supervisors' meeting and filled up the whole office. We had a spokesperson. It was beautiful.

Even before the election, we had a big meeting to discuss what we should ask for in the contract. I'll never forget a young man who got up and said, "I work in the book store twenty-four hours. Then I go to work in the warehouse twenty hours. And I don't get time and a half." And then Louise Dennis got up and said that she had worked at the University for a number of years, got pregnant, and asked for a leave of absence for a year. And when she came back they couldn't find her record!

Going to work became a pleasure. We were stewards. We were stimulated. Helping our colleagues became our mission.

The First Contract

The election was held in November 1978. About 75 votes were challenged. We were ahead by only 15 or 20 votes. It was April or May, six months later, before we were recognized.

The stewards then became the bargaining committee. Let me tell you, when more than twenty of us were sitting at the bargaining table, and they had about ten on the other side, they didn't know what was what. They'd make a statement and we'd counter it! I can remember telling one of them, "Sir, you have the wrong information." I didn't call him a liar. And I remember Maggie would say, "You know what? We can run this University better than you can."

Another thing I'll never forget was said in negotiations, after we won the election. Someone in management mentioned that Chicago was a "prestigious" university. And we responded, "When I go to the store to buy a loaf of bread, they don't ask me whether that dollar is from a prestigious outfit, or from Woolworth's. We can't live on prestige."

CHARLOTTE: I think one of the factors that made the Teamsters effective was that we did a lot of research. We knew what the problems were at the University. The wage scale was very, very low. Working conditions were not good. The place had about a hundred different departments, and every department was like a little fiefdom, with a director who determined whether you got a quarter raise or not. It was so uneven.

VICKY: I remember that when we petitioned for an election the University brought in over 2100 job descriptions for 1800 jobs.

CHARLOTTE: I think the greatest contribution that we made to the union, and to the people there, was to classify all those hundreds of jobs. We gave each job a price, we gave it parameters.

VICKY: We reduced the number of job classifications to something like 300. There was one steward who felt that because she had a degree she should be able to get a job that she wanted, at higher pay. But the job description did not require a degree. We debated that. We decided that she had no right over anyone else. I remember talking about it on the basis of experiences I had in the Packinghouse Union. Our jobs in the stockyards were manual. So it didn't matter how much education you had.[4]

I raised the question before negotiations that our contract should not only prohibit discrimination based on race, religion, and all that, it should also prohibit discrimination because of sexual preference. We had a big debate amongst the stewards.

CHARLOTTE: So many things were left undone. For instance, we talked about day care, but it never really materialized.

VICKY: One of the things I suggested and that we got into the contract was that when a new person came to work, and the secretary had to train that person, the secretary would get fifty cents an hour more for doing it. It wasn't carried out.

I was there for another ten years after we got the union. I was able to

---

4. Just before the NLRB election in November 1978, a leaflet was issued entitled "University of Chicago Employees Speak Out." The first employee to be quoted was Vicky Starr, who said in part: "After 11 years in the same department, I am still 60 cents below the maximum rate.... Further, most jobs haven't been re-evaluated in years, and job duties have been added with no raise in pay."

take a personal leave of absence for six months to travel with the film *Union Maids*. I came back to a job at the same pay rate.

The faculty are glad that the union is there. They now have a stable office staff. People want to stay. Before, women would come to work there, they would learn the ins and outs of the job, learn to operate different machines, and in no time, take off: go downtown and get twenty percent more.

CHARLOTTE: But I think the University has been successful in taking away the power of the union. Our original union was all clerical workers. Now they've divided it, and that always diminishes the strength. And I don't think the Teamsters have done such a good job in the last few years.

VICKY: Our initiation fee was fifty dollars. All of a sudden we found that it had been changed to seventy-five dollars. We didn't know about it. Even the stewards didn't know. We asked for a meeting with Don Peters. We went down there, we fought, and actually won! People got money back.

CHARLOTTE: I don't know how you keep that spirit alive.

VICKY: We have some complaints about union policy. But this should not diminish the great contribution the union made to University of Chicago employees. Charlotte, remember how you and I went down to the hospital recently on medical business and talked to the secretaries? We asked them how they were doing. We said, "You're a union member. Well, we helped to organize the union." And they said, "Thank you, thank you, thank you."

Marshall Ganz

"David conquered Goliath with five smooth stones. So it was with the Farm Workers"

Marshall Ganz grew up in Bakersfield, California. In 1964 he went to Mississippi as a volunteer in the civil rights movement. He stayed until the fall of 1965, registering black voters in dangerous Amite County as a field secretary for the Student Nonviolent Coordinating Committee (SNCC). He recalls that he learned a lot about listening, about paying attention to what was going on around you, and that he learned how to operate in a culture very different from his own.

From 1965 to 1981, Ganz worked with the Farm Workers as an organizer, organizing director, and national officer. Unlike the typical trade union, the Farm Workers under César Chávez required equality of sacrifice from leaders and led. During a strike its officers and organizers were paid no more than strike benefits. The Farm Workers did not view the "service model" and the "organizing model" as alternatives. For them, servicing individual needs was a form of organizing. And because federal labor law does not cover agricultural workers, the Farm Workers were free to use the boycott and ordinarily had to strike for union recognition. Self-appointed committees, and boycott campaigns staffed by rank-and-file volunteers, made possible a series of Farm Worker victories.

This account is drawn from an interview conducted with Marshall Ganz in September 1998. The narrative has been enriched by consulting Marshall Ganz, "The Paradox of Powerlessness: Leadership, Organization and Strategy in the Unionization of California Agriculture (1959–1966)," an unpublished paper, and the transcript of an interview with Marshall Ganz recorded by Frank Bardacke in April 1996.

From Mississippi to California

Even though it was a union, for me the Farm Workers was a California version of SNCC. It was almost incidental that it was a union. It was an extension of the Movement. It was "more than a union." The bridge was a very natural one.

The Farm Workers was about economics, and we had already come to the conclusion in the South that that was really important. And it was a way to keep going. This was a time when a lot of people were dropping out of the Movement. I count myself really lucky to have wound up in the Farm Worker setting.

In the Farm Workers I re-learned grassroots organizing. In SNCC I had learned by osmosis. In the Farm Workers, organizing was taught as a discipline. There was a method, and you could learn it, and be good at it, and then you could teach others. That consciousness of organizing as a craft, and an art, was something special to the Farm Workers.

When I first went to work with the Farm Workers, I was assigned to Bakersfield, where I had grown up. Even though the strike was going on in Delano, César wanted me to begin by learning how to do personal service work. I opened a little office. César sent his cousin Manuel to train me in holding house meetings. I held house meetings in which everybody spoke Spanish. There was always a local rep with whom you would work, the dues collector for that particular community.

It was all built around a lot of personal service. These were immigrant communities, and they had all kinds of problems: on the job, with drivers' licenses, with the Immigration and Naturalization Service, with this, that and the other. You made the organizing credible by beginning to do something about those problems.

In the Farm Workers, people paid $3.50 a month dues for a family membership. A kid six months old got a union card. In return for their dues, the family got a death benefit. They got a newspaper, *El Malcriado* ("the upstart"). They got help with personal services and they could join the credit union. It was the Asociación de Campesinos, an ethnic community association.[1]

By the end of the year I got involved in the Delano grape strike.

---

1. In "The Paradox of Powerlessness: Leadership, Organization and Strategy in the Unionization of California Agriculture (1959-1966)," pp. 11–13, Ganz compares the Farm Worker approach to that of the AFL-CIO Agricultural Workers Organizing Committee (AWOC) which functioned in the first half of the 1960s. "AWOC's timing was short term, focused on visible results. . . . The intent was to produce immediate membership growth." Farm Workers leaders believed that a critical error of AWOC and similar efforts was trying to strike and organize at the same time.

The Delano Grape Strike

The strike was begun by Filipino workers, not by Mexicans. They struck in the Coachella Valley, which is where the grape season begins, and won an increase from $1.20 an hour to $1.40 an hour. Then they came to Delano and struck. César had been organizing for three years in Delano, mostly among Mexican workers. He had been planning to organize for two more years without striking. But he was confronted by the strike. There was a crucial choice to be made as to whether to join the Filipinos. César had the foresight to see that if the strike had been allowed to turn into a racial thing at that point, the union would never have recovered.

The Farm Workers decided to test support for the strike among the 2500 Mexican grape workers by holding a strike vote meeting. It was held at Our Lady of Guadalupe Hall in Delano on September 16, Mexican Independence Day. The people were very enthusiastic, because there had been a long period with no wage increase. But César wanted to be sure that if they got into it, they would not just play with it, they would come out the other end.

So he put out three conditions. One was nonviolence. That was a new thing. Nobody had ever heard of that before. It was a condition that people had to accept, or the Farm Workers would not lead the strike. The second condition was that the strike would not be just for a wage increase, it would be for union recognition, and people would agree to stick it out, whatever it would take. And the third one was that there would be shared sacrifice. He explained that there was no strike fund, but every one would share the same level of sacrifice.

There were about 1200 Mexican grape workers at the meeting. They unanimously approved a strike with these conditions. But as time went on, it became more problematic. Lots of people went on strike and then went elsewhere to work. We had a relatively small group of highly-dedicated people, farm workers and non-farm workers, a hard core of about 150[2] We had to learn how to turn that into a capacity to affect the growers. We had to learn how you manage the internal politics of a group in struggle, how you sustain morale. We had to keep coming up with new ideas. Nonviolence isn't not doing anything. Nonviolence is constant action. Inaction will produce violence.

We had to work in a multiplicity of cultural settings. Mexicans were the largest group, but there were Chicanos, there were Filipinos, there were the Anglo volunteers. The Farm Workers were grounded in a deep sense of cultural pride. Mexican identity was very important, and a source of

---

2. The core of about 150 activists devised the "roving picket line" tactic to compensate for their numerical weakness. Ganz, "Paradox," pp. 18–20.

tremendous commitment and courage. But César was determined that it would not turn into an anti-white or anti-Filipino or anti-black attitude. If it did, there couldn't be a union.

Of course there were tensions. Volunteers came in. There were farm workers and students. There were young men, young women. At one point the wives of a number of young farm workers were very upset about the white volunteers. So César had a meeting just with them.

There was a lot of history between the Filipino and the Mexican communities. There was a lot of potential for feelings to boil up. To his great credit, César wouldn't give an inch on that. It was put out in the open that people were different culturally, but we had to work together. Otherwise there wasn't going to be a union. The union was able to articulate itself as having a powerful cultural identity, yet at the same time maintain a balance between different groups. Filipino-Mexican joint committees were formed, and eventually a joint board was formed and leadership was drawn from both groups. The Filipinos were actually over-represented on the merged board if you compared their seats on the board to their proportion of the work force.

Money or Independence?

When the grape strike began in September 1965, it was clear that you couldn't have a strike without money. The Farm Worker leadership including César, who had been getting $50.00 a week, received only strike benefits during the strike. The strike benefit began at $1.00 a week, then went to $2.00 and eventually to $5.00. Every one lived in the same way. The idea was that if there was no money, you couldn't pay your leadership.

But the union couldn't sustain a strike without getting help from some place beside workers. There had to be some compromise with the idea of being self-supporting. We drew support mainly from churches and student groups, who organized caravans. These were Protestant churches and some Jewish groups, not many Catholics until later. There were also a few maverick labor groups.

César had applied for an OEO [Office of Economic Opportunity] grant three months before the strike to set up service centers. This was an alternative future that could have happened. César was known to the Kennedy people, who tried to recruit him for the Peace Corps in 1961. A grant in the amount of $270,000 came through a month after the strike began.

César turned down the OEO money. Two things were evident. First, you couldn't take the OEO money and continue the strike. If all the energy went into setting up service centers, there wasn't going to be a strike. It had to be one or the other. And secondly, taking the money would have tied the hands of the strike leadership.

In December 1965, Walter Reuther came to town. The Filipino group was affiliated with the Agricultural Workers Organizing Committee, AFL-CIO [AWOC]. We were an independent association, in loose coalition with the Filipinos. Reuther had the sense to see that the Farm Workers had the potential to put out a different idea of what labor was about.

We did some very intense lobbying. The word was, Reuther was going to give a pledge of support to the strike from the UAW [United Automobile Workers]. We wanted half the money, even though we were unaffiliated and independent. We got that. Reuther announced at a big meeting that there would be $5,000 a month, half for AWOC and half for us.

That was a big victory. The labor movement had recognized that we were real. But that night we got a bottle of Christian Brothers wine and went over to the house of César's brother, Richard. We sat there drinking. And César said, "Tonight we lost something that we'll never get back." "What's that?," we asked. He said, "We lost our independence."

I think it was the right choice. We were able to maneuver by avoiding dependence on any one source of funds. It was an alternate strategy for maintaining autonomy. We had labor over here, we had the churches over here, we had liberals over here, we had Chicanos over here [pointing in four different directions]. Any one group could only get so pissed off at you. If they cut you off, they pushed you into the hands of the others. The original strategy had been, depend only on yourself. This strategy was multiple sources of support.

The Schenley Boycott and the Sacramento March

The first boycott, the Schenley boycott, began in December 1965. It was almost accidental. Somebody thought the Kennedys owned Schenley. They didn't, but it turned out that Schenley owned 5000 acres of wine grapes in Delano and distributed highly boycottable products, including Cutty Sark whiskey.

I recently found the phone list that we used in the Schenley boycott. The first boycott calls were to friends of SNCC and SDS [Students for a Democratic Society] offices around the country. The boycott featured a march in Harlem organized by CORE [Congress of Racial Equality] to get Schenley products out of Harlem liquor stores.[3]

I was assigned to coordinate the march to Sacramento, which took place the next spring. The march grew out of a concern to keep workers

3. Ganz points out that because farm workers are not covered by the National Labor Relations Act, Farm Worker boycotts were not subject to legal prohibitions against "secondary boycotts." The Farm Workers asked consumers not only to boycott Schenley *products* but also not to shop at *stores* being picketed until the stores removed Schenley products from the shelves. Ganz, "Paradox," p. 24 and n. 17.

from returning to Delano in the spring when work in the grapes resumed. Chavez gathered a leadership group at a supporter's home in Santa Barbara to spend three days figuring out what to do. According to my notes:

> As proposals flew around the room, someone suggested we follow the example of the New Mexico miners who had traveled to New York to set up a mining camp in front of the company headquarters on Wall Street. Farm workers could travel to Schenley headquarters in New York, set up a labor camp out front, and maintain a vigil until Schenley signed. Someone else then suggested they go by bus so rallies could be held all across the country, local boycott committees organized, and publicity generated, building momentum for the arrival in New York. Then why not march instead of going by bus, someone else asked, as Dr. King had the previous year [in Selma, Alabama]. But it's too far from Delano to New York, someone countered. On the other hand, the Schenley headquarters in San Francisco might not be too far: about 280 miles which an army veteran present calculated could be done at the rate of 15 miles a day or in about 20 days.
>
> But what if Schenley doesn't respond, Chavez asked. Why not march to Sacramento instead and put the heat on Governor Brown to intervene and get negotiations started? He's up for re-election, wants the votes of our supporters, so perhaps we can have more impact if we use him as "leverage." Yes, someone else said, and on the way to Sacramento, the march could pass through most of the farm worker towns. Taking a page from Mao's "long march," we could organize local committees and get pledges signed not to break the strike. Yes, and we could also get them to feed us and house us. And just as Zapata wrote his "Plan de Ayala," Luis Valdez suggested, we can write a "Plan de Delano," read it in each town, ask local farm workers to sign it and to carry it to the next town. Then, Chavez asked, why should it be a "march" at all. It will be Lent soon, a time for reflection, for penance, for asking forgiveness. Perhaps ours should be a pilgrimage, a "peregrinación," which could arrive at Sacramento on Easter Sunday.[4]

The march was timed for March 17, when the Senate Subcommittee on Migratory Labor was to hold hearings in Delano. The AFL-CIO wouldn't join us in the march. It was led by a farm worker carrying a banner of Our Lady of Guadalupe, portraits of campesino leader Emiliano Zapata, and banners proclaiming "peregrinación, penitencia, revolución" (pilgrimage, penitence, revolution). The 82 original farm worker marchers reached Sacramento accompanied by 10,000 farm workers and supporters.

During the march to Sacramento we won the first agricultural workers' contract, with Schenley. It was an incredible breakthrough. It showed that it was possible to get contracts with growers. There was a substantial wage increase, hiring halls to replace labor contractors, medical benefits. It

---

4. Quoted in Ganz, "Paradox," p. 25.

went right to the heart of what the abuses were. It happened just four days before we got to Sacramento. All of a sudden everything was possible.

What we learned in the Schenley boycott was that we weren't going to win boycotts in Delano, we were going to win boycotts in New York and Boston. As long as the struggle was local, there was no way we could win. Farm unions had always been destroyed by fighting it out on local turf. By re-defining the struggle as national, we had leverage, because the growers couldn't do much in New York, Boston, or Chicago, but *we* could. They could run the police and the courts and everything else in Delano, which they did, but we could get Stop and Shop in Boston to cooperate.

It was exactly the same thing the civil rights movement did: to re-define the arena of struggle. Gandhi did the same thing. South Africa did the same thing. Power is often a lot more unequal locally than it is on a broader scale.

DiGiorgio Farms and the Teamsters

Then we got into a fight with DiGiorgio Farms. This was a big corporate farm that had defeated an earlier effort to organize farm workers in the late 1940s. We threatened a boycott of Tree Sweet Juices and S & W Fine Foods, which were owned by DiGiorgio. We pressured Pat Brown, the governor, who was up for re-election, with the help of MAPA, the Mexican American Political Association. He intervened, and mediated, and DiGiorgio agreed to have a representation election.

In the midst of that organizing, the Teamsters appeared. DiGiorgio had contracts with the Teamsters in food processing and trucking. One night we were out making house visits, and people all of a sudden had cards from the Teamsters.

DiGiorgio supported the Teamsters, so we had to out-organize the Teamsters and the employer together. This drove us closer to the AFL-CIO, because we needed their support.[5] One of the results was that we negotiated a merger with AWOC and became the United Farm Workers Organizing Committee (UFWOC), AFL-CIO. That was in August 1966. We remained an organizing committee until 1972 when we became a national union.

One of the DiGiorgio ranches employed about 1200 workers. The other had about a thousand. The whole campaign was like a school. Except for Fred Ross, who was in charge, all the organizers were new. There were a lot of young farm workers. We probably trained 50 to 60 organizers during the DiGiorgio campaign. And we beat the Teamsters in DiGiorgio.

5. At this time the International Brotherhood of Teamsters was not affiliated with the AFL-CIO.

The wine contracts took us all over California. By July 1970 we had signed 200 contracts with the grape industry, covering 70,000 workers. We got contracts in 1970 with grape growers of whom we had never heard. We swept away the whole industry.

We went from a membership of 3,000 to 70,000 overnight. That was High Point Number One, no question about it. By 1972 we had expanded into Oregon, Washington, Arizona, Texas, Florida. We had citrus workers, hop workers. We had a contract with Coca Cola in Florida. The boycott put the fear of God into a lot of employers.

The Teamsters and the Vegetable Industry

On the eve of our signing with the whole grape industry, the Teamsters went over to the Salinas Valley and signed up the lettuce growers. We didn't even have our victory party before we had to deal with the Teamsters, once again. We had gotten them out in 1967. They came back into the picture in 1970.

We wound up having to do two things at once. We had to bring all the grape workers under contract. Many of them had never been on strike. They weren't unionized workers. There was no culture of contract enforcement or hiring halls. At the same time we were in a battle with the Teamsters over the vegetable industry. This led to a strike of 7,000 workers in Salinas in August 1970 and to a lettuce boycott. It was a whole Second Front.

One issue with the Teamsters was race. There was economics but there was also a lot of racism. The growers thought that César was a crazy Mexican. The workers wanted their "own" union, not one run by Anglos.

Also, the vegetable industry was much more commercially organized than the grape industry, and much more vertically integrated from harvesting to processing. Grapes take seven years to grow. The grape growers were mostly Armenian, Italian, and Croatian. The vegetable growers were Anglo business people. They had contracts with the Teamsters in processing operations like canneries, in trucking, in coolers. A lot of it was covered by the NLRB, because these businesses were defined as commercial operations that shipped for multiple growers.

The vegetable growers had a friendly relation with the Teamsters. The Teamsters had made their reputation in California agriculture as the responsible union, pro-private property and anti-Communist. The background was in the 1940s when a Communist-influenced union had tried to organize the California canneries. The Teamsters made common cause with Del Monte and the cannery council and they had a series of Red-baiting elections and the Teamsters took over 40,000 workers in the canneries.

So the Teamsters had a way of operating in which they benefitted from the existence of a more militant union by providing an alternative.

Another factor was that a lot of work that had been in the sheds was moving to the fields, to a field-packing, field-production operation. These had been Teamster jobs. The Teamsters didn't want anybody representing field workers other than themselves.

In 1970 the Teamsters and the growers in the vegetable industry signed a five-year contract. Lettuce workers were getting 32 cents a box. The contract gave piece-work workers an increase of half a cent a box per year, with no benefits and no representation.

. We had begun organizing lettuce workers along the border in 1968 by opening a service center in Calexico, across the border from Mexicali, and beginning to do medical and other services on a small scale. These workers followed what was going on in Delano. A delegation had come in 1969, wanting to strike. We said No, we had to win the grape strike.

In 1970 the lettuce workers figured it was their turn. When the Teamsters signed their contract in Salinas, and the growers went out to the fields and told the workers that they had to become Teamsters and have dues deducted, the workers said, "What Teamsters? What do they have to do with us?" The Teamsters were white. The Teamsters were with the boss.

We organized a meeting for lettuce workers. We had leaflets printed. We went on the radio. We had contacts. We had the use of the upper floor of a poverty program office. Two hundred people came from all over the Salinas Valley. César explained what had happened in Delano, and what the growers were trying to do with the Teamsters. He said they could have their own union but they would have to fight for it. They said, "Yes!"

We didn't quite believe that, so the next thing was a series of marches that were organized to converge on Salinas and protest the Teamster contract. About 5,000 people showed up in Salinas.

The talk in the rally was, "OK, what you need to do now is to form committees. Every ranch, form your *comité*. Every crew, form your *comité*. When you have formed your *comité,* come to the office." We had set up temporary union headquarters on the main drag in the Mexican part of Salinas. We asked the committees to come in and get cards to sign up with the union.

All these committees started arriving! "Hello, we're from so-and-so. What do we have to do?" It was one of those moments! It was a combination of the pent-up discontent from years without a pay raise, and the grape strike which showed the possibility of victory.

We rented an old post office with a huge open space and started to have meetings there every evening. Only committees were allowed in these meetings. What it did was to create a community among the grassroots leaders in the vegetable industry. There were people there from tomatoes and strawberries as well as lettuce. The resistance to signing with the Teamsters was sustained by these meetings.

Then three lettuce crews were fired for not signing with the Teamsters. We called everybody on strike from that company, a subsidiary of Purex named Freshpict. Freshpict was the first strike. The next day we went around announcing through loud speakers, "Don't work at Freshpict. Freshpict is on strike." There were about 300 workers at Freshpict.

There was also a huge strawberry company in the area named Pic N Pac. It had 1200 workers, who lived in a big family camp called La Posada. They heard the announcements and they thought "Freshpict" was "Pic N Pac." And so we got a call at about eight o'clock in the morning. "Aquí estamos. Donde están?" ("We are here. Where are you?") "What do you mean?" "Estamos a huelga." ("We're on strike.")

So we hustled over. There were several hundred workers milling around the big trailer park. We elected a committee, and pulled out the rest of the workers in the fields. Pic N Pac was the second strike.

About two weeks later, August 24, 1970, we took a big strike vote. On Friday, the committees voted to recommend a strike. The strike vote was to take place on Sunday, in a big field.

It was decided that to go on strike you had to take a vote of the people on your ranch, and report what the vote was at the big meeting. Secondly, you had to have your own flag that identified what company you worked for. One of the male lettuce workers stood up and said, "Tenemos un problema." ("We have a problem."). What is it? "Nosotros no podemos coser." ("We don't know how to sew.") At that point, some of the women from the family camp of strawberry pickers said, "We have lots of women. We're great sewers. Just bring us the cloth and the pattern, and we'll sew flags." For the next three days you'd see little delegations of *lechugueros* (lettuce cutters) going into the camp with cloth. The camp became a flag factory.

On Sunday they voted to go on strike, and the next day it began. It was over 7,000 people, the biggest strike we'd ever had. Really, it was a general strike, from north of Watsonville all the way south to below King City, a coastal area of about 120 miles. Companies were going on strike that we didn't know existed. People would come and say, "We're the brussel sprouts workers. Help us strike." "We're the radish harvesters."

It was led by committees of workers, and we were trying to coordinate it as best we could. Harry Bernstein of the *Los Angeles Times* drove in and said, "I've never seen anything like this. There's a hundred miles of red flags."

The very first day the growers got injunctions, claiming it was a jurisdictional strike. We figured we had to turn a strike, which could be enjoined, into mass discharges, which could not. We picked Mann Packing, a broccoli company. The workers decided that they would force the company to fire them. They decided they would all go to work in the morning, and at ten o'clock the leader would jump up on the broccoli machine. He would pull out a flag. And then everybody would sit down and refuse to leave, which would cause them to be fired.

So they went to work. At ten o'clock we were all at the edge of the field. We couldn't see what was happening. We kept waiting, and eventually we saw a yellow spot in the distance. (They wear bright yellow rubber suits, because broccoli is very wet in the morning.) It was all these guys marching out, waving their red flags.

There were pickets and counter-pickets. The Teamsters brought goons to town. The AFL-CIO brought in members of the Seafarers. The workers would say, "Los gorillas han llegado! Por favor, mándenos los gorillas buenos!" ("The gorillas have arrived! Please send us the good gorillas!")

At the end of the first week we got our first contract. Inter Harvest was the largest employer in Salinas. It was a subsidiary of United Brands, owner of Chiquita Bananas. We threatened a boycott of bananas. Inter Harvest rescinded its Teamster contract. They signed with us. There was a 30 percent wage increase. Instead of half a cent we won 12 cents.

At the end of the second week we got a contract with Freshpict, the Purex subsidiary. Then a final injunction issued on the 16th of September. Again we faced a choice.

Since it was the 16th of September—Mexican Independence Day—we took the whole strike to the seashore and we had a big celebration. We decided we needed to focus on the boycott, end the strike but sustain our organization. People went back to work, but it was an organized work force.

Within a month we'd gotten two more major contracts. One was with Pic N Pac, owned by S. S. Pierce. The other was with D'Arrigo Brothers, an outfit that had outlets in Boston, New York, and Chicago. By November we had four major contracts.

A New State Law

In 1971–1972 the growers tried to pass legislation to take away the boycott. We went through a series of defensive legislative battles, in California, in Kansas, in Oregon, in Washington. They got it on the ballot in California as an initiative, Proposition 22, but we beat them in November 1972.

We went back to the boycott. We put everything we had into reorganizing the boycott of grapes, lettuce, and Gallo wine in 1973–1975. We took the strikers to the boycott in a big car caravan across the country. We took about 300 people. We went to Phoenix, to Albuquerque. We had a mass at Ludlow, Colorado. We went across to St. Louis, up to Chicago. Every place we would drop groups of people, members of farm worker families, who were going to launch this second boycott.

Then in 1974 Jerry Brown was elected governor of California. Up to this point we had resisted any legislation, because we knew that so long as

Reagan was governor any state legislation—no matter what it said—
would not be what we wanted. We didn't want federal legislation, either,
because it would take away the boycott.

By 1974 we were beginning to make a lot of headway. In the summer of
1974 we had short, disruptive strikes all over California. There were
strikes in melons, tomatoes, you name it. By 1975 there was a great deal of
pressure for legislation. National supermarkets came to Sacramento and
said they wanted legislation, because they didn't want boycotts. Law enforcement in California wanted legislation. We were demanding jury trials
for all our several thousand arrests and literally bankrupting rural counties. The Teamsters thought that legislation would confirm *their* contracts.

So we negotiated the California Agricultural Labor Relations Act and
got it passed in June 1975, to go into effect in August. It provided for elections in seven days. Brown appointed a board that included Leroy Chat-
field, a long-time supporter of the Farm Workers, and was chaired by
Bishop Mahoney, presently cardinal in LA. The Board agents they hired
were like what I've read about the first NLRB people. Many were Chicanos, young lawyers. They were all for us. It was our law.

During the summer of 1975 we did intensive organizing. The law went
into effect in late August, and within about a month we had 300 elections.
I was still working in Salinas. Every day we had ten, six, eight elections.
We learned a hell of a lot about how to win them and how to lose them.

The Teamsters won some elections. Every election that they won we ob-
jected to. Our attorneys organized a massive free lawyer consortium to pursue all these hearings. The Teamsters were paying through the nose for everything. We were able to use the law to make it uneconomical for the Teamsters
to stay in the field. We also had launched a major anti-trust suit against the
Teamsters and the growers, which was costing them lots of money.

The law worked so well that by the spring of 1976 the Board ran out of
money and was shut down. The legislature refused to renew its funding,
because the law had turned out to be a pro-farm worker law. We had to
put an initiative on the California ballot in 1976. We lost the initiative, but
the struggle removed the resistance. The Board was refunded and went
back into operation. So, we had a law.

We had built the union back up, not to 100,000 but to 40–50,000. The
first peak was 1970–1971. The second peak was 1977. We were all set,
ready to go again.

Whom the Gods Would Destroy

It took four years to undo what had taken almost twenty years to build
up. I think there were several factors.

In the spring of 1977 we negotiated a five-year jurisdictional agreement with the Teamsters. They got out. I think our situation turned a corner when we signed that pact. Until then we had to compete with the Teamsters. And in retrospect, it was a damn good thing. The competition between the Teamsters and Farm Workers meant that a lot of farm workers got organized, wages went up, and conditions improved.

Second, in 1972 we were chartered by the AFL-CIO as a national union. We never developed regional structures. Power always remained very concentrated, within the Board and, particularly, with César.

Every ranch had its ranch committee, every crew had its steward. But there wasn't sufficient concentration, such as a regional entity would have provided, to make the committees and stewards a power base. No ranch was strong enough to be a power base. You would have had to have regional local unions. We never created that.

César used to resist creating locals, because as he liked to say, "Once there are locals there is politics, and once there is politics we won't be able to continue the struggle, because we'll consume ourselves in politics." There's some truth to that. But institutionally, we never created enough diffuse points of power to have real accountability.

Further, as I think often happens to charismatic leaders, César became isolated. César was an amazingly gifted and talented person. But the more his aura grew, the more people told him what he wanted to hear. César knew that that was happening. From one standpoint, the distrust that he came to feel was rational. On the other hand, there's a line between distrusting what you are told and thinking that everyone is lying to you. By 1975–1976 it was as if he had lost his confidence. It's hard to describe. He became very inward, much more reticent, and began to lose his sense of humor. It was a whole personality change, a kind of breakdown.

There had always been the danger of agents. But by 1976 there started to be unreal stories about agents, about Communists, just very bizarre stuff. The first people started to be purged. I didn't fully grasp what was going on. It seemed that something very strange was at work, and I kept thinking that César would get on top of it. I was close to him, as you are with a mentor and a teacher. It was hard for me to accept what was happening to him.

About this time, the Secretary Treasurer of the union got on the road and said to different ones of us, "We need to do something." Nobody quite believed him. César had governed with a spoke system. There was more connection between you and him than between the people around him. There wasn't the kind of trust that it would have taken for us to respond.

Finally, people began to want to get salaries. All this time we had been functioning as a strike community. When we got the contracts in the 1970s, we immediately wound up in this other fight with the Teamsters, and everybody continued with no salaries. You got $5 or $10 a week. You got food stamps. We didn't pay rent, we could put gas in the car, and the union took care of medical problems if we had them. Basically it was a subsistence deal. We did pay our lawyers something like $7,000 a year. We had a couple of doctors to whom we paid $12,000. Some of the field staff began to want salaries, too.

César felt really threatened by this. He thought that once you started to pay salaries, you lost your community, you became professionalized and bureaucratized. There's an element of truth to that. But on the other hand, how were we to stabilize the organization? Is there a point at which people need to be able to live whole lives?

The effort to make the Farm Workers into a total community became a year-long campaign. Along the way, the union got rid of its lawyers. The Board split for the first time over whether to abolish the legal department. We had a 5–4 split, with the four younger members including myself voting against César. People started leaving.

We had no tradition of legitimate opposition. A group of workers I helped to organize in the late 1970s tried to run their own candidates for the Board at a union convention. They were run out of the convention.

By 1981, the capacity that we had created over the years for leadership at all levels was gutted. It was just gone. By 1982 the union leadership was mostly César's family.

Five Smooth Stones

I call the doctoral dissertation that I am writing about the Farm Workers, "Five Smooth Stones." The Farm Workers are like David when he fought Goliath. When David volunteered for individual combat with the Philistine champion, the king of Israel armed David with a helmet of brass and a coat of mail. But David put off the king's armor, because this was not the style of fighting natural to him. David was a shepherd. He fought lions and bears to protect his father's sheep, but he did so with a shepherd's weapons. And so, "he took his staff in his hand, and chose him five smooth stones out of the brook, and put them in a shepherd's bag which he had . . . and his sling was in his hand." Thus armed he went forth and conquered (1 Samuel 17 4-51). So it was with the Farm Workers.

Mia Giunta

"Working-class people have a very deep culture based on solidarity and trust"

Mia Giunta (pronounced "Junta") grew up in a working-class community in eastern Pennsylvania. It was a union family, the kind of family that formed the backbone of the emerging CIO. As a young adult, Mia Giunta went to college in Connecticut and became an organizer for the United Electrical, Radio and Machine Workers (UE).

To be hired as an organizer for the UE at that time you had to come out of a factory. Mia Giunta started organizing as a volunteer. And in the UE the organizer took part in negotiations at the place that he or she had organized. This was because the organizer stayed in one community, putting down roots. It was a practice consistent with what Mia Giunta calls "women's style of organizing."

Among Mia Giunta's memorable experiences was a factory where women workers insisted on sharing the work equally during layoffs. Later, she was present at the scene of a building collapse, waiting with an Italian immigrant family for news of a family member who didn't make it. She believes that this event gave rise to Workers' Memorial Day, now celebrated each year on April 28.

How I Was Raised

Both my maternal grandparents came from the southern part of Italy. My father's family came from Sicily.

I never met my father's father. My grandfather came to this country in the 1890s because of the Ethiopian War. He came not to be wealthy, but to be free and independent, and so as not to fight in a war in which he did not believe. He peddled fruits and vegetables and olive oil from door to door. He died of influenza in 1918.

My father's mother worked in a cigar factory after her husband died. When I was in college and opposing the Vietnam War, my grandmother loved the hippie movement, because it brought out something in her that she remembered as a young girl. She told me that my grandfather didn't want to work for anyone because he didn't want to be a slave. And he didn't want to employ anyone, and have them become a slave. The only thing that suited his temperament was to go door to door.

He couldn't read or write, but he kept a notebook in which he drew pictures to keep track of his accounts. My grandmother and my aunt say that he would throw a pocket change purse to the children, and let them play with the money, because he hoped that some day there would be a world where people didn't have to have money, and didn't have to work for it, because everything would be provided.

He was a man of contradictions, though. He wanted his family to have absolutely the best, and worked very hard for that. My father and his brothers were very proud that they were the first family on the block to have an inside toilet and electricity.

This was in Scranton, Pennsylvania, which is an anthracite coal mining region. I became aware of unions at a very early age. My father was a plumber, partly because his older brother was a plumber. While working at the trade as a teenager my father found an old, old plumber, who was a member of the Knights of Labor. He learned about the labor movement from this old man.

It was part of the family tradition not to trust the boss, to be suspicious of authority. My father wanted to join the plumbers' union. He was not allowed in because he was an Italian American. The story my father told me is that one day the plumbing inspector, who was also president of the union, came to my father's work site to inspect a job. My father waited until the guy was in the bath room, met him at the door, and said, "There are three ways out of here. One is the window. One is over me. And the other is by letting me in the union." My father joined the union that day. When he passed away last year he had been in the union fifty-eight years.

He was a building tradesman, so there was a certain elitism. But there was also an understanding that the union should be open, and he saw to it that other people who had not been allowed into the union were admitted. His nephew became business agent for the same local in the 1970s, and my cousin fought to have women admitted and also recruited African Americans.

Once my father got into the union, he was upset that everything was so secret. He found out that there were some other guys who didn't like it, either. You never knew how the money was spent, you never knew what was going on. So he was part of a rank-and-file movement. As a kid I didn't know what was going on, but I knew it was deadly serious. They met in my parents' living room or in the basement to talk about how they could get rid of the corrupt officials. There was such energy there! You just knew it was good stuff.

I got addicted to it. Once when I was only three or four I was listening intently, and at the same time, shaking a ginger ale bottle with a stopper in it. The bottle suddenly went "boom!" They all hit the floor.

They won. My father went on to be treasurer of the local, and representative to the Labor Council and the Building Trades' Council.

My uncles were coal miners. They went into the mines when they were eight years old, and were put into spots where grown-ups couldn't fit. They never learned to read. I remember with great sadness how I came to realize this. I had begun to figure out words and when I went to my uncle and asked him to read a story, I found that he wasn't reading. He was making things up.

My mother's father was a stonecutter. He eventually left stonecutting because he developed silicosis. Then he opened up a grocery store which was something that a lot of people did if they were blacklisted, or became disabled. When my grandmother died a few years ago, someone came to the funeral who said he wanted to thank her, because during the Depression she and her husband had helped their family to stay alive by giving them stuff to eat. Nobody knew that but my grandmother.

My father had a little cottage somewhere near the Poconos. There used to be a lake there, but the lake went during a hurricane. We still used to go up there. The whole Giunta clan would come. You had coal miners. My aunts all worked in garment factories. There were people who worked on the railroad. You had the whole AFL-CIO represented.

Naturally when anybody came the first question was, "Where do you work? Who do you work for?" My grandmother used to say you can always tell who somebody is by what kind of work they do. So one time they asked a man, and he said he worked for a certain company that was on strike. So they said, "Oh, you poor man. You've been on strike all summer," and they really laid the food on him. And he said, "Oh no, not me, I go to work every day. I'm in management." They took the food back! Nobody would speak to him. They fed his wife and daughter, but not him.

Then there was another time I got a Judy Bond blouse with a little bit of money I had saved. It was all I could afford. This blouse had the Peter Pan collar, and the little buttons, and all the things that blouses were supposed to have in 1960. But Judy Bond was on strike. My father made me take it back, and apologize to everybody on the picket line. I was mortified.

That's how I was raised. I don't think my background is anything special. It's part of a working-class experience that can make us very strong. But in the process of becoming Americanized, we run the danger of forgetting who we are and what our families taught us.

Becoming a UE Organizer

I hated Scranton. I felt so confined. It's in a valley, and there are all these mountains, and I used to have fantasies of flying over the mountains to the other side.

I was encouraged by my father to think for myself, to look beneath the surface. Somehow I couldn't do that in Scranton. The world was too rigid. I wanted to get out. And school was the way to do that. I went to the University of Bridgeport and studied sociology. But the reason I went was not to study sociology, it was to get out of Scranton.

I found out about the UE [United Electrical, Radio and Machine Workers]. I met some wonderful UE organizers. I found that rather than say, "Oh, you're a woman, you can't do that," they were happy that I was a woman, because I could reach other women and help them to organize.

I didn't go to work for the UE right away. I used my social work background and in 1975 got a job with the Bridgeport Labor Council, to help unemployed union members during the recession. Then a big strike hit one summer and I said, "Striking members are unemployed members!," so the job became doing strike assistance. I became known as the "food stamp girl." I would show up at a picket line and they'd say, "Oh, you're the food stamp girl!" It became more than helping people to get resources. I was helping people in one factory to get in touch with people in another factory, encouraging people to go to each other's picket lines.

One strike was at the Bullard machine shop. Racially and ethnically it was a very mixed shop. So during the strike they had different kinds of nights, when they would show films. On "Hispanic Night" they showed *Salt of the Earth*. When people were on strike there was a different kind of community. People were on the picket line together, day in and day out. At Bullard they got a very good contract offer but people didn't want to go back to work!

I did get in trouble with some of the Labor Council officers. They didn't think it was right for me to be doing this. But the people on strike got wind of what was coming down, so they showed up en masse and it didn't go very far.

I knew I wanted to do organizing. But the UE wasn't hiring college kids. You had to come out of a factory. I was willing to go into a factory, but by that point, no one in Bridgeport would hire me. My picture had been on the front page of the local paper. There was a very long strike at Jenkins Valve, and the company was bringing in scabs. John Del Vecchio, a member of Steelworkers Local 7528, and I showed up one morning to try to dissuade the scabs from going in. There was one really young guy who just didn't know what was happening. John and I were talking to him. We weren't being nasty or threatening, but we were both Italian, and we were talking with our hands. The photographer took a picture of us with our hands in the air! Eventually I went to work for the UE as a volunteer.

F-Dyne Electronic

There was a place I had heard about when I worked for the Central Labor Council, an awful, awful hell hole. Its name was F-Dyne Electronic. The plant made little products, less than an inch long, which held electrical charges. Most became parts of a razor or a pencil or a tape recorder.

I told the international rep that I wanted to organize this factory. He said, "Well, go ahead and do it. But please understand that places like this can move out very quickly, and it's a tough work force to organize, because of all the different nationalities."

The place was fascinating. There were African Americans who had lived in the city a long time. There were African Americans who had come from the South fairly recently. There were people from Africa, from Puerto Rico, from Portugal, from Cuba, from Mexico. There were people from countries like El Salvador, who didn't want you to know they were from Latin America. There were over two hundred hourly workers, and less than a dozen were men. In Bridgeport at that time there were trucks that would come around outside the plants and serve breakfast: awful coffee, awful chile. People would get that cup of coffee before they went into the shop. I would go and ask questions. "What's it like working here? Are they hiring?" People started complaining. I met one Portuguese guy whose name was Manny, and asked him, "What's it like here?" He said, "It's terrible. We need a union." I said, "Oh. I'm from a union." He said, "One minute please." He came back with a bunch of women, and said, "I go now."

I took the women's addresses and said, "I'll meet you after work." That's how it started. Some of the people weren't interested, but you ask around, and you find out who the organizers and the leaders are.

In the process of organizing, by department and by issue, the barriers started to break down. Many of the women could not read and write in their own language. Certainly many of them could not read and write in English. As they got to know each other, they found they all had something in common as working women. They were willing to take a chance together to better their lives.

The women had different political experiences. The women from Portugal said about elections, "Oh sure, you get to vote Communist, Socialist, whatever." But you also had women from Cuba who were anti-Castro.

There was a woman in the factory named Marguerite. She was a Cuban immigrant. Marguerite's goal was to become a citizen. She was terrified she would be sent back to Cuba. One day Marguerite, who was very active in the union drive, was suspended. She was upset because she thought she would not get her citizenship. She left the factory in tears.

An African American woman put out a leaflet about what had happened to Marguerite. She wrote it in the voice of Harriet Tubman. The leaflet more or less said, "Harriet Tubman rides again." At that time

Jimmy Carter was president and he was talking about human rights. The leaflet said, "Mr. Carter is talking about rights, but not rights for everybody. Mr. Charley is in the North and won't let us have our union. Harriet has to come again, and organize her people, and help Marguerite!"

People loved it. Harriet began to become different people. Harriet was Puerto Rican. Harriet was from Pakistan. The woman who started this was not a political woman. She had stayed home, raised her kids, found herself with a husband who didn't love her any more, divorced, went on welfare, and then worked at the plant. Her name was Louise.

After the union came in, and we got our first contract, some of the women went to college, got better jobs, ended abusive relationships with husbands and boy friends, and I think it was because the collective experience had transformed them.

I get really angry when it is said that working-class people don't have culture. They have a very deep culture. It's a culture that's based on solidarity and trust and helping each other, and a dream for a better life for your children. These people were tired of the way they were being treated.

Sharing the Work

We won the election. People were jubilant. People got caught up in thinking that they had transformed their workplace.

It took us most of a year to get a contract. There were all kinds of legal delays. I was a part of all this, because at least in my day in the UE, the organizer took part in negotiations at the place that he or she had organized. This was because the organizer was viewed as part of the community. You could be transferred within the same community, or asked to work on special projects, but you had a base. I was a better "organizer" because I was also a "servicer," and a better "servicer" because I was also an "organizer." I can't imagine not doing it that way.

We came very close to striking. We would have lunchtime meetings, to inform people what was going on in the contract negotiations. Sometimes the meetings lasted a little longer than the half hour lunchtime. People wore stickers, buttons, T-shirts. Workers spoke to organizations in the community about their struggle for a first contract. We formed a strike committee.

Finally we had a lunchtime meeting and people voted not to go back to work. The company told them they were all suspended. They let in only a few people who didn't go to our meeting. We acted just as if it was a strike, and the company settled shortly afterward.

It was an interesting contract. The company claimed they didn't know what they were signing. We got voluntary overtime. We got a year's maternity leave. While you weren't paid during the leave, you accrued vacation and seniority and your health benefits continued. The average age of the women in the shop was about twenty-five.

Then came the day that the contract was all typed up and we were going to have the signing. The company wanted to reneg. People walked out of the factory, with signs that said, "Mr. K. [the company president] won't sign the contract." He signed.

There was a clause in the contract that provided a cost-of-living increase in the third year. The company said they were not going to pay. The women were furious. They created such an uproar, the bosses went to the only place they could think of, the men's room. The women wouldn't let them out. Finally the bosses came out and the women said, "You broke the contract!"

So we filed a grievance, and the company had to pay a lawyer, and before the arbitration hearing the company settled. The average worker got maybe $75 a few weeks before Christmas. People went out and bought a winter coat or whatever, and said, "This is my union coat."

People in the shop were very supportive of each other. I remember when the local was going to get its charter as Local 210, UE. A woman in the shop was going to go to a meeting to pick up the charter. She was embarrassed, because she didn't think her clothes were dressy enough to go. The women were all making minimum wage at the time. They took up a collection and got her a whole new outfit.

One woman had a horrible absentee record. We went in and said, "She has children, and it's very hard when you have children that you're raising by yourself." We got her job back.

The company had an operation in Florida. Mr. K. was from New York, and as long as he was president, the Bridgeport plant was kept open. But there were layoffs. There were layoffs in 1978, 1979, right after the contract was signed.

Under the contract, the layoffs went according to seniority. We felt terrible, thinking of some of the workers who would be put out on the street. There was a Portuguese woman named Albertina who had little children. She was crying, but she said, "It's OK. It's all right." The other women said, "That's unfair."

The workers took up a collection for her. I felt very guilty, and tried to talk to Albertina to make sure that she and the kids would be all right. We just didn't want to see her go.

When the next bunch of layoffs came along, somebody suggested, "We'll all work a few hours less each week. That way everybody can stay. Everybody will have health insurance." And they took advantage of the vacation and maternity leave, and that became the tradition in that factory.

The contract was never amended. Every time there was a layoff, we would sign a side agreement that everyone would agree to cut back. When the factory finally closed at the end of the 1980s, I think people were working four and a half days a week.

Varieties of Organizing Experience

There was a plastic factory down the street which used chromium and nickel and mercury. About 175 men worked there. They had a horrible union. Someone got hurt in the factory once, and they called the union collect and the union wouldn't take the phone call. They never got to see their contract.

Someone who worked there heard about the UE, probably from someone at F-Dyne. We had a discussion, "Are we going to raid this place?" We concluded, "Maybe we can give them some tips about how to make the union work better for them." This was going on while we were trying to get the F-Dyne contract.

We arranged a meeting with the workers for a Sunday afternoon. It was a very cold day in February. People walked from all over the city to come. After they told their story it was decided then and there that we would work with the people for the UE to take over.

We started with a very militant committee. But as workers were lining up to vote, the National Labor Relations Board called off the election, because the company had said something in a leaflet the day before that they weren't supposed to say. The incumbent union filed charges.

People said to me, "Everybody knows that we are voting for the UE. Mia, we're going underground." There were a lot of people there from Latin America and they had experience in working underground. They said, "You won't know. We're not going to speak to you. You're just going to have to trust us." It was going to be nine months until the election.

I remember a day outside the factory, early in the morning. These guys in suits drove up in a huge Cadillac. The workers weren't even there yet. There was nothing except these guys, me, the garbage dump, Long Island Sound, and a public housing project. I said to myself, "This is it. I could disappear, and nobody would ever find me again." They walked up very menacingly and muttered obscenities. The wires in my car were pulled out.

When the election finally came the UE won overwhelmingly. There was such celebration! We went to the union hall that night. People brought salsa records. We danced, and we danced, and we danced all night long. We stayed up making a flier saying, "WE WON!," as if people didn't know!

That factory, too, had to overcome differences. It was harder for me to work with because they were mostly men. There were Jamaicans in the shop who didn't get along with the Puerto Ricans. There were Dominicans who didn't get along with some other group. You show people their common needs, common interests. You work with them to believe that they can do it together, and not alone.

There was another factory outside New Haven, Bridgeport Plating, which we heard about from the son of a UE member in another plant. We set up what was supposed to be a small meeting. But instead of four or five workers coming to McDonalds for a cup of coffee, half the factory came. The McDonalds wasn't big enough for me to speak to the people and I didn't have any other place to go. I got up on a chair and the McDonalds manager started to get really nervous. So we went out in the parking lot and continued our discussion. I asked people from different departments to get together in different parts of the parking lot, and make a list of their problems, while I would rotate.

From that day, through the organizing drive, through the election, to the day we went out on an unfair labor practice strike, we had exactly the same amount of people. We called it "the grandmothers' strike." They were older women, who had never stood up for anything before in their lives. They made harnesses for jet aircraft. When you shook hands with them, you realized that their hands were deformed.

Our strike headquarters was a tent, like a tent you would use for a wedding. The women decorated the tent with artificial flowers. They cooked delicious meals. People were always meeting people: "Here, have a slice of cake, we'll tell you why we're on strike." There was a quiet woman, who at the beginning of the campaign wore her union button to work under her apron, in a skirt pocket. Her union button evolved. I had to work with her to get her confidence up, to say, "It's OK to be who you are, and believe in this. This is part of you. It is you. You can make it yours." She got up out of her chair—I'll never forget this—and she had her fists clenched up tight, and she said, "That's right." She was crying, and shouting at the top of her voice. "This company sucks! I've been waiting 28 years to say this! It sucks!"

Burnout

I burned out. I was in my mid-thirties. There were strikes in between organizing campaigns, national negotiations, immigration raids. There were campaigns that didn't take off, because for every one that did there were at least three that didn't go anywhere, and people got fired. And at the time, there weren't many women organizers, either.

Hugh Harley, the director of organizing, wanted me to take a leave of absence. In retrospect, I probably should have taken a leave of absence and gone to work for a florist somewhere, and just taken it easy. But when you're in the midst of a burnout, you don't know your own abilities. I said, "No, no. I'm a terrible organizer. I can't do this any more." So I left.

It was awfully hard! I didn't fit in anywhere. I worked at a shelter for battered women. I did an OK job but there wasn't the same passion as in organizing. I worked very briefly for the hospital workers in New England. They had an organizing model with which I did not feel comfortable. From my point of view, it was too manipulative. It worked for them but it didn't work for me. And my age affected me, doing hospitals and nursing homes twenty-four hours a day, seven days a week.

There have been some things written about women's style of organizing versus that of men. Women tend to be nurturing, to look at the cycles: the cycles of the seasons, the cycles of life, the cycles that every organization goes through. Men tend to be, "Bam! Let's get it done!" Women are more patient. We look at things differently.

Workers' Memorial Day

Local 1199 sent me up to Waterbury to work on a long hospital strike. We did some creative things during that strike. We offered free health screenings to anybody in the community. The nurses did things for free to show that we weren't against community health care. We had a food bank. The maintenance people settled but the nurses were still out. So the maintenance people stayed out to support the nurses.

There was a luxury apartment building, L'Ambience, being built in Bridgeport. I came home from work at 7:30 one night in April, and got off the bus, and I was told, "The building that [my husband] Peter told the city council not to give a tax break just collapsed. And there were men inside." A little later an aide to the mayor called and asked me to come up to the school, just across from the building site. He said, "The Red Cross is here but we need help with the families."

I went. It was the end of the week, pay day. People had been there to get their checks when the building collapsed. I immediately recognized a family that I knew from the Waterbury hospital strike. It was an Italian family, born in the same province as my grandfather on my mother's side. I remembered the family because I used to go to the picket line at Waterbury hospital very early on Sunday morning. And I recalled a time when the whole family was sitting around a fire at the entrance to the hospital. A member of the family had just had a baby. They were celebrating with homemade wine and espresso in thermos bottles. One of the old men had gone into the woods to get mushrooms. My uncles who were miners also collected mushrooms. I felt very connected with them, and their celebration of their grandchild, or great grandchild.

And there they were again, six months later, waiting for news of someone who didn't make it. I stayed with that family. It had been a warm spring but had turned very cold that day. The men who were digging for their co-workers in the rubble were chilled and wet to the bone. We went crazy looking for warm clothing, and long underwear, and wool socks. These guys did not stop digging. Their hands were bloody but they kept on digging. They were incredibly tough.

There were wonderful things that happened. Like anyone else, Italians can be very racist. By the end of those two weeks people had become long-lasting friends. Once they found the last body, the construction workers built an impromptu memorial for their co-workers. Poems and notes were written all over the walls. People took their tools, their hard hats, and laid them in a row.

I talked to the families, to the construction workers. They put it to me that they didn't want to talk to the shrinks but they had to talk to somebody.

You've heard of Workers' Memorial Day. This was how it began. The building collapsed because the wrong kind of bolts were used.

I never could figure out what to do with that experience. The best that I've been able to come up with is, looking at these people who have the same kind of look and build as my grandfather whom I never knew, and sitting with them by the firelight, and thinking, is this what I would have been doing if my grandfather had lived? Would we be talking, and drinking coffee and aniseth together?

I still plant bright blood-red tulips every fall. I think of life and joy and the baby who was born that fall. When the tulips bloom in the spring, and as the petals drop, I think of the workers' blood in the ground that spring.

Gary Stevenson

"The freight industry is going to be organized by members in freight"

After many years of organizing for local unions, in 1996–1998 Gary Stevenson coordinated the campaign to organize Overnite Transportation for the International Brotherhood of Teamsters (IBT). Overnite was the largest non-union LTL (Less than Truck Load) trucking company in the country, and the campaign was one of the largest organizing efforts in the AFL-CIO. In the next account, Hugo Hernandez tells the story of the Overnite campaign as seen by one of those organized, from the bottom up.

Gary Stevenson was inspired to become a union organizer by the idealism of the 1960s. He found that the best way to organize was not by leafleting or wearing buttons, but by direct action. When workers asked what they would have in their contract, he responded, "Well, what do you want? It's your union." Gary Stevenson believes that when an organizer talks about the union, weaknesses as well as strengths, failures as well as successes, must be put on the table. He resigned from the IBT shortly before the election of James Hoffa, Jr., in 1998.

The following interview was taped at the Meany Center near Washington, D.C., in September 1997. We have also drawn on remarks by Gary Stevenson at a conference on "solidarity unionism" held at the hall of Teamsters Local 377 in Youngstown, Ohio in June 1998.

Growing Up in Brooklyn and Queens

I was born in 1951 in Brooklyn. My grandparents lived upstairs with my uncle. My grandfather was a member of the bookbinders' union. In fact, I still have his withdrawal card from 1903 on the wall in my home. My relatives—cousins and so forth—were mostly painters, brewery workers, machinists. I come from a very conservative Catholic background. My whole family was very much involved with the Church in Brooklyn, and then later in Queens when we moved to a place called Richmond Hill. I went to parochial school. There was one time when I was being directed toward the priesthood.

When I was growing up, my father worked as a machinist at a defense plant on Long Island. My mother passed away when I was nine. I remember that while she was alive my father went on strike a couple of times, and that when there was a strike, my mother would go to work as a secretary. When the strike was over she would quit and return to the house.

The way my father spent his life was, he went to work early every morning. He'd always wear a white T-shirt, gray khaki pants, and work shoes. No matter what season it was, it was always a white T-shirt. He had a funny habit: he'd eat breakfast wearing his army hat from World War II.

He came back, like clockwork, at five o'clock in the afternoon. I knew exactly what street he would come from and sometimes I'd run to meet him. Then he'd have dinner, and sit in front of the television, half dead, in the easy chair in the living room that was designated as his chair.

For as long as I remember growing up, my father never once talked about work. Every once in a while he'd come home with parts, which were magnificent. He built a chess set out of metal parts. He was a superb machinist.

The guy was working all the time. He was working his ass off in the 1960s, which was supposed to be a time of prosperity, just to maintain the house and the family. Neither my mother or my stepmother worked, because he didn't believe in that. So he did it. And he never complained.

My uncle was also a World War II veteran. He was like another parent in the house, a very warm, close parent, always at hand. My uncle had a very profound influence on my life in the 1960s, when I was in my late teens. He had a son who was exactly a year older than myself. This son enlisted in the Army around 1966 or 1967. My uncle threw a fit. He was terrified that my cousin John would be sent to Vietnam. He told me that you could replace your country but you could never replace your son.

My father, on the other hand, was a conservative, far Right Republican. He was for Vietnam. He supported Nixon. He thought the Army could make a man out of you.

In my junior year of high school I discovered reading. There were never any books in my house. My parents never talked about books. It was usually daily newspapers and *Life* magazine. I began to build my own book collection. I burrowed in my room after school every day and just read.

The first book that influenced me was *The Autobiography of Malcolm X*. I noticed a friend of mine was carrying it around with him. It was incredible. And then, Henry David Thoreau, Ralph Waldo Emerson. I started to take school more seriously, particularly social studies and English. I read everything. I participated in class every day. I had discovered an insatiable thirst for knowledge.

The anti-war movement was going on. There were activities at Columbia University in New York. As we were sitting at the dinner table, my father would go on about "these damned students. Their parents should take them by the hand, and bring them home, and slap the hell out of them."

My thoughts were heading in another direction. I was intrigued by all this. There seemed to be more to it than my father's simplified explanations. There was an SDS chapter at my high school, which put out a student newsletter. I thought it was incredible that a group of my fellow students could put out a newsletter. And then there was something at the school called the East Meadow High School Students for World Peace. I started gravitating towards the kids that were involved. I was drawn to the new kind of student who had ideas about the way society should be.

College

No one in my family had ever been to college. We didn't have any money. So obviously the state system was the most accessible. I applied to a state school in New York and I got accepted. I picked the school furthest from my home on the map, Oswego State College. It was a small teachers' college on Lake Ontario in upstate New York.

My first semester was fall 1969. I got wholly involved in the student movement and the anti-war movement. I started to go to meetings and demonstrations. I did a lot of reading on American foreign policy. I became highly politicized. I was a political figure on campus. My classmates all came from working-class, suburban communities, and were introduced for the first time in their lives to things that seemed to be beyond their mere existence, things to believe in and to be willing to fight for.

The Newman Center was the Catholic organization on campus. It so happened that an activist priest headed the Newman Center. He was a priest that I had never imagined existed: a priest who actually cared about what was going on in the world. I began to see that there could be a moral foundation for opposition to the war in Vietnam, and for opposition to poverty and social injustice.

The Berrigans came to town. Dave Dellinger spoke on campus. I joined the War Resisters League and Fellowship of Reconciliation. We had a "we won't go" group. We started a massive letter writing campaign to the local draft board. We figured we'd jam them up with tons of letters.

The first national student strike was in the spring of 1970, after the killings at Kent State in Ohio. I was involved. Everybody on campus was involved. The dean sent letters home to all our parents, telling our parents that their children were troublemakers. So my parents came up and met me at the Holiday Inn at the end of the spring semester.

My father was heated. I had begun to grow my hair long. He cursed the professors at the school. He thought they were responsible. He said, "We're going to take you out of this school. Come back to live with us. You'll go to a community college."

I said, "No way. That will never happen. Furthermore, I might even join the Peace Corps." I had already burnt my draft card. I said I was not going to the war. I said I had found something in my life that had meaning, and I was not going to go back to live with them, to live that stupid existence of believing in nothing and doing nothing.

So we had a total break. He disowned me. To this day, we have never spoken. I met him once at a funeral.

Getting Started

When I graduated college, my friends and I had all decided that we were going to go on to organize for a better society. I was never career-oriented. My thinking was, it doesn't matter what you do in this society, the point is to change it. Those changes had to occur at every level of society. I felt that since I came from a working-class background, and I had a college education, I had an obligation to remain in the milieu from which I came, and bring to it a whole different perspective about life, and about the way life should be.

I had an apartment on Long Island. Whenever a demonstration was announced anywhere, I'd go. There was an alternative movie theater in the neighborhood, where things were posted on a huge bulletin board. I found out that there was a local chapter of NAM [the New American Movement] on Long Island that met maybe once a week, with a phone number. So I joined. That's where I met my wife. This was about 1975.

When I met my wife, I was working as a warehouseman and truck driver for a book company based in New York that had a branch on Long Island. It was called Brentano's. The warehouse was not automated. Everything that moved in that warehouse moved because somebody carried it from Point A to Point B. We referred to our work as "humpin'," humpin' boxes of books.

I worked there for about four years, just to make some cash. A representative from Local 810 of the Teamsters named Ted Bloom showed up. Local 810 represented three other Brentano's locations. I said, "Yeah, give me the cards. I'll talk to some people." But I couldn't do it. A lot of the young people were interested but the older folks in the warehouse were not.

Then a friend of mine got a job there. He was also a very political guy who came out of District 65 of the Distributive Workers. When my friend got a job it became easier to sign people up. More work was being done and we had a lot more young people.

It was decided that we would go out on a recognition strike with Local 810. There was a tradition in that local that they would strike for recognition, rather than go to an NLRB election.

We picketed every single location. We demolished trucks like you wouldn't believe. We chased trucks. We went to many of their stores all over the Northeast. We picketed inside malls and got attacked by customers: everyone was slugged one time or another.

Had it been just Brentano's we might have stood a chance of winning. But Brentano's was owned by the Macmillan Corporation. (For some reason I always get stuck in these situations where a company is never just a company. It's always owned by a conglomerate!) The company hired lots of scabs. Eventually the NLRB ordered an election, and the scabs won. We continued picketing. After nine months we were ordered off the picket line by a court injunction. We never surrendered.

I still tell people about that strike. The strike was lost, but in the course of those nine months every single one of the strikers became deeply politicized. For example, one person went on to become a labor reporter in Mexico. Another guy became an activist in another local, which the workers at Brentano's joined sometime later. Every one of those individuals went on to do something good in their own lives to promote social justice.

During the course of our strike we got a lot of support from Local 810. Some people felt let down in that they had greater expectations about what the union could do. I never had any false impressions about what the union could do, because I felt that the union was the folks who were picketing, who were striking. That was the union. The larger organization, Local 810, was giving us money to stay alive on the picket line. I also felt that the Teamster picket sign was powerful. It stopped a lot of companies from delivering. No union driver would cross that picket line.

Organizing for Local 810

I went on to work in a steel company organized by Local 810. I was elected shop steward. Then I became an opposition force over the death of a particular guy I worked with on the night shift who was crushed by a steel coil. The business agent never showed up. I went to the next meeting of the local and screamed and yelled and shouted. I said, "This is a sell-out operation. This is a bullshit union. They don't represent anybody. There's a death, and nobody shows up. This is outrageous!" Finally, the local sent someone down to meet with everyone, and we had a safety meeting with management.

It was a family-dominated local. The family patriarch asked if I was interested in organizing. I said, "Yeah." He said, "I'll give you $150 a week, $50 expenses. Here's a stack of cards." That was the extent of the training. He said, "If you bring in members, this will be your job. If not, see you later."

So for weeks, I went out to industrial parks early in the morning, every day. I went to all the five boroughs. I button-holed people on the street at six o'clock in the morning when they were going to work, getting off the subways. I asked, "Where are you working? What are the conditions like? How's the pay? Do you have a union?" I went through this over and over again, everywhere.

One thing I learned is that people will talk to you. That's why I always teach organizers, "Just jump into it. You'll be surprised how much people have to say." But you have to have some chutzpah to get out there and talk to people.

This was a local that always had strikes going on. I learned that the Teamster picket sign became an advertisement to other employees in the area. They would drop by and talk about their own particular place, and what was happening, and the fact that they might or might not need a union, or they had a union and needed a better one.

There were an awful lot of disgruntled union members out there. Many people hated their own union. I went to dozens of places where people would tell me, "We haven't seen the union in a year." Or they didn't know the name of the union. They said that the union representative would come to the shop and walk into the boss's office. If the contract had to be renewed, they would wake up one day and all of a sudden there was a new contract. That was it. They were told, "This is what we got for you." I learned that it was almost impossible for people to change unions. I thought that was outrageous. Why should people be held hostage by a particular union if it's not doing the job?

I found out that communication among the members was much easier in some Teamsters locals than in others. In a drivers' local, for example, there was a unity of interest among the members. People related to each other in the terminals.

Local 810, on the other hand, was a huge amalgamated local. At one time it had 15,000 members. They were scattered throughout New York, Connecticut, and New Jersey. There were something like 170 contracts, representing all sorts of workers: immigrant workers, steel warehouses, something called the wire display industry, trucking, chemicals, small manufacturing, metal stamping, warehousing. This local picked up anyone who walked, as long as you were breathing and there was more than one of you. It seemed an impossible task to figure out who was a member.

The guy who ran this local had founded it above a garage on the Lower East Side. He had eyes and ears in all 170 shops in the system. He had a massive control mechanism. Even if you developed a base in five shops, forget about it. When there were meetings, a flood of people would come in from all over the metropolitan area who knew this guy.

At that time my interest was to learn as much as I could about organizing. I needed to figure out how I could apply in the labor milieu the things that I had already learned about organizing as an activist. That was my focus.

Every business agent in Local 810 was required to organize. There were staff meetings held once a week. The old man would go around the room and say, "What are you working on now?" If somebody said he wasn't working on anything, they'd get rid of him. That place was the biggest revolving door I've ever seen in my life. They'd hire people, give them a stack of cards, and wouldn't let them have more than a month to start bringing people in. In order to get a raise, you had to bring in a shop. There were no automatic increases. In fact, you could never consider yourself a permanent employee. If you stopped organizing you were gone.

I was building lists of contacts. Whoever I met I took their name and home phone number, and I wrote down the place where they worked. I figured, "All right. I now have a contact in this plant." Even though nothing was going on at this moment, I would call these people regularly, just to talk.

I worked like a dog, early mornings, midnight shifts, traveling in my own car. Eventually I started hitting some small, 25- or 30-person shops in Brooklyn. I'd meet with one or two people on the street. Then I'd say, "Let's meet down the block at the diner, later, when work is over." They'd bring a few more people. And I'd say, "So all right, you've got to bring more people to a meeting."

They'd ask me, "So how do we bring the union in? What's it going to take?" Then I would tell people, "There's an easy way of doing it or a hard way. Which way do you want to do it?" And I would say, "The hard way is to file for an election. It would take so–and–so many weeks to do this. Then it may take so–and–so many months to do that. In all probability it will take six months to bring in this union."

Everybody would go, "Oh my God! That's too long. We'll never be able to hold out. What's the other way?" I framed it in the simplest terms. "Well, the other way is we get everybody to sign up secretly, right, and they designate a committee to represent people on the inside. We go see the boss the next morning, at the morning break. We walk in with a recognition demand." Local 810's recognition demand was unique because it asked the employer not only to recognize the local, but to agree to the pension plan, the health and welfare plan, binding arbitration, union security, and a couple of other things. They'd say, "Let's do it the easy way."

I would tell them to meet me the next morning on the street in front of the place, or on the corner, at break time. Then I usually got in touch with another guy in the local, so there'd be a couple of us to go in there with the committee. And we'd march into the boss's office with the committee, and say, "Mr. So–and–So, we represent Teamsters Local 810. We represent a majority of the employees of this place. This is the committee right here." I'd have the committee introduce themselves. "This is the recognition demand. We'd like you to sign it today." Sometimes we'd give him till the end of the day, but more often we'd give him till the following morning.

Only once did the boss sign it then and there. In most cases the boss would say, "I have to contact my attorney." At break time the following morning, we'd go into the office with the committee once again, and ask to see the boss. "What's your answer?" "No. Go file for an election." We'd look at the committee and say, "All right. Everybody out." And everybody would walk out and set up the picket line.

The strikes took three hours to six weeks. We stayed out until a contract was signed and ratified. We won 80 percent of them, I'd say. These were small companies of 25 to 200 people.

The strikes we lost were where it became a personal thing for the boss. It didn't matter if his house burned down, he was not going to sign. There was a guy who owned a scaffolding outfit in Staten Island. We had the whole place out. We demolished his whole company, trashed his whole operation, destroyed all his trucks, smashed his car. I've always insisted that no one should ever get hurt, but as to property, let it rip! But the boss took the position, "Never."

The theory was that we needed to remove the people from the workplace, where the boss could meet with them day in and day out and work on them through captive audience meetings. If you brought people on the street, you thereby put them in the union's hands. The only thing left to the boss was to send supervisors out and try to convince people to go back to work.

Our message to the people was, "We're never going to win this just by walking up or down." In an urban setting it's much more feasible to carry on a street war. People duck into subways. There are all sorts of nooks and crannies, places where people have to walk, turn corners. It's conducive to urban guerrilla warfare. On a minor scale, that's what would occur.

The organizing was very secretive. We never handed out leaflets or flyers. We never wore union insignia. I would dress in jeans, flannel shirt, Army jacket, work shoes or sneakers, and just talk to people on the street. I looked like anybody else walking around who might work in the area.

The willingness to strike was a powerful message to people. Today a lot of union people say, "Don't talk about strikes. It's not a very popular thing." At that time all we talked about was strikes. The strike translated into the message, "There's some willingness to fight back here. There's some chutzpah to take on the boss."

The First Overnite Campaign

I got to know Vicki Saporta, the director of organizing for the Teamsters, when I was organizing for Local 810. Way back in the early 1980s I had mentioned to her that I would love to work on a national organizing campaign for the Teamsters. In the fall of 1989 she told me that the union was gearing up for a national campaign against Overnite Transportation, the largest non-union LTL [Less than Truck Load] trucking outfit in the country. Eventually I got a call from Vicki, saying to come to a meeting in Washington. This was in April 1990. After the meeting, I was told that I was hired.

Between the time of that meeting and the day I started, Vicki Saporta was taken off the campaign. A guy from Ohio was put in charge who was one of Jackie Presser's ex-bodyguards.

I was told that my location would be the Carolinas. I had never been there. I came from New York, and there were Overnite terminals in New York and New Jersey that I could have handled. I found out later that nobody knew who I was; everybody was suspicious. Everybody else was related to somebody or had some connection to the Old Guard. So I think they figured, "Let's give him the worst location in the entire system." I said to myself, "This didn't turn out the way I thought. But what the hell, let me give this a shot."

I was assigned with two other guys. Talk about pork! One was the husband of the daughter of Roy Williams, a former Teamsters president. He was the sleaziest Old Guard pork chopper I had ever met in my life, second only to the other guy, who was classified as an international organizer. He'd been on staff for fifteen years. If he had ever worked a day in his life I would be shocked.

Technically the three of us were equals, but each of these guys reported to someone else at headquarters. I remember having a discussion with them about, "Well, here we are, what shall we do?" I suggested getting some names and phone numbers of Overnite drivers in the area. The guy who was related to Roy Williams said, "You gotta understand. This is the Carolinas. First you have to get to know these people. You can't meet with them. You can't phone them." I said, "How do we get to know them?" He said, "We'll go in front of the gate and eventually over the course of time they'll recognize you, and that's how they'll get to know you."

I said, "Jesus Christ, this doesn't seem too sound." We were going to go in front of the gate, without having made any connection inside the terminal, thereby notifying management immediately that we're there. What made him think that anyone would seriously talk to us in front of the terminal? He said, "That's the way you do it down here."

Then I got a call from the guy who was running the campaign. He said, "Look, this guy you're working with knows exactly what he's doing. He's got a lot of experience. Follow his lead."

We didn't even begin by going in front of the terminal. He said the first thing we had to do was to get into a car, park near the terminal, stay there from six in the morning until nine at night, and count how many trucks were coming and going throughout the day. We did it. I said, "What are we gaining from doing this?" He said, "We're getting to know the area." He insisted that we do this at three other Overnite locations.

Then something happened. Some guy in the Northeast dives into a garbage can some place, and we get a master list of all the Overnite employees throughout the entire system. The three of us received a list of about 2500 employees in the Carolinas. I said, "Wow! We can housecall everybody."

These two guys refused to do it. They said, "They'll shoot you down dead. You'll never get past the front door. This is the South." One of them came from the West Coast, the other one from Kansas City.

So I started housecalling myself. The door always opened. I went around housecalling for five months in Charlotte and the surrounding rural area. As it turned out, there was not a great deal of support for the union. But I felt that these were good conversations. This was the first time that anyone from the union had even communicated with people.

The whole national campaign turned into a disaster. Only fifteen to eighteen full-time organizers worked on it. They were not serious. They were golfers. None of the local unions were on board. All the literature cranked out for the campaign came from national headquarters. It was totally top–down. After six or seven months, only 15 percent of the workforce was signed up, and the international called it off.

I got a complete bird's eye view of what the international was all about. It was a wholly bogus operation. There was no grassroots anything. There was no committee-building. All the ingredients for a successful organizing drive were missing.

I went back to my old job at Local 810. There seemed to be big changes coming in the Teamsters, and I had a premonition that someday I would be back there. Instinctively I knew that in order to do that you had to come out of a Teamster local.

The Second Overnite Campaign

After Ron Carey got into office I got a call from Vicki Saporta, and I was hired again. I came on board as one of four organizing coordinators. I had the Eastern region.

Vicki Saporta's idea was that applicants for organizer should go through a three-day screening at the Organizing Institute. I had serious doubts about this way of judging people. After the election, there were many rank-and-file Teamsters who had worked hard in the Carey cam-

paign who applied for a job as organizer. They couldn't make it through
the Organizing Institute! Vicki Saporta's view was that an organizer had
to be able to travel into any area and function anywhere. That meant being apolitical. You had to have all the skills, but organizing took place at a
local union level, so you had to be able to work with all the locals. In order to be able to work with the locals, the locals could not perceive you as
a political operative. That was the basis of her recruitment of organizers.

My first involvement with the Organizing Institute had actually come
before the first Overnite campaign. It was the first or second three-day session that the Institute ran.

I criticized it based on the following incident. A guy came to the session
whom AFSCME [American Federation of State, County and Municipal
Employees] was considering hiring in Montana. He was a huge man. He
had worked in the Laborers for many years. He did organizing all over
Montana. He was involved with some bloody strikes. His life was threatened. He took on a corrupt local union and ran as a reform candidate. He
had dynamite thrown at him. He was a middle-aged guy. They rejected
him! The ones they accepted were Ivy League kids with little or no workplace experience. And I said, "Wait a minute! What about this guy from
Montana?" I was told, "He can't communicate." I said, "Here's a guy who
spent half his life fighting for the union movement. And he's dodged bul-
lets. He was part of a reform movement in a local. And you're saying he
can't cut it?" I felt that there were serious class problems, serious cultural
problems in the evaluation process. I felt the program was doing a disser-
vice to the labor movement.

So I had to go through this OI [Organizing Institute] process again as a
Teamster coordinator. There was a young woman from western Pennsylvania. She was a mother of several children, she had just become politicized, and was so thirsty for political involvement. I went to bat for her. I
said, "This woman is a gem." They shot her down. Not only did they
shoot her down, but what they would do, they would have exit interviews
in which they told people, "The labor movement is not for you." I felt that
this was evil.

Dozens and dozens of rank-and-file activists were rejected as organizers.
I came to hate those sessions. It seemed to me the judgments and evalua-
tions were so arbitrary. I had learned organizing on the job. I didn't learn
it by having an instinct for organizing. I learned it by doing it.

In February 1996 I got the assignment of coordinating the Overnite
campaign. I thought a great deal about what needed to be done. I figured,
first, that the number of people working on the campaign had to expand.
Second, we had to build an army of organizers who came out of the ranks.
We had to identify rank-and-file freight activists from local unions around
the country, because I thought it was important that people come out of
the industry, that they know the language of freight, that they could walk

it and talk it. So I recruited about thirty people by speaking to local union officers in freight locals and to other people around the country. As a way of leveraging resources out of the freight locals, we had to make sure that the principal officers of the locals supported the organizers who were being hired.

Finally, part of the job of these organizers was to cultivate leadership among the rank-and-file Overnite employees. We had to build an activist list. The role of the organizer would be to support and provide resources to organizing campaigns that Overnite employees would be engaged in. This could not be looked at as a top–down organizing program. There were 170-odd terminals. We were doing a long march through the terminals, one by one.

This is a very different thing from the blitz model. We don't believe in the blitz model. We don't believe in parachuting folks in from somewhere else to run a fast-paced program. Somebody referred to blitz organizing as "junk bond organizing." We believe that the freight industry is going to be organized by members in freight.

A Struggle for Citizenship

Union organizing ultimately is a struggle for democracy and also a struggle for citizenship. That theme rings very strongly for these Overnite guys. I've found that if we engage people around the fact that we live in a country with a Constitution and a Bill of Rights, that our parents have gone off to wars for certain things, that we have something called the American flag, the struggle becomes: Whose flag is that? Does it belong to the CEOs, the corporations, or is it the flag of the people?

Some Overnite workers are Latino, African American, women, but they are predominantly white male workers. If you look at all the things that have been coming out of the AFL-CIO recently, the AFL-CIO has been talking about organizing immigrants, women, African Americans. They don't mention organizing the white male worker. They've given up on him. Here we have a campaign that is seriously engaged in organizing white guys across the country, *with* blacks and Hispanics. Most of our victories have been in the South.

The voting patterns of white males in this country have been becoming steadily more conservative. We have to stop saying that white guys don't mean anything any more. They are a serious voting bloc. It's either we organize them into unions or we lose them.

Hugo Hernandez

"Instead of letting me go out alone, they went with me"

Hugo Hernandez worked at the Overnite terminal in Miami during the national organizing campaign described by Gary Stevenson. He tells the Overnite organizing story from the bottom up. Hugo Hernandez decided to side with the union rather than to become a foreman. Later he became chief steward for the terminal, and later still, a full-time organizer.

The union's strategy at Overnite was to seek recognition in one terminal at a time, then to negotiate a national collective bargaining agreement. The result was that terminals where the union was recognized early in the campaign might go for years without a contract. Organizers had to figure out a way to help Overnite members build their own unions inside those terminals. The union had to demonstrate that you can win victories without a contract. Hugo Hernandez tells how he used the statutory right to have a union representative present when a member fears discipline to overcome the absence of contractual protection.

Hugo Hernandez shared his story, on both audio and audio-visual tape, at the Highlander Research and Education Center in April 1997. Those narratives have been supplemented by his remarks at a conference on "solidarity unionism" held at the hall of Teamsters Local 377 in Youngstown, Ohio, in June 1998.

I was born in El Salvador, in the city of San Salvador. I came over to the United States when I was about four years old because of the civil war. That was in 1971.

My mother was concerned about the civil war, and she and my father were having problems. So she came to Los Angeles and started a life for herself, thinking that she could bring all of us children after she settled down, which she did. She moved from LA to Miami, came back, and brought four of us to Miami. She left three of my brothers with my father and one of my other brothers in Costa Rica. Later on—she is a strong woman—she was able to bring everybody over to the United States.

As far as I can tell my family never had anything to do with unions. Everything I know about unions came from the Overnite organizing campaign, during the past two, two and a half years [1995–1997].

Organizing Overnite: The First Time

I was employed by Overnite for about eleven years as a city driver. We tried to organize the first time around 1990. I wasn't one of the leaders in that first campaign.

At first I was very skeptical about the Teamsters union. There was the stigma of mob influence, and corruption, and sellouts. I wasn't that well in tune with unions at the time. I had a lot of questions before I was going to get involved.

We had a meeting with union officials. There wasn't any organizing. It was "sneak around, don't say nothing, sign cards." We didn't know anything about organizing, about unionism, about solidarity. We did as we were told. We signed the cards. A man came out to the gate a few times. After those few times he was nowhere to be seen.

Two weeks later about ten guys got fired. We put two and two together, and figured out what had happened. We had enough cards, over 60 percent. But something went wrong. Somebody got bought off. Some people were fingered. Others got promotions. We saw that we were going to be on our own.

Trying Again

Five years later we had a big overturn. Guys would get fired for just about any reason, guys who were family-oriented. That was one of the first things that led me to come forward as maybe a leader in this movement.

I was working in the office at the time. I was what you call a "lead man," who helps the supervisors. Because of that nobody trusted me. But I was getting some reliable information to them, underground.

We called the international union. They sent a lady in by the name of Doreen Gasman. This was around February 1995.

The campaign became visible in March, about three weeks before the election. When we filed we had about 65–70 percent. I was still underground, still getting information from inside. We got an election date. I came to work the next day in a Teamster shirt and a Teamster hat.

This was one week before they were going to send me to supervisor school. I weighed everything. I made my decision. As a result, I took a pay cut. I was going to make more as a supervisor. I was going to have more benefits. But I didn't think that I was fit to be a supervisor because of my way of thinking. I saw that I would have to be a robot, and think the way they thought. I wouldn't have my own thoughts and opinions. It wouldn't have worked out for me.

So I gave up what they had offered, and came out in my Teamster shirt and hat as a show of solidarity, to show that I was going to help in the campaign, physically now, instead of undercover as before. At the time there were only three or four guys wearing shirts.

I walked down the dock. It was funny, because my knees started shaking. I was very scared. It was the first experience that I had. But it was something that we as a committee, supporting one another, thought we should do. My fear was the fear that every worker in the campaign went through, and had to overcome.

The company offered us all kinds of positions in Richmond, tried to buy us off, tried to scare us. But after a while it began to feel real good. I started being very vocal, and investigating, and bringing Doreen Gasman some of my ideas.

Solidarity

We were divided in our terminal. The divisions were between races. We had blacks, Anglos, and Spanish. The Spanish had the highest percentage.

The organizing committee saw that right away, and we went to the leaders of each group. We told them that we needed their support, that if we didn't come together as one we were not going to win this. This was right before the election.

The reaction was good. People voiced their concerns about stuff that was going on that they didn't like. Some of the blacks and Anglos didn't like it that some of the Spanish guys spoke Spanish around them. So we went to the Spanish and said, "We have to curtail this. They feel that they're being left out. They don't understand, and sometimes they feel threatened. To win this election, we need to cooperate."

All three groups came to be represented on the committee. Even to this day, we have a black shop steward, an Anglo shop steward, and [in April 1997] I am the chief steward. When the company sees us together they think twice about firing someone. During the process we became very aggressive, very focused. We knew our limits but we knew that we had to confront management to win the campaign. They were doing a lot of one-on-ones. They were doing a lot of backroom deals.

We had our game plan. But if somebody in your workplace all of a sudden is in trouble, you don't look at the game plan and say, "What do I do?" You look at what's right, at direct action, inside. When there was something wrong we would start going after it until we fixed it. One person's problem became everybody's problem. It wasn't just one person any more. We gained a lot of respect that way.

For instance, during a critical part of the campaign a lot of supervisors from different places came in: the CEO, the vice president, the regional vice president. They were targeting our weak link, seven or eight workers who handled the inbound freight at night.

They decided to come in one afternoon and stay all night. They would help the guys on the dock unload their freight. They were trying to buy these guys, to put them up on a pedestal and make them feel, All of a sudden you mean something to us.

We didn't have any strong leaders in this unit. Most of our strong leaders were city drivers. So we decided that in the morning we had to do something.

What were we going to do? We decided to march in with the American flag. We made up some signs real quick that said, "OUR DIGNITY, OUR HONOR NOT FOR SALE."

We started with a group of I'd say twenty. They were gung ho. We walked in, and when we got to the steps going up to the building, there were about ten minutes left before work. Management was right in plain view. Our guys got weak in the knees. They said, "Oh Hugo, we're going to get fired. Let's just do it some other time." I said, "No, these guys need us now. These guys can't wait for tomorrow. The damage was done last night. We must act now."

I took the flag, and I started to march. There were two guys who saw that I was going to do it alone, and instead of letting me go out alone, they went with me. One of the guys was who did it Avelino Gonzales, a guy who was so quiet, who never spoke out. But when he saw that I was going to go up there by myself, he grabbed a sign. Another guy, Pedro Perez, grabbed a sign also. They walked with me.

The three of us proceeded down the dock, holding these signs, walking very, very slowly. We marched with pride, saying, "Guys, we're with you. Stay strong." The guys were looking at us. Everybody was looking at us, like, "They're doing it! They're doing it!" The guys in the trucks turned around as they were working. They smiled, and they applauded.

We went all around the dock and came back, and we were met by management. They were very pissed off. They said, "Why did you do that? You can't be walking down the dock with the flag." I said, "You got something against the flag? It's my flag." They were ticked off that we were holding up production. We said, "We're not holding up production. We were just getting our hand trucks so as to be ready for work." It was something that we weren't supposed to do, but we did it. It was a little thing, but we felt that we had to do it, to give support.

We went on a roller coaster. Sometimes the company would gain ground. Sometimes we would gain ground. We were always trying to stay one step ahead of them.

One morning they were all standing there: the vice president, the head of human resources, the terminal manager. About fifteen of us went right up to them on the dock, where everybody could see us from the break room. We formed a circle. We held hands—these were grown men—and we got our heads down. A black preacher, Keith Davis, started giving a prayer. The prayer was, "We need strength, God. Please Lord, give us strength to go through this." It was good.

The big shots were right there. They didn't know what to do. They didn't know how to react. How were they going to fight God and the American flag?

The workers were determined, and finally we won the election by a 2 to 1 margin, 42 to 20.

Winning and Weingarten

After we won the NLRB election, we found that the terminal manager was just as lost as we were about labor laws. I think that by playing a bluffing game with the terminal manager, and using the support that we had with our people, we put him in a position where he was afraid to make a move.

Here is how we used our *Weingarten* rights.[1] We saw that Overnite would appeal things, and take every case to the extreme, so we tried to go to the extreme even in the smallest things.

For instance, when I was fighting on behalf of somebody, I would go into the manager's office and ask for the write-up. He would give me a copy of the write-up, I would then go to the worker, and we would talk about the write-up as long as we wanted: 45 minutes, an hour. We established the right to do this.

Once the worker and I had established our strategy, our game plan, we would go into the terminal manager's office. Instead of having a closed meeting, we would leave the door wide open so everybody could hear what was going on. We would bring people in to witness, so it was almost like a court. Workers were waiting around to see what was going to happen. We purposefully got into loud conversations so that everyone in that part of the terminal could hear.

When we got to a point where we needed to ask a question to the worker, we wouldn't ask it in front of the terminal manager. We would ask

1. In *NLRB v. Weingarten, Inc.,* 420 U.S. 251 (1975), the Supreme Court held that in a workplace where a union has been recognized, an employee whom management seeks to interview and who reasonably fears that the interview may lead to discipline, has a right to request the presence of a union representative.

to caucus. One day the terminal manager said, "Wait a minute. You're asking to caucus? This is ridiculous." So we said to him, "Are you denying us our right to caucus?" He thought about it. He said, "Wait a minute. I'll be right back." So he went inside his office and called the company attorney. He must have been in there fifteen minutes. He came back and said, "Go ahead and caucus."

So we went outside and caucused. And we took a *long* time. We did it on purpose. The management guys were standing around, waiting for us to come back in. They didn't want to disrupt us. They wanted to make sure that whatever they did, they did right.

We finally went back in. I think they just wanted to give this guy a verbal warning! But I stuck to the position, you have to prove this to me and that to me. Finally the manager said, "Look, just forget about it. Just go to work."

We did that even with a verbal warning, even if the supervisor only wanted to ask him a question. We took it to the extreme, because when we got into a situation that was more severe, they were going to think about it. They were going to say, "Wow, they gave us a rough time for a verbal warning. Imagine if we really want to go after somebody!" So we didn't have write-ups in that terminal for years.

Without a contract, you can establish a grievance system on the basis of past practice. From before the election, we would take notes on how they treated their pets, the company supporters. We compiled a master list, so I could defend the pro-union guys on the basis of disparate treatment. If one of my guys was going to be written up, I would have everything there to defend him.

We filed our own NLRB charges. During the time that we were organizing, the local union went through three trustees. We were forced to fight on our own, because when a new leadership came in they were not familiar with our cases.

Our steward is involved in every negotiation. He has a right to speak, like everybody else on the committee. He even has a right to question the union.

This is the democracy that has come about. Whenever there is a new leadership in our local, they have to come to the leadership of that barn in order to get guidance.

Getting Fired

I got fired in 1995 after the election. The inbound workers were getting picked on. They were being written up. I confronted management. I was able to resolve a lot of issues, but the terminal manager thought that when he wanted something in return, I wouldn't give it to him.

I filed against him with the NLRB for retaliation against the inbound guys. I started putting a case together. I'd been given access to the files, and one Friday I told the supervisor, "I need some information." He called his immediate supervisor, the assistant manager. The assistant manager got me on the phone and said, "What's going on?" I said, "Well, you know what's been happening here, the manager has been retaliating against the inbound guys, and we need some documentation to build the case." He said, "Well, Hugo, do what you gotta do. No problem. Go ahead and get what you need." I gave the phone back to the supervisor, and the assistant manager told the supervisor the same thing.

The door was wide open, the supervisor was right there, everybody was looking at me going through the records. I was there for two, three hours. I saw that the brothers on inbound had been working there for seven or eight years with no write-ups, and all of a sudden you see a rash of write-ups. So I had what I needed. I took it, made copies of it, and went home.

This was a Friday. Monday morning I came in to work and the same supervisor that gave me the authorization said, "The terminal manager wants to see you." I went inside and the manager said, "Look, I understand you went through the files, and you didn't get my authorization." I said, "I got the assistant manager's." The assistant manager didn't say a word. The manager said, "I don't care, you didn't get mine. You're fired."

I left. The guys asked me what was going on. It was very excited in the terminal, very emotional.

I went to my house. I called the organizer. We immediately filed an NLRB charge.

We told the workers we would meet early the next morning outside the terminal, at 5:30, 6 AM. They all showed up. Everybody was wearing their union shirts. We gathered them around, and explained what was going on. They rallied around me. They gave me a lot of support. It really touched me.

We turned that place upside down. We disrupted the radio transmissions of the dispatchers, jamming their system. We got a lot of drivers and their spouses to call in bogus pickups from different customers, and tied up the lines. The company had to bring back freight.

Volunteer activists who had helped us in the election campaign came out again. Their friends came out. Truckers from all over the community would park in front of the terminal before going to work. People from different unions would come and rally with us, the workers would stay out after work and rally.

We marched inside with petitions demanding my reinstatement. The second time we marched into the manager's office, the security guard padlocked the gate behind us and called the police. When we came out, we climbed over the barbed wire fence. The police were lined up. It was a very hostile situation.

We had a big rally every day. There were five or six police cars there each morning. All of a sudden the FBI began showing up. They started taking pictures of people.

We disrupted the company's operations so much that we backed up fifty, sixty trailers a night. They felt it. They didn't know what to do with the freight coming down from West Palm Beach. They were holding freight up in Atlanta. You had the customers complaining, the salespeople complaining.

The IBT sent down organizers, including Doreen Gasman, who had left after the election. Together they put out faxes to all the other Overnite places about what was going down in Miami. Joe Reeves [a rank and filer] in Atlanta rallied their bunch.

We threatened to go out on an unfair labor practice strike. We took a strike vote, by secret ballot, out on the picket line to make sure the company would know about it. Only one guy was against it. After the vote, we went ahead and planned the strike.

Monday is the heaviest day of the week. Three weeks after I was fired, and two days before the Monday when they thought we were going to go on strike, the company settled. Their lawyer faxed a letter to us Saturday morning. (You know, lawyers for a corporation don't work on Saturdays.) He faxed us an agreement from his office that same morning, saying they would reinstate me with full back pay, take it off my record, everything. I was the first person ever fired by Overnite who came back to work with full back pay. And the managers who were responsible were fired.

We all walked back in solidarity. Everyone was behind me when I went back to work. There was a police officer in front of me, as an escort.

The Productivity Package

In 1996 the company introduced the "productivity package." The package stated that all the terminals in the company would receive a wage increase, but they would have to accept this productivity agreement, which was to reclassify you, to change your starting times, to bring in sub-contracting, and so on and so on that the company wanted to do. They presented it to the national bargaining committee. We said, "The past practice is to grant wage increases with no strings attached. That is the status quo. Why should we give up our rights to get a wage increase?" So we didn't accept it. We told the Teamsters we didn't want to do it, and filed an unfair labor practice charge.

The company tried to sell us the agreement. We got a letter from Overnite CEO Leo Suggs saying that he wanted to visit us, and talk to us about this "interim agreement." He came down. We were ready for him with a petition from former employees of his at a company called Ryder P.I.E. (Pacific Intermountain Express). Back in the early 1980s, Suggs had convinced them to buy a productivity package, and some of those workers lost $25,000 during a five-year period.

Leo Suggs came in. All of our guys were wearing stickers that said, "Blow on this dot until it turns blue, and all the company promises will come true." Here he was introducing himself to everybody, and they were all wearing the sticker. This was a very loud sticker, bright yellow, bright red. The dot was black.

After he greeted everybody, he walked down to the room where we were going to have the meeting. He waited for us. We stopped everybody. Our stewards got the big banner that said, "Overnite Teamster. An Injury to One is an Injury to All." About forty of us gathered behind the flag, all wearing the stickers, and we marched down, synchronized, to greet him. Our guys put the banner against the wall without saying anything, and we sat down, and the meeting continued. It was very successful. He lost a lot of credibility.

This has been a long struggle. At our terminal, and at other terminals where the union has been recognized, the people utilize the Labor Board,[2] they utilize the local union, they utilize spontaneous solidarity actions to get the job done. When you put together all these things you have a better environment at your workplace. You're not dependent on your local union, so that every time you have a problem you call up your business agent. You take it upon yourself to address the questions at your workplace.

We emplace committees. Even when we lose, we don't lose. Because why? When we leave there, even if we lost the election, we have established democracy, we have established a sense of empowerment through those committees, through the education process, through the bonding of brotherhood, the bonding of doing solidarity actions and depending on one another.

Back in 1994 Overnite was one of the least well paid companies in the non-union LTL [Less than Truck Load] industry. That all changed when this campaign started. Overnite had the question, How are we going to stop this drive? They started giving raises, they started raising benefits. We've won about $2.55 an hour in the last three years and increased pensions, even without a contract.

Looking into the Future

I've been fired by this company two times. I've been put in jail by this company. I'm on top of the hit list. It's a tough fight. Sometimes you find yourself not only fighting the corporation, but also fighting your own union.

I'm twenty-nine years old. I have no clear vision of the future. Right now, it's really a gamble. I'm probably blackballed from every trucking outfit in Miami, maybe the country. I'm doing this just in belief, in faith, that something good will come from it.

2. At the Overnite terminal in Milwaukee, the company changed the prices of snacks in the snack machine. The workers charged that this was a unilateral change! Overnite restored the old prices.

Kay Eisenhower

"Certain folks call me a permanent rank and filer"

Daughter of an airline pilot, Kay Eisenhower was born in Texas and lived as a child in Guatemala, New York, and Florida, before moving to California when she was in her teens. She was very active in the Methodist Church as she was growing up.

Kay Eisenhower became a feminist and carried feminist values into her organizing with hospital workers. This meant "a lot of solidarity and sisterhood" and also a commitment to do whatever it took to make it possible for women with children to function fully. It meant a unionism that sought community support, rather than going it alone. And it meant "collective decision-making, trying to build a group and to get away from reliance on a particular person."

For twenty-five years Kay Eisenhower has been a rank-and-file member of a local union of public employees in Oakland, California. Presently she works as a part-time reference librarian for the main branch of the Alameda County Public Library.

We interviewed Kay Eisenhower at her home in Oakland in August 1998.

Movements

When I was a sophomore at Stanford University in late 1962, I got kicked out because I became pregnant. (They don't do that any more.) It was a major experience in my life. It got me out of Stanford, which I've always felt was a really good thing. The child was adopted out.

Next I went to San Jose State College, where I met my first husband. San Jose was a very different environment from Stanford. By and large the classes were smaller. Professors socialized with students: we'd go out drinking on Friday nights. A lot of education went on outside the class room.

By then I had left the church, and begun to get involved in Left activity on campus. I was in the Student Peace Union. My husband and I went to Selma to march with Martin Luther King in 1965.

We came to Berkeley for my husband to do graduate work, and I completed my senior year at the University of California—Berkeley in 1965–1966. That was the year after the Free Speech Movement. I jumped right in. We were particularly involved in anti-Vietnam War stuff.

In 1967 there were a series of anti-war marches when the cops beat people up, brutally. I didn't get beaten. But I was in a group kneeling on the pavement, and I remember seeing a comrade come toward me with blood streaming down his face. I've never forgotten. It was Stop the Draft Week. After that came People's Park in 1969. It was one thing after another.

My husband and I joined the Independent Socialists (I.S.) together in 1967. He left the fold because of a disagreement. I stayed in much longer and helped to manage its newspaper, *The Independent Socialist.*

My husband and I got divorced in 1970 after we had a child. I spent a while being the office manager for the I.S. I would work at the office in the afternoons. The I.S. paid for child care for my son.

I became more and more involved in the women's movement. I was a single mother, and all the issues of being on welfare, a father who couldn't pay much in the way of child support because he was a student, control over my body, happened to me immediately. I was celibate for a while, but I ended up getting pregnant when my IUD failed, and needed an abortion. I was able to get one, but I had first to see a psychiatrist and get him to say that I would go nuts if I had the child, which I wasn't happy about doing.

It was obvious that even in an organization as committed to internal democracy as the I.S. was, it was men who by and large were the leadership. I found it more comfortable to be in an all-female group.

The feminist organization that I worked with primarily was the Oakland Women's Liberation Group. Several comrades from I.S. worked in that group but it was not itself a socialist organization. There were a lot of women who had similar problems. There was a lot of support, a lot of solidarity and sisterhood. We were committed to doing whatever it took to make it possible for women with children to function fully.

I carried this into clerical organizing. It was what I knew. Why would I do anything differently? In the Oakland Women's Liberation Group I met the other women who eventually went to work with me at Highland Hospital. The Oakland Women's Liberation Group had various collectives within it, one of which was called the health collective. That's where my two friends came from. They were focused on women's health issues. We became the core of the hospital organizing committee.

Going to Work for the County

Berkeley had a wonderful pre-school system, cheap and very well organized. My son could get in when he was three. So I started looking for
work.

I.S. was sending people to work in certain fields, but I had a child and I
was single. I was too short for United Parcel Service. They had a height requirement, and I'm under five feet. I didn't see how I could manage doing
shift work at the auto plant and still give my son the attention he needed.
I wanted to work as much as possible in an 8:30 to 5:00 environment. It
was logical to look for work with Alameda County.

I took the entry-level clerical exam at the hospital. I was hired in December 1971 to do hospital billing. Marnie and Ellen, the other two
women who had been in Oakland Women's Liberation, came soon after.
They ended up in direct care jobs. One of them worked in the clinic.

Almost immediately it became obvious that the thing for us to do was to
organize a union. Ellen's husband had been a long-time activist in the office workers' union at Kaiser. It was apparent that there were a lot of
things wrong, and clerks had common complaints.

There was an old employees' association. Like most employees' associations, they basically did legislative lobbying and trips. It was male-domi-
nated and pro-management.

There were three locals of the Service Employees International Union
(SEIU) already in the county. They had carved it up, depending on which
local came to which part of the county first. The employees' association
had about half the county, and the three SEIU locals had most of the rest.

SEIU was one of the more progressive trade unions and had come out
against the Vietnam War. So we knew people in SEIU, or knew of them.
Initially we worked mainly with SEIU Local 535, the social workers'
union. SEIU decided to go for a clerical unit that would include about half
of the membership of the employee association.

Clerks' County

We called ourselves "Clerks' County." This [showing it] is one of the issues
of the newsletter by that name that we put out. Marnie, Ellen and I all had
college backgrounds, and movement backgrounds, and women's movement backgrounds, and some acquaintance with socialism. We recruited
other people who were not like us at all. The first two people were my
friend Cathy, who is now a nurse at Highland Hospital, and Pat, who
went on to become an international vice president of SEIU. Cathy was a
white clerk, and definitely from a working-class background. Pat was a
black clerk, and came from a middle-class black background in Oakland.

It was a very interesting combination. It made the group thrive. We really liked having these different backgrounds, and teaching each other different kinds of things.

Then those five eventually recruited another three people, one of whom was a male, the only male we were ever involved with for very long. He ended up in the October League, a Maoist organization. And at one time or other there were a lot of other women, mainly clerical people, who were involved with us.

SEIU assigned us an organizer, a former member of I.S. We said, "sure," but we wanted sole control over our newsletter. They agreed. We didn't realize that this was somewhat unusual.

We were supposed to have a bargaining unit election for the clericals in the spring of 1973. It was quite clear that we were going to win. The association had nothing going. Our people were really excited. Until then, nobody was doing clerical organizing. We got interviews. We were in books. We were on TV.

We focused both on issues broader than the workplace and on specific workplace issues. People in one unit used to have to turn in a used pencil before they could get a new one; we would write about things like that. There were a lot of problems with the clerical job descriptions. There were pay issues. There were more dignity and respect issues than anything else. A lot of single women needed to take care of their children when the children were sick. There were issues around discrimination, lots of problems with management favoritism.

We had a great group. We had international union support. But SEIU, typically, did not trust its rank-and-file members to do the right thing. Behind our backs, they negotiated an affiliation with the employees' association.

SEIU could have come to us and said, "You guys have done a great job. And because you're going to win, the association wants to come over altogether. Then we wouldn't just have the clerical unit, we'd have the nurses and everybody. Wouldn't that be swell?" We probably would have said, "Well, yeah. We just want to get a few things nailed down first."

But they never had enough respect for us even to ask us. We had a big meeting after the fact. A representative from the international told us that the affiliation was settled, and we could not have our election.

So here we had this warmed-over association calling itself Local 616. There were non-bargaining unit managers on the executive board. There was the same old rinky-dink staff. But they were very motivated to integrate us. They put me on the bargaining team in 1973. Most of us became stewards. For a year or so they let us use the union's mimeograph machine. And that's where we made our first important decision. They wanted us to make "Clerks' County" the official newsletter of the clerical bargaining unit. We said, "No thank you. It's ours, and we'll keep publishing it."

We spent the next few years trying to turn this warmed-over association into a real union. Our instrument for doing that was "Clerks' County." We had been an SEIU organizing committee for an election. Now we became, and called ourselves, an organized caucus within the new union.

The 1975 Contract Campaign and 1976 Strike

We were able to force them to do a number of things that made the organization more open. In 1975 we were leaders in an incredible worksite campaign in support of the SEIU locals that were bargaining together for a new contract. Three SEIU locals were involved: Local 250, which had a number of hospital people; Local 535, with social workers, eligibility technicians and mental health therapists; and Local 616, with everybody else—RNs, technicians, clericals, professionals.

We spent seven or eight months preparing for a strike. Our contract was to expire in June, and we started in November to build worksite committees. We did a zillion worksite meetings, signing people up as if there might be picket duty, getting people to agree to do a number of different things. At the hospital, since we had three shifts, you usually had to have a number of different meetings. We made mini-picket signs with the tongue depressors that are all over a hospital, and half sheets of paper. People would stick them on their desks, or on the bathroom door, or wherever. The one I've got at my desk says, "Justice for part-time workers."

We put on Clifford Odets' play from the 1930s, *Waiting for Lefty,* as a fund-raiser. Rank and filers acted in it. We took ferries to Angel Island. Somebody said the ferry looked like the last boat from Danang, with people hanging off the sides.

We called it the strike support committee. We didn't have much of a strike fund. Under the guise of fund-raising, what we were really doing was organizing. We had a strike vote in 1975 and 1976. Until 1997, part of every field campaign for every contract we've ever had has been at least one twenty-four-hour walkout at the hospital.[1]

---

1. The "Clerks' County" approach is suggested by the following extract from a lead article in one issue:

> We believe that the decisive force in negotiations is the employees themselves. It is the demands we tell our representatives to put forth and how strongly we are willing to back them up with action which will provide the answer to the questions "How much will we get?" and "What will the contract be like? . . ."

> We must be very wary of those in Management, and even more important, those in the Union, who attempt to hide the basis of our strength from us. This is done by placing too much emphasis on the importance of "expert" negotiators, by quietly hinting about our "friends" on the Board of Supervisors, or by building up hopes of Central Labor Council action.

We were acutely aware of the importance of community support. All of us had been involved in movements where you try to work with the community, so naturally, now that we were in unions, we wanted to do the same thing.

This stand unnerved the county so much that they settled in 1975. That year Alameda County public employees got the best public sector settlement in the State of California. What was special from our point of view was that instead of the usual percentage pay increase that gives the higher-paid employees more, we settled for $60 and three per cent. Lower-paid people ended up getting a higher percentage increase. We were pretty proud of that.

And then the next year, 1976, we went on strike. The Board of Supervisors had a very arrogant attitude because of the contract we had won the year before. They thought, "You guys got it last year. You can sit it out this time."

We approached several community organizations. One of the groups was opposed to building a jail in their neighborhood. We had a button that said, "Bread and jobs, not crumbs and jails." We sent delegations various places.

The Central Labor Council was very militant but very old-line, and they were very nervous about these efforts. They said, "To approach the community is a sign of weakness. Labor should be able to do this on its own." We said, "We don't see it that way. We're public sector. We depend on community support." There was no law that permitted California public employees to strike but there was a court decision that said we could. The county never tried to get restraining orders. They did start suing us when we stopped the races at the fairgrounds! That all got settled when the strike got settled.

It was a 49-day strike, the longest public sector strike in the history of California at the time. During the strike, our two supervisory bargaining units decertified. It was a wonderful experience, because it completed the process that we had initiated of trying to turn this old association with a pro-management orientation into a fighting union.

The strike was run by the rank and file. I was chair of a rank-and-file strike council. It met every evening, and made decisions about what to do next.

The guy who is now the head of the Labor Council (he retired subsequent to this interview) was a staff person from my union then. He tells me every year that our 1976 strike taught him the importance of developing community support in labor struggles.

Then in 1978, when Proposition 13 was on the ballot, half the layoffs in the State of California occurred in Alameda County. We formed a labor-community coalition that included community-based, non-profit health services, such as the Asian Health Center and La Clinica de La

Raza, most of whom got money from the county to run their services. We wanted to make sure that we weren't at each other's throats, fighting over the same pot.

Seeking an Organizational Model and a Personal Role

We built a core of progressive persons from all three local unions. We developed bylaws for this tri-local relationship. It consisted of a negotiating committee and a strike support committee. Now it's called "the contract action team": people don't want to use the word "strike" all the time. We haven't had a strike since 1976.

We have had a three-local contract from 1973 to this date. We bargain tri-locally every two or three years. Acting as three locals sometimes feels unworkable. We certainly experience antagonisms, as do our members. At times the locals get tired of being hooked together. Yet we recognized in 1975, "This is the only way we are going to make it." Between the three locals, we have three-quarters of the county's employees. We feel that we all need each other.

John and I got married in 1975. He had come out of the Local 535 rank and file but by then he was employed by the SEIU Joint Council of Northern California as a research person. Our marriage made some of the conservatives in SEIU very nervous. The executive director of my union tried to keep John out of bargaining, because he felt it would enhance my position, and I was already a "red hot" about whom they were very nervous. I had turned down a couple of jobs that SEIU had offered me, or hinted that I could get. I was often the spokesperson of the rank-and-file caucus.

One of the things that drew me to John was that, although he's not a socialist, he has a very pragmatic belief that if it ain't democratic, it don't work. And he's a low-keyed kind of guy; he doesn't have the male ego that you usually see displayed in bargaining, on both sides.

In marrying John I entered a social circle that included a lot of staff, and very few rank and file. I discovered that staff socialize mainly with each other. There were many parties when I was the only rank-and-file person there. And I was only there because of my marriage, not because they thought that I should be included.

So I saw early on the difference between rank-and-file activists and staff. What I noticed first was who staff hung out with. After I thought and read about it a little bit more, I realized how different are the material conditions of the two groups.

I agreed to run for president of Local 616 in 1977. I was the first woman president. In my local all the officers are rank-and-file volunteers who are elected. That's true of many public employee unions. You have a "city manager" model: the local union executive board hires a full-time executive director who in turn hires and supervises full-time field representatives.

We had gotten rid of the conservative executive director. We had hired a close friend of myself and my husband, who worked for Local 535 and had a Left history from Detroit. Son of a gun, within three or four weeks he was making sarcastic comments about "the royal rank and file."

We had one-year terms at that point. Throughout the year I was president, the executive director and I were very close personally and used to go out after most meetings, but there was constant personal pressure on me to do things. I finally said to him, "You're always using our personal relationship to pressure me to do things that I don't agree with." And he said, "Isn't that what friendship's all about?" I said, "I guess not."

I refused to run again. The staff were all trying to get me to run again. I said, "No." I've been secretary several times, vice president several times. I never ran again for the presidency.

It happened with several executive directors. I played a key role in hiring the woman who succeeded my friend, and the man who succeeded her. Each of them was a person I had worked with when they were on staff, and whose work I really liked, and whom I respected. But they became EDs and suddenly there was a loyalty thing. It was hard to disagree without things getting personal. Finally I had the sense to realize, it's not that all these friends are going bad. It has to do with this role. It does something to everybody who gets there.

When I was president I got the bylaws changed to take most of the president's powers away. All the appointment power was transferred to the executive board. This is something I brought from the women's movement: collective decision-making, trying to build a group and to get away from reliance on a particular person. So over the years we have de-fanged the president, and all the officers for that matter. But that in turn has made the officers less powerful in relation to staff.

We're turning to the organizing model. The way it's working out for us, we're trying to train our stewards better so that they take on a lot more of the work that the reps used to do. Stewards got pretty de-skilled in the last ten years. Because I've been there since 1973, I have more skills than most of the stewards and I can do departmental-level grievance hearings by myself.

It isn't just to get the stewards to take servicing work off the backs of the staff. It's to get the stewards to think of themselves as workplace organizers, and to look for organizing solutions to problems for which we used to file grievances, or where there might not be grievable language. Stewards will tell you that most of what people are upset about at work isn't covered by the grievance procedure or by the contract. It has to do with crap like how you get a new pencil.

We used to do a lot of workplace problem-solving in "Clerks' County." One of the things we did back in the 1970s was help to defend the boyfriend of one of our members, who was a black housekeeping service worker. He got into a hassle with a Deputy Sheriff who was stationed at the hospital and who maced him in the elevator.

We organized like crazy. We developed a black caucus, in which I was the token white person. We had press conferences. We mobbed the office of the hospital administrator. None of that would have been possible through the grievance procedure. And even if it had, the grievance procedure only involves the people immediately concerned with the grievance.

We're trying to move beyond the grievance procedure. SEIU says it wants that. Everyone agrees that we need to be more organizing-oriented in our union work, rather than spending 90 percent of a union's resources defending the 3 percent of the work force who get in trouble.

But so far the organizing thrust has come from the top. The national unions have realized that they can't hire enough organizers to organize the unorganized fast enough to keep up with plant closings and everything else. So they have to turn us all into organizers in order for the "organizing model" to work. And they're not going to be able to control everybody. As more and more of this thinking gets around, it's going to be a lot harder for the internationals to keep tabs.

Still Organizing

Labor activists have trained people to believe that the union as an institution can take care of things. The labor movement, in the United States anyway, has taught workers that they can pay their dues and rely on their union staff to take care of their problems. Even though there's a lot of rhetoric that goes in a different direction, I think that most of our members feel that way.

We've done it to ourselves. And then we turn around and blame the members when they don't come to meetings. I hear a lot of complaining about members who don't get involved. But why should they get involved? For years we in the leadership would say that we could not get a decent contract without a strong field campaign. And then the last couple of years we've had weak field campaigns and we still got good contracts. What does that teach our members?

The SEIU international is notorious for grinding up its organizers. It's a terrible employer. Everyone prefers to work for a local union. The locals are still fairly autonomous. But it was wonderful when the locals in Northern California had their own regional research department. You had huge locals like Local 250, with scads of money, and then you had a tiny local up in Napa Valley that needed assistance with negotiations. The whole concept of the joint council was that every local would pay a per capita tax, and the research department would staff the negotiations of unions that were too small to have their own negotiators or research staff. Local 250 saw it as their role to support locals that didn't have the same financial resources.

That got wiped out, because that was building alliances and loyalties between SEIU locals in Northern California. They weren't dependent on the international. Sweeney changed all of that. It used to be that the international would give an organizing subsidy to a local, and the local would hire the organizer. So the local would be in charge. The organizer would be an employee of the local. Now the international often controls the hiring of the organizers. They decide who goes to which local.

For several years we've been organizing homecare workers. It's a difficult jurisdiction. There is one worker per work site. A quarter to a third of the workers turn over every month. They receive only minimum wage. Many are immigrants, and don't speak or read English. It's been an eye-opener for our county local of white-collar, public sector workers. Compared to homecare workers, we're pretty privileged.

We did have a lot of help from the SEIU international. There were a couple of very competent organizers who worked with us. But we also used member resources. SEIU has a program of "every member an organizer," which we have really used. We had special training for member organizers. We set up a workers' center, which did literacy work, helped people get jobs. It's not yet a hiring hall but over the long term that's what they want to get.

Now we have a public authority that is the technical employer in about four different counties in Northern California, and that's who we bargain with. There's no way that full-time union staff could keep up with that kind of work force.

The differences between the homecare workers and more traditional workers in the union are so profound that most of the homecare workers' meetings are quite separate. One of the homecare workers gave a presentation at an SEIU conference. She cried when she talked about what the union means to her. She used to be ashamed of the work that she did.

They put in a lot of volunteer time. They staff the workers' center when they're not working. These are all rank-and-file people doing this. My hope is that, despite the differences, we can import some of that feeling about the importance of being in a union, what it can do for you, what you can do for it, and what we can do for each other.

Summing Up

Certain folks call me, with disdain, a permanent rank and filer. It's obviously not the case that I have refused to take leadership. I have run for office. Most of the time I win, although I have lost occasionally. People can't accuse me of not having done that. Only one of our old clerical caucus has ever gone on staff, and it was a big decision for her, because she knew I wouldn't do it. I explained to her, "I don't want to do it, I'm a socialist, and I don't see going on staff as the way I want to help make changes in this union. But you don't have those politics, and it's something you really want to do, so go for it." Then problems developed with her that were absolutely predictable.

As I said earlier, when I came to Berkeley I was recruited by a socialist group (International Socialists) and was a member for seven years. During that time the group took a turn toward going into basic industry, which I didn't feel able to do, partly because by the time it came up I was a single parent. I felt from at least the Bay Area chapter of I.S. that the focus on basic industry was more important to them than working with women.

I found myself feeling really good about what I was doing in "Clerks' County," as well as grateful for what I had learned in the socialist organization, much of which I was applying. But I felt that my work didn't matter to them and that they weren't really helping me. I found that I was much more comfortable with my new colleagues in the labor movement than with the members of the socialist organization whom I had known for years.

So I quit in 1975. It was friendly. I still participated with I.S. in multi-union and movement-type activities. And then seven years later, I rejoined, mainly because I was so impressed by the project of starting *Labor Notes*, and the intent that it not be controlled by the politics of any socialist organization. That and the labor work that some people were doing in the Teamsters and other unions was very impressive to me. And I found that, as buried as I was in the labor movement, I needed some external pull to keep me from succumbing to the day-to-day pressures of the labor movement. For me that was the socialist organization now called Solidarity. For somebody else it might have been a church.

Part of what I've gotten from that long-time connection has been a much more international view than most union members have. I've hosted a lot of tours for Japanese, Korean, and Filipino workers, and some Central American trade unionists.

At various times I feel that pull is more important than at others, or that I need it more than at other times. When I was brought up on charges in my local several years ago, that was a period when I was so buried in the day-to-day struggle that I didn't do anything external.[2] But that's not a good place to be. I remember going to a *Labor Notes* policy committee

2. The charges against Kay Eisenhower and two rank-and-file colleagues were filed by a defeated opponent in the previous local union elections, in the hope that the charges would prevent Kay and her friends from running again. Allies of the charging party were cited by dozens of members for illegally possessing and distributing blank union ballots and/or actually submitting ballots in the names of members who had not in fact voted. SEIU had to repeat the election given the level of election fraud discovered, and Kay and her slate won all the seats for which they had originally run.

meeting, and realizing, "Oh my God! There are really good people doing really good work out there, and I'm part of that."

I don't have a clear sense of the trajectory for going from what I'm doing to a society that is more fair economically. All I know is that if people like myself don't do what we're doing to mobilize workers at this level, I don't believe anything can happen in the absence of that. If I don't do it then things will get worse.

Bill DiPietro

"They're not scabs any more"

Bill DiPietro was president of a small local of the International Association of Machinists at a Buick dealership in Youngstown, Ohio. He led a strike in 1992–1993 that lasted almost a year. Throughout the strike, Bill DiPietro insisted that no settlement would be acceptable unless it included a union shop. After the strike only a handful of the strikers chose to return to work, and DiPietro rebuilt Local 1519 with former strikebreakers. He hurt his back lifting a tire and is now disabled.

Bill DiPietro was interviewed at his home in Hubbard, Ohio, a suburb of Youngstown, in April 1998.

I was born in 1950 and grew up on the North Side of Youngstown. I was one of seven kids. My father worked in the mill, and my mother stayed home. She had her hands full.

I went to St. Anthony grade school and then to public school. My first job was working in a bowling alley. There was no union there. I worked for a Rambler dealer on Rayen Avenue. Then I worked for a while in the steel mills, at the McDonald Mills of U.S. Steel. That was my first union job. I was nineteen then.

I filed my first grievance at the McDonald Mills. I burnt my hand at the mill, working hot wrap. We were working midnights, and the boss didn't want to give me a doctor's slip. So I went to the doctor myself. The boss got mad and wrote me up for not asking for gloves. But we did ask him. He never gave them to us. He gave those gloves out as if they were gold.

So they wrote me up, and I filed a grievance. Somehow the discipline got dropped. We went to the office, and I told them my side of it, and a union representative was with me, and the superintendent said to forget about it.

This was in the 1970s. I noticed that the mills weren't getting any better, and they weren't fixing them. I used to be real good friends with the electricians who would come out on the line when things broke down. They liked me. They told me, "Get out of here. They're just wrapping this place up to close it down."

So I quit and went back into the mechanical business. I went to a school through the Manpower program, and learned my trade there. I worked for Taylor Olds for a while and got laid off. The mechanical business was up and down back then. Then I got a job working for a Ford dealer right here in Hubbard. I got married and we had a baby.

A friend of mine said, "Let's go to Buick Youngstown. They're hiring." I got hired, and then I really got into the union stuff.

A New Boss

There was a union already there. To get sworn in, you had to go to a meeting. So I went to the meeting, and because it was an amalgamated local, there were forty or fifty people. There was the bus company, International Harvester, Schwebel's bread, a lot of little mechanical shops at the auto dealers on Wick Avenue. State Chevrolet was in our union. Valley Pontiac was in our union. The president, Carl Agnone, worked out of our shop.

I started to get interested. Our contracts were almost all the same, and it was a pretty good contract. It took care of any special tools you needed. It was a really strong union then.

When you used to go on strike, you would strike for maybe three weeks. Then the boss and the union rep would settle something. The weakness of the union was that contract expiration dates were not coordinated among the different shops. But if State Chevrolet went on strike, we would go and give them some relief. And if they got a 3 percent raise, every other dealership would get that, too.

Mr. Hopper, our boss at Buick Youngstown, was a nice guy. He was close to ninety, but he would walk through the shop and he knew everybody's name. He wanted workers who took care of the customers. He didn't care about speed. He didn't want flat rates.[1] He paid you a decent hourly wage. He didn't want to hear of a customer having any problems. And he handled his own contracts; he didn't have a lawyer.

Mr. Hopper died, and Bob Sweeney took over. Sweeney wanted to

---

1. A flat rate is so much money for each kind of job, such as changing a muffler or installing a new fuel pump, regardless of the difficulty of the job on that particular vehicle. Thus doing a tune-up correctly might take two hours but the flat rate might pay you for an hour and a half.

change things his way. He didn't like hourly rates. We tried to explain to him that hourly is the best way to go, because if you're trying to be a flat rater you're not trying to do a car right. He didn't want to hear that. He kept reading papers about flat rate shops, how they were producing. The men who were union officers in the 1980s kept explaining that numbers on a sheet of paper don't mean that the customer is going to be satisfied. That's where we locked horns.

Sweeney and his lawyer introduced the flat rates through a bonus system. They kept everybody working forty hours a week, at (let's say) ten dollars an hour. They said that most of the people weren't really making their money. What they meant by that was that a man might work forty hours, but only complete jobs worth twenty hours under a flat rate system. They checked every mechanic's work each week. The lawyer would say, "Such–and–such a mechanic isn't pulling his weight." And the steward would say, "Well, what did he do in those forty hours? Maybe he had a broken bolt. Come on, you're not giving the guy a chance. You just throw it out there as if he's a bum." And Sweeney and his lawyer said, "He *is* a bum."

Then they said, "Here's what we're going to do. We're going to give you your forty hours. We'll give you your raises over three years. But we're going to introduce an incentive, a bonus." If a man completed jobs worth twenty-two hours, instead of twenty, they would give him a little extra money.

We all got together and the union officers said, "Look, they're trying to make you go faster." But I don't care how you explained it, there would be some guy who saw that money, that carrot, and go after it. They were killing themselves. We had half an hour for lunch and two fifteen-minute breaks. People started working through their breaks. The other guys would say, "You don't have to do that. You're making forty hours straight. Why get involved? You're playing right into their hands." We had debates at lunch time!

Then at the next contract the boss would say, "Look what happened here. George used to do only twenty hours a week, now he's turning thirty-five." Next they wanted a guaranteed wage of only thirty, thirty-five hours. We went on strike for eight weeks to keep the forty-hour guarantee. That's when Bob Sweeney decided he didn't want the union.

The lawyer would call six of us upstairs at a time, and say, "I don't want to tell you how to do your jobs. I want to help you." One guy said, "You're a union buster." "No, no, no, I don't bust unions." This was maybe 1982, 1983. All the mills were going down, and they thought this was the time to make their move. It was like bringing a cannon in to shoot bugs.

When I first was hired there, you did all kinds of mechanical work. You did brake jobs, you did transmissions, you had to do everything. Our mechanics were very close-knit. We looked after each other. We were almost a family.

In the old days, you were really hired in as an apprentice. You followed the journeyman around for at least a while. If you had problems, the journeyman was there to help you out. They used to hire a lot of kids from Choffin Vocational School who would come in to the shop and learn. If you wanted to learn something at Choffin, you could go at nights and the company would pay for it. It was in the contract that we had to go, to keep up on things.

After Sweeney took over, he started cutting corners and said, "Let's specialize." Somebody did transmissions. Somebody did motors. I did alignments. Sweeney wanted everybody to take the ASE test to be licensed. I had no problem with it, but there were a lot of older mechanics who were very bright, but couldn't pass the test. So we resisted putting the ASE test in the contract. We said, "It's great to be knowledgeable on a test, but it's also nice to have a guy with fifty years of experience on whom you can rely."

They wanted a 50 percent profit from everybody. Well, guys who did tune-ups made their own profit and other people's profits, too. They didn't want that. The shop steward would say, "It's impossible. The guy who does transmissions is not going to make a profit."

We had a wash department. After we got through working on someone's car, we'd send it to be washed. It was a nice thing. They started saying, "Why do we need a wash rack?" They got rid of the wash man. The guys got mad, and started leaving greasy fingerprints all over the cars. They called us in. We said, "You got rid of the wash rack. That was never a complaint until now." Then they wanted *us* to wash the cars: to pay ten dollars an hour for a job they used to pay five for.

They used to have a man who fixed interiors. He did beautiful work. They couldn't take away the job because it was in the contract, but they moved the man around until he had a heart attack.

Then they started working on the paint shop. The men there were older, but they were good painters. The lawyer called us in and said, "We're going to cut out the paint shop." The shop stewards, Joe Vasko and Bill Stevens, said, "Why on earth would you do that? That's your bread and butter, for collisions, everything." The lawyer pulled out a big chart and said, "You don't understand business." One time I said, "I'm just going to sign my pay check back to you, I feel so sorry for you."

Becoming a Union Spokesperson

We had three people on the negotiating team: one from the body shop, one from the parts department, and one from the mechanical. They were the elected shop stewards in the different areas.

Our union would send around a paper saying, "January 1st is the election for shop stewards. If anybody is interested, come at lunch time and we'll nominate you." It was so small a shop that if you wanted to run for shop steward, you could do it. There were shop steward elections every year.

I never wanted to run for shop steward. I saw that the men who were elected as shop stewards had a hard time with Sweeney in negotiations. And it seemed like everybody who became a shop steward got fired. I was getting madder. One day I just put my hand up and said, "I'll run." I won. This was in the late 1980s.

What I did, I went around and asked everybody what they wanted in the contract, and I would put it in the pot. The business agent didn't know mechanics. He didn't know what was going on in the shop.

The company wanted to close the body shop. I said there was no reason for that. They said, "Could you talk the men into taking a cut in pay?" I said, "Are you crazy? They'd cut me up into little pieces." I said I wasn't going to do it.

The lawyer looked at the faces of the other shop stewards, trying to find someone who would agree with him. We took a break. The body shop steward told me he wouldn't mind taking a cut, if the company was having a bad time. I liked the guy: we had worked together for fifteen or twenty years. But I said, "If you take a cut, that doesn't mean you'll stay. You'll stay for maybe a year or so. Then he'll cut you." He said, "Oh no, I've known Mr. Sweeney for a long time. Mr. Sweeney would never do that." So those guys took a 50 cents cut in pay.

When the company closed the body shop, I *wanted* to run again for shop steward. The men who worked there had forty years' seniority. They had done everything for this company. Sweeney called them in right before Christmas, and told them he was closing them down. He was going to subcontract the body work.

We wanted to call a wildcat, because the bargaining unit defined in the contract included the body shop. The union lawyer said, "You can't do that." We said, "Why can't we?" He said, "Because all these years they've been doing some subcontracting during busy times, and now it's past practice."

Then the company started in on hospitalization insurance. I said, "That's a cost of doing business. If you don't want to do business, shut the doors, turn it into a meatpacking place." I took it back to the men and told them not to vote for a co-payment. They voted it in.

By this time Mr. Sweeney had given the business to his sons, Dave and Doug. The company brought in an accountant. I asked him, "What do you do? What are you for?" The man said, "I'm here to explain something about insurance to you." I said, "Why do I have to hear this? That's the Sweeneys' problem, not mine." He said, "You don't understand. There are two people back there who have had heart attacks." I said, "You're nothing but a bean counter. So what?" He said, "You have a guy with Parkinson's disease." I said, "I don't care what they have. I don't want to get into that." He said, "Our insurance rates are going up and I can't find you good insurance."

I said to Dave Sweeney, "What about when your mother had a heart attack? Didn't that make your insurance rates go up? And you took her to a hospital in Texas. I'm not condemning you. I'd probably go for the best, too. But we paid for that ride." Sweeney said, "You guys are getting older. How about paying more for your insurance?" I said that wasn't going to fly but our new business agent started hemming and hawing. I suggested they just close the place down and open up an ice cream joint.

What triggered the strike in 1992 was that the company abolished the positions of the men who had had heart attacks. I told them they were looking for a strike, that they were bargaining for a strike. I asked, "What are those men supposed to do?" They answered, "Let them become mechanics at flat rates." I said, "One of those men is sixty-two years old. He has just come back from a heart attack. He's a good mechanic but you're not going to be able to give him engine jobs." They said, "That's *his* problem." I said, "No, that ain't right." All the stewards told them, you're just looking for a fight. I looked at Randy, and he looked at me, and we said, "We're not taking this contract back to the men."

The business agent said he would take it back for a vote. So we met at the union hall, and all three of us stewards said we wouldn't vote for this contract to save our souls. The men voted it down.

We went on strike. The company started hiring strike replacements right away.

The Strike

This guy came by the picket line and blew his horn. He said, "Hey, my name is Jack Walsh. You want some help?" I said, "I'll take any help I can get." The guys didn't know who he was. I told them, "Well, we're out here on strike. The business agent is not coming around that much."

Jack said, "Why don't you come to a meeting?" I said, "What meeting do you want me to come to?" He told us about a retiree group that met in Hubbard, Solidarity USA. I went there, and started listening, and it sounded right.

Bob Moore, our lawyer, said we had to go to court. I asked the business agent, "Do you think the members should be there?" He said, "Nah, we'll take care of it." I said, "I think we should go." He said, "Nah, you don't need to." And here we got an injunction because we didn't go and explain our side of it. I asked the business agent, "How many strikes have you handled?" He said, "None. This is my first big one." I knew we were in trouble then. Here I am a mechanic, and I don't know too much about strikes, and I've got a greenhorn for a union rep that doesn't know anything.

Then we came up with the idea for a Beep-A-Thon. Under the injunction, we weren't allowed to march on the place. One Saturday Jack O'Connell was there from the Mahoning County central labor council, UAW people were there, Local 800 of the Food and Commercial Workers, Teamsters, and they all wanted to march. But I had a president and a vice president who didn't want to march. I had a lawyer calling me up at night telling me, "Don't march." So I think it was Staughton Lynd that came up with the idea of driving by Buick Youngstown, blowing our horns.

We did say some things about the judge. The lawyer called me again that night and said, "You can't talk about the judge." I said, "Why?" He said, "Because you have to go in front of him. And don't put up a sign which says, 'Don't cross this line. The judge says you might be arrested.'" I said, "Why not? It's the truth." He says, "I don't want to see a sign out there saying that." I said, "He's only going to arrest the president and the vice president. I'm just a shop steward."

The Beep-A-Thon was great! We started with the big one that Saturday. There were seventy-five cars, driving real slow. It went all the way from the school, up the back, and around. The cops were so tickled that we weren't marching that they held up traffic for us. We went back and forth. People were in the cars, holding up signs, driving one after the other. The signs said "Scabs," "Sweeney's a union buster." We honked and honked. I burned out two of my horns. But it was well worth it.

After that, we did it two nights a week. It was good for morale. You didn't need very many cars. We tried to pick times when they did a lot of business.

Those Beep-A-Thons drove the company nuts. One time I was in Sweeney's office after the strike. He had a little reading light that was all busted up. I said, "Did you throw that at the lawyer during those Beep-A-Thons?" He said, "Those Beep-A-Thons!" He started going off about the people in the Beep-A-Thons. He said, "Where did you find those people?" I said, "Those are good people. They were better than anybody I ever had on the strike line." He knew all the names. "Where'd you get Bob Schindler? Where'd you get Staughton Lynd? Where'd you get Jack Walsh? Where'd you get Greg Yarwick?"[2]

We started in April and we were still at it in December. The vice president left the picket line and I became vice president. Carl Agnone, the local union president, was dying. I went to see him. Nobody had bought him anything. I got some cards and said, "These are from the men." Carl said, "You have to promise me one thing." I said, "Carl, I can't promise you

---

2. These are all names of members of the Workers Solidarity Club of Youngstown.

anything. What do you want me to promise?" He said, "Make sure it's a union shop." The men felt the same way.

I was fined $3500 for violating the injunction. That very evening the president of the UAW Lordstown local called and said that they would cover any fines.

One day we were on the line, and Dave Sweeney pulls up in his truck. He said, "Let's go have some coffee." I said, "If it was the last cup of coffee in the world, I wouldn't drink it with you." He said, "Come on, Bill." All the guys were telling me to go. I said, "OK, I'll go, but only because these guys want me to." He said, "Where do you want to go?" I said, "Someplace expensive. You're paying." So we went to Arby's.

He tried to get me to say who would come back. I said I wouldn't play that game. So I met with the men, and we met with the lawyer, and in the end we agreed that up to ten of the eighteen strikers could return. But a good half of the men had gotten other jobs, and Sweeney was offering money to buy people out. In the end, only three of the men who had gone on strike went back to work in March, eleven months later.

Representing the Scabs

I was the only mechanic who went back. The other two were parts men. Sweeney and I agreed that after thirty days, all the strike replacements who had not been discharged would be in the union.

Before the thirty days were up, Sweeney fired one man. As that man was walking out the door, I told him that if he wanted, the union would file a grievance and fight for him. He said he didn't want to be bothered.

There was a kid in parts who was really slow. The boss approached me and said, "I want to fire one more person." I said, "No, you can't do that." He said, "Why? You don't care about these scabs." I said, "They're not scabs any more. They're paying union dues. They're union brothers. I've got to help them out."

We went in the office. All the men were watching. The supervisor told the kid he was slow. The kid replied that he was still learning the computer, and I backed him up. Finally the supervisor said, "Well, I just want to warn you." After that the kid was our best union man. He came to all the meetings.

I started going to the lunch area and talking with the men who had been scabs. They said, "Why did you stick up for this guy?" I said, "Because he's in the union. That's what unions are about. It's not because I like you, or don't like you." I also said, "I don't want you to follow me. I want you to come up and tell me, 'Bill, you're wrong.'" They liked that. They really liked that.

It's a terrible thing to say, but I wound up with a better group of men coming to the union meetings than I had before the strike.

Two Kinds of Organizing

The international unions want to do good, but they don't know how to organize. You can't organize the way they want to do it.

The Machinists international had a class in Berkeley. They brought people in and said, "Here's how we figure we're going to organize." I gave them a good listen. I want to organize, too.

Then I went up to the man who made the presentation and said, "It's never going to happen." He says, "Why?" I says, "Because you're not going to bring maybe ten guys in, and zoom into this town, like maybe Youngstown, and say, 'OK, we're going to organize this. We're going to talk to people about why they should be in the union.' " Those are great words. But if you aren't there every day, you can't do it. People will tell them, "I don't want to talk to you. I want to see what you can do."

I told those professors in Berkeley that if I were doing it, I'd have the staff man open up an office in Youngstown, where he could help people who were fired, and that sort of thing. That would do more than bringing guys into town and going door to door. It's nice to have people come and talk. But people remember more what you did for somebody.

II

THE ASHES
OF THE OLD

Ed Mann

Elly Leary

Elly Leary

"I was devastated when the plant closed"

Before becoming an industrial worker, Elly Leary worked as a paralegal in a women's law collective. In 1974, she and two friends were hired at a box factory where she met another new hire who became her husband. Together they read Rank and File. *Elly Leary went to work for General Motors at its Framingham, Massachusetts auto plant in 1977.*

Twelve years of struggle to build a rank–and–file caucus at the Framingham plant came to an end when GM closed the facility. After the plant closed, Elly Leary continued organizing, first among workers in homeless shelters and then among clerical workers at Boston University (BU) where she found work as a secretary.

At the time of this interview, June 1998, Elly Leary was vice president of the United Automobile Workers (UAW) local at BU, and one of four co-chairpersons of New Directions, a reform movement within the national union.

My story illustrates the deindustrialization of the Boston area. I was an auto worker for twelve years and now I'm a secretary. When I worked in the Framingham auto plant, we were "the anchor shop" in the regional UAW. Now the secretaries' local at Boston University is the anchor shop of the region.

GM's Framingham plant was constructed in 1947 and opened in 1949. None of the original hires lived within thirty miles of the plant. There was no natural community. There was never any CIO history to draw on or any union activists who were former Reds.

We had a completely ineffectual, do-nothing union president. The real power in the shop was the shop chair who had been in office for more than twenty years. By the time I got hired, his fighting days were long over. He was in the plant for five minutes a day, from 6:00 to 6:05 A.M. The rest of the day he was at the track or tending to his various business interests, among them fencing diamonds and reselling cars. The incumbents were pretty lax. The newspaper hardly ever came out and grievances were rarely filed.

I was fortunate to be in an auto plant that was run by gangsters. It forced us to realize that you could do nothing alone. We had to work collectively.

We decided to create the union in absentia. We went about developing a second political party in the plant. We would have caucus meetings at lunch or during the hour between shifts. This was a shop that was 1 percent women and 1 percent African American. The caucus was mostly white women and African American men, with a few white men.

Styles of Organizing

Before I came to the Framingham plant, a Marxist group called the October League had sent some members there. The plant had run on one shift for five years and didn't open a second shift until late 1976, so a bunch of them got hired at that time. In the spring of 1977, three months before I came, there was an election for delegates to the national UAW convention. The folks from the October League put out a flyer that basically said: "You stupid fucking workers, why are you following the bureaucrats? Why don't you listen to the communists? We'll tell you how to build a good union and this is what you should look for in the delegates." The October League called for a demonstration at the plant gates in order to bolster their position and sell their newspaper.

Well, quite naturally, the workers were absolutely enraged! The October League appeared at the gates and the union organized members to go out there. The result was a pitched battle in front of our plant with baseball bats and lead pipes.

The company found out who all the radical intellectuals were and they were fired before the day was out. The remaining working-class members were unbelievably harassed. One of my best friends, a former organizer for the October League, later said to me, "It set back any radical work in the plant ten years."

This mistake, by some of the first political organizers in the Framingham plant, made all the other political people in the plant say, "You know, we have to sink in. We have to develop roots in the working class, and just become regular people and be part of everyday life, and talk about everyday things." It became really important to listen. The way you framed your issues and the way you talked about your ideas had to be in a way that people could hear them.

You have to be part of the working class, swimming in the sea of the people. That was the lesson that my group took from Mao: *From* the people *to* the people, in that order. We learned the importance of democracy, of continuing to have revolution so that people don't get stagnant and bureaucracy doesn't set in.

"Let a hundred flowers bloom": that was an important thing to me as a young "communist." It's important to hear other voices. That's how you come up with something new.

Some of the smartest people I ever met in my life worked in the Framingham plant. Their intelligence wasn't geared to our learning system, but they were very smart and cunning people, and very good strategists, excellent tacticians. They were people you definitely wanted on your team.

I would say, "Hey, did you see the news tonight?" And I would pick out something I wanted to expound on. It was much more effective than selling a political newspaper and trying to talk to people about issues when they were already turned off or didn't know the person at the gate. At least, doing it my way, I could gauge the conversation with a particular person and figure out what to say next.

Personally, too, proceeding one on one, talking to people and listening to them, was simply physical protection. Our plant was scary. Two of us had guns drawn on us. Others got tires flattened or hot coffee thrown on them. People got spat at too. Verbal abuse was constant. I had to have bodyguards for eight years because it was too dangerous to walk around alone. I had to have protection. And the only way I could get protection was to be someone people wanted to protect.

Red-baiting

At first we thought that everyone in our group would work separately, because it was so dangerous to get together. There were spies. People would scream "communist bastard" at you. My husband used to get phone calls all the time threatening our kids and me.

We had a couple of people drop out of our caucus. My hardest moment was when a guy I had worked with for ten years, who had a lot of respect in the shop, came into work one day literally crying and said, "I can't do it any more. My wife said it's either me or the caucus." He said he had to drop out of the caucus because his wife couldn't take the threats.

Red-baiting was a constant thing. All you had to do in our plant to be called a Red was to raise your hand at a union meeting.

After the concessionary contracts and the beginning of jointness in 1981, job actions became impossible at Framingham. People knew that they could count on the caucus if there was an overloaded job, that if they were working next to us we would get that problem resolved, but we were completely on our own. People were so intimidated by the way the union was run that we couldn't pull off shopfloor actions like they did in Lordstown. If we tried, we would be pulled off our jobs by the union, and put on tougher jobs.

Elections

Our caucus was called the Standup Coalition, and had an agenda about democracy, and ending jointness and concessions.

The only democracy that Americans have even the remotest experience with is elections. They so equate democracy with elections that they see that as the vehicle for their expression.

Workers would tell me, "If you keep working on the issues and doing all that stuff on the ground, when are you going to put your money where your mouth is? When are you going to stand for office?"

So when our caucus talked about, "What are we going to do first?," the obvious place to begin was local union elections. One huge issue was corruption. Old-timers told us that the union had never run a straight election. They would bring in shoe boxes full of ballots from the back room when things weren't going their way. People talked about the crooked elections all the time.

We put out a four-page flyer that talked about why we needed democratic elections. We put it out two days before the election of the union election committee. This was usually a ho-hum affair. People that the union picked went down to the union hall and voted for themselves. We caused a stir.

There was a big snow storm the day of the election committee election, so they had to reschedule it. Then we put out a second flyer. We said, "Don't be deterred. They're going to have a meeting down at the union hall, and no matter what you have to do today, you really have to come."

We got 750 people from day shift to turn out. But we hadn't completed the job, because we hadn't encouraged anybody to run for election committee. So we learned, it's not enough just to agitate. You have to be prepared. You have to have a program.

In the 1986 election for convention delegates, the person we decided to run in the Framingham local union was an African American man who came from a union family, and had worked in the plant for twenty-some years. He had been a steward, on the local union election committee and on the executive board. He was a well-respected guy who had hung in there all these years. He won.

He went to the international union convention, and the first night he called up on the phone. He said, "You're not going to believe this. There's a whole other region of the country that has the same political program we do, and they're organized!" This is the story of the UAW: nobody knows what's going on outside their own plant.

Newspaper

We decided to put out a newspaper. When we first started it, we handed it out just inside the doors, before people went through the time clock. It was the most physically intimidating experience I've ever been through.

So we said, "Now what are we going to do?" We decided that we wouldn't make people decide in front of the guards, and in front of the union officers, whether they were going to take the paper. We would come in early, put the newspaper on work benches and talk to people about the paper then.

We began to talk to more and more people before we put out an issue: "What do we want to discuss this month?" We always gave news from other plants, and our lead article every month was an analysis of the auto industry.

Before an issue of the newspaper hit the shop floor, the articles had been reviewed and critiqued by fifty or sixty people (sometimes more). Sometimes it would take us six weeks. We knew that if we didn't have a core of fifty or sixty people who felt that they'd had some input, everybody would trash the newspaper.

I remember one article, after we had been publishing for six or seven years, that was on Red-baiting. One hundred and fifty rank and filers critiqued the article before we put it out. We felt we couldn't put it out unless enough people had ownership of this thing to say, "Yeah, I read it before. I know what's in it. I'm going to talk to people about it." We involved them *before* we put out the newspaper.

It changed the balance of power in the shop. After a while workers would come up and say, "When's the next one coming out?" About every three months we would go around the plant and ask people to pony up a buck. So we were self-funding, and on a voluntary basis.

Everyone in the group had a little something to do. It spread the risk, was how we looked at it then. Now I can look back on it positively and say, this is how you build an organization.

Maternity

I had both my kids while working at GM. The first time, 1978, there was no maternity leave at the Framingham GM plant. They tried to fire me when they found out I was pregnant. I had to fight to get my job back.

The more pregnant I got, the fewer jobs I could do. I lost three good jobs because I couldn't reach the car.

The last two weeks I was in the plant it was six weeks to my due date, and we were working ten hours a night. There wasn't a chair in the plant. They put me on fender welding in the back with all these noxious fumes. The men there didn't know me from anybody. They said, "You, go sit over there. If you see anybody in anything but work clothes, get up and come over here." For two weeks they did my job. They all pitched in.

More good came out of this situation. About two months before I left the shop I had seen an article in the *Boston Globe* about how some women got maternity leave covered under their union short-term disability contract clause. I went around the shop and found three other pregnant women and showed them the article. They all wanted something done about it, but they wanted me to take the lead. I approached my committeeman. He didn't want to hear about it. His attitude was, "women don't belong here." I then went up the chain of command. Finally I talked with the day shift benefits rep. I told him that I would do something about it whether or not the union did. He immediately asked me to get the other pregnant women together and he arranged a meeting at the hall. Some international reps came too. With me as the "plaintiff" the union would sue GM for maternity leave. So ten days after I had my first child, I and the rep and the international staffer filed a law suit. GM settled immediately. And everyone after me got maternity leave. When I had my second child, I was laid off. I was called back when she was three months old.

Plant Closing

One of the best political conversations I had at General Motors was near the end. I was sitting in the cafeteria with a group of workers. A union representative came by and asked them why they were sitting with a commie bitch. The workers told him to get lost. Then one of them turned to me and said, "Elly, I apologize for being one of the people who was in that fight out front with baseball bats and pipes. You were right about the union and you had the patience to stick with us and explain and hear us out and win us over, and we're sorry we beat up on you." I reminded the guy that I was not yet hired in at that time. And then we talked about anti-communism, how communists in an anti-communist environment can do good work and become leaders either in spite of or because of their views, how the union leadership didn't really have our best interests at heart and wasn't going to make this a democratic union. We were all crying at the end.

I was devastated when the plant closed. I had just spent twelve years of my life there. These were my friends and our caucus was at the height of its success. I was 43 years old.

Every one of us was injured. My two closest friends took medical retirements.

My family refused to become GM gypsies. One kid was in junior high. She said, "We don't have to move. Go get another job, Mom." But when I did get another job, my thirteen year old daughter said, "Why can't you get a good job, like you used to have in Framingham, and we could really go and buy stuff?"

After the plant closed, I worked part-time for three years as an SEIU organizer. I organized workers in homeless shelters. When I was organizing shelter workers, they said, "When are you going to make house calls?" I said, "I'm not making house calls. If I can't go in there and meet people at lunch, or arrange to have coffee with them before or after work, then we're not going to win this thing anyway."

I don't believe in house calls. Every night at supper time, when the salespeople start calling, you resent it. So if I'm coming knocking on the door, it's the same thing. If you want to bend my ear about the union, do it at work! You're so stressed out when you get home, from doing two jobs if you have a shitty job, or being overworked if you have a higher-paying job, the last thing you want to do when you get home is to hear more about work.

When I went to work at Boston University I had been blacklisted by the UAW so I had to be totally underground until my 91st day. The international union found me on my 91st day and tried to get me fired.

Vision

We built a fabulous caucus at the Framingham GM plant, but we erred on the side of getting caught up in the trade union crap. Ironically, just as the plant was closing we began to talk much more politically. Everybody knew that we were socialists and communists. The Red-baiting was so intense you couldn't hide who you were. But we spent so much time trying to defend ourselves, and trying to build a power base, and trying to build a democratic union in place of no democracy, that we really neglected the long-run vision of a different kind of society.

We need to talk about the vision.

Since BU is a university, the permissible scope of discussion is much wider than it was in the plant. It's much easier to say, "You know, what we're doing through the union is only a stopgap. This isn't all there is to life." You can talk about vision much sooner.

You can't get anybody to want to be like you if you look like a one-dimensional person. I coach in an all-girls baseball league. This is the best thing I do all year.

The example of Vicky Starr a.k.a. Stella Nowicki[1] meant something to me on a couple of levels. You remember how she said she was fired, and then she went to the beauty parlor and dyed her hair, and then they kicked her out again. She kept going back. She didn't give up. She had a vision. She could have just gotten a job, and said, "Screw it. I'm just going to make a living." But she didn't do that. And that really inspired me.

And the second thing about her story was that it was absolutely clear to me that Vicky/Stella was able to do what she did because she had a party, a group of people, an organization behind her, that offered her all kinds of help. The organization gave her a place when she didn't have one, conversation, a place to meet new people, a place to talk about more problems than just the kill floor [in meatpacking]. All that enabled her to be an all-dimensional woman. It spoke to me.

We have to begin to model today, to the best of our abilities, the society we want after we get through the eye of the needle of the revolution. If we want workers to take control and be empowered, then we have to begin to create those situations in small ways while still thinking about the larger questions. How are you going to pull all these small things together? How are they going to cohere? How are they going to build up to more than the sum of their numbers? If people know what it looks like on a small scale, how are we going to get from here to there?

We don't have a deep enough sense of vision. There's not one group out there that can do it. It has to be all of us, figuring out how to begin to work together, to create enough "density," ideologically, in people's minds. People today have a pretty good clue that they're getting the short end of what's going on. They just don't know what to do about it.

Since I left the plant I've had the privilege of studying Freire and going to the Highlander Folk School, so now I have a framework for all these things. People come with a lot of experiences. They have tons of knowledge. They may not know they have it. They may not have any way to categorize it or make it useful to themselves. The role of union and political organizers is to help people understand how much they already know, help them to put that knowledge to good use, to get a view of the world and to analyze the world, big and small, and chart a path from there.

1. See Vicky Starr's accounts in this book, in *Rank and File,* and in *Union Maids.*

Ed Mann

"I'm going down that hill"

Ed Mann was a long-time activist at the Brier Hill mill of the Youngstown Sheet & Tube Company in Youngstown, Ohio. He was president of Local 1462, United Steelworkers of America, at Brier Hill from 1973 until the mill closed in 1979. After his retirement in 1980, he was a vital member of the Workers Solidarity Club of Youngstown, Solidarity USA (a militant retiree organization), and the Industrial Workers of the World (IWW). Ed died in 1992.

As he explains in his account, Ed Mann believed that unionized workers have "too much contract" and can better solve their problems through direct action, such as wildcat strikes. This was also Ed's approach to the challenge of plant closings. After his own mill closed, he led the occupation of U.S. Steel's Youngstown headquarters building.

Ed Mann speaks often and vividly in Shout Youngstown, *a 45-minute video by Youngstown natives Dorie Krauss and Carol Greenwald Brouder about the closings of Youngstown's steel mills. It can be obtained from The Cinema Guild, 1697 Broadway, Suite 506, New York, NY 10019, tel. (212) 246-5522.*

What follows is excerpted from We Are The Union: The Story of Ed Mann, *published by the Workers Solidarity Club, and based on oral histories recorded by Pat Rosenthal, Bruce Nelson, and Staughton and Alice Lynd.*

Treating People Fairly

I was born in 1928 in Toledo, Ohio. Treating people fairly was the undercurrent in our family. There were a lot of people we would call "homeless" today. In those days they were called "on the bum," and my mother always had something to share at mealtime if they came around.

My grandfather on my mother's side was a custom tailor. He came from what was Prussia at the time because he didn't want to fight for the Kaiser. He lived with us. He had been all over the world.

I remember how when I was a kid the old-timers in the neighborhood would come to our house on Sunday afternoons and discuss current events. The kids sat and listened and the old-timers talked. I can remember folks coming around recruiting for the Spanish Civil War. I think there was a socialist tendency, which probably came out of the 1848 period in Germany. I got this just listening.

It was primarily a Jewish neighborhood and all the kids were raised Jewish. I went to a Reform temple, which is probably about as liberal as you can get in the Hebrew tradition. I saw some anti-Semitism as I was growing up. Toledo had a large Polish population. The kids would get in fights. During World War II we were very much aware of the Holocaust. I felt the attitude was, "Don't make waves. We don't want to create any more anti-Semitism than there is already."

I had an uncle who was somewhat of a hustler. He helped me to get an egg route. I could keep 5 cents a dozen. I had to fight to keep the boys in my neighborhood from breaking my eggs.

I never finished high school. When I was seventeen, I enlisted in the Marines and spent two years there, 1945–1947. After getting out of the Service I got a six-month membership in the YMCA. In Toledo, as in many other places, they had a black YMCA and a white YMCA. I met this black fellow. His name was Bell. He was going to box and he said to me, "Ed, I've got to take off four or five pounds" to get in a certain weight class. I said, "I've got this membership in the Y. Let's go down. They have a steam room."

So we go down there. Here I am, a returned veteran from the Second World War, black fellow with me, and I went up to the desk and I said, "I want a guest pass." They looked at me like I was crazy! They said, "You better talk to the manager." So I said to the manager, "Hey, I want a pass for my buddy here. We want to work out." He said, "Look, don't cause any trouble. He's got his YMCA and this is yours."

I think it's things like that that politicize people. I was at an age where I was like a sponge, wanting to participate in society. Then I found out what society was like.

Youngstown

When I was in the Service I met some folks from Youngstown. They said, "If you want to earn good money and go to school, you can do both in Youngstown." The steel mills were paying well and the university would take anybody on the G.I. Bill.

It was so easy to get jobs in Youngstown at that time. I had eleven different jobs in one year and never got fired from any of them. They were decent paying jobs. The reason I quit was because the conditions were horrendous. They were all union jobs but unions were just starting to feel their oats. Unions had not yet settled into job descriptions and bonus systems and crew sizes.

I got a job in the cafeteria at the university. I was batching it and I wanted meals. That's where I met John Barbero.

John came from a family that had steel mills in their blood. His dad and mother were strongly involved in the 1937 Little Steel Strike. His dad was one of the folks who was blackballed at Republic Steel in 1937 and one of the I don't know how many who got their jobs back through the Supreme Court.

John was a very literate guy. He'd been in the Marine Corps during the Second World War. He was an interpreter. He learned to speak Japanese and married a Japanese woman. He felt strongly about what happened with the atomic bomb. He was sympathetic to many different ideas.

The Korean War started and in October 1950 I got a telegram: "Be in Philadelphia Navy Yard in ten days." I had a wife and a baby. I was going to college, had a job and no money. I had to quit school and quit my job. I got out in December 1951.

Brier Hill

A friend of mine worked in the machine shop at Brier Hill. He said, "They're going to put on some more apprentices there." John Barbero was working in the Brier Hill Open Hearth.

I went to the employment office. I said, "I want to be a machinist in the apprenticeship program." He said, "They're going to give the test this month. I'll put you in there as a rigger helper." This was in 1952.

You got a thirty–day probationary period. In that thirty days I took the apprenticeship test, and the fellow who gave the test said, "I can tell right now that you passed it." After they graded it, he said, "You got the highest score in the company."

In the meantime, the guys in the shop got me appointed as steward. Nobody else wanted the job. Going through the job descriptions, I found that a machinist working in the shop gets one rate, and when you're out in the mill you're supposed to get a nickel an hour more. I filed a grievance for all the machinists. I won the grievance! And I never heard a thing about the apprenticeship program after that.

A fellow with whom I'd gone to college said, "Look, if you want to make some money, come on up in the Open Hearth and get all the overtime you want." So I went up to the Open Hearth. A week later they put on two new apprentices in the machine shop.

I really liked that Open Hearth. I think the first three months I was there, they must have had ten wildcat strikes. The guys wanted better working conditions. We'd say, "We want rubber-tired wheelbarrows," because the ones they had been using were steel-tired. They'd hit a rail, it would twist, and guys would get hurt. "We want a relief man!" "We want cold water!" The refrigerator system would break down, and the superintendent was too cheap to buy ice. "We need safety masks today! Hey, somebody got burned. We want safety jackets or we aren't going to work on those furnaces!"

The grievance procedure wasn't working. That's why we had wildcat strikes. We weren't going to get tied up in paperwork. The wildcats didn't last long: a day, two days at the most, maybe eight hours.

Rank and File

When I started at Brier Hill it was a big plant. It was an integrated plant in the sense that they started out with iron ore and made a finished product, electric weld pipe. In that plant there were three local unions. Local 1462 was the biggest, with about 3300 members when I started there. It was the first place I worked that had even the facade of a big union.

We had some strong young people with ideals. We believed in what the union was supposed to be like.

Before the local was organized, a lot of Italians lived in the vicinity of the plant. They were discriminated against as much as blacks were discriminated against. They got the lousiest jobs. They did track labor. They were helpers in the mason gang. They could not aspire to the jobs in the shops that the Germans or the English had. Most of the Italians were of limited formal education. They couldn't express themselves as well as those that they called "Johnny Bulls," the English, Irish, and Scots.

There was a young guy who was very literate named Danny Thomas. He was tough. If a foreman was mistreating an old Italian guy, he'd grab the foreman by the shirt and say, "Leave that old guy alone!" So he got a lot of respect in the Italian community. Danny Thomas was president of Local 1462 from the late 1940s until the early 1960s, when he became a staff man for the international union. He was a real dictator as president. He made all kinds of deals.

We had the most dishonest elections you can imagine. One time they had a bottomless ballot box and they set it over a cold air return in the old house that we used as a union hall. As you voted you put your ballot in the box. It would drop down into the cellar. There were two people down there. "This one's OK." They'd put it aside. "This one's no good." They'd throw it in the furnace. (We heard this after these guys retired, years later.) We'd wonder, "There are three thousand people in the mill but we only got eight votes? Our caucus is bigger than that!" That was the game that was played. We learned early: if you don't have the power to count the votes, you don't have the power to win.

We knew we had two battles to fight, one with the company and one with the union. We weren't interested in breaking away or destroying the union. But we felt that the union had to be more responsive to what the members needed.

The union thought that what was good for the company was good for the union. I don't agree. I think the union should look out for its members. The company can look after itself. I got involved with the union because I thought it was the best way to be represented. You're on an equal footing with management. I always thought you had to demand your rights. You had to fight for them.

We spoke up in favor of union officers working at least one year in four in the mill; that no official should take more than the wages of the highest paid member he or she represents; that staff be elected, not appointed.

One of our main issues was, "We want to elect our stewards." Back then the local union president appointed all the stewards. In a 3300-person plant, Danny Thomas had over 100 paid people, like precinct committeemen. They had control over overtime and days off. We wanted stewards to be responsible to people who elected them.

We won that issue many times on the floor. We'd bring a group of people to the union hall and we'd vote for electing them instead of appointing them. Next meeting, our people wouldn't show up, he had a majority, they'd vote it down. This went on for years until we took office in 1973.

Race Discrimination

Blacks got the worst jobs. They worked in the coke plants, blast furnaces, track labor, plate mill, scarfing yard. There were very few blacks in the skilled trades. The only blacks I can recall in a skilled trade during my early years in the mill were bricklayers. There were none in the shops. No electricians. Maybe a few millwrights and motor inspectors but not many. Even in the black departments, the top job was usually held by a white man.

Blacks did not get the jobs where there was a chance to promote. Maybe he became the truck driver, but he could never become the roller. Maybe one could become the craneman but he could never become the charging machine man.

Blacks had been brought in as scabs in 1919 and 1937. This gave any white racist an excuse to say, "The blacks are going to take your jobs. They are scabs. They'll work for less." And it's an excuse because there were many blacks who, when they found out they were being used as scabs, came out of those mills.

Blacks had their place and whites had their place. Nothing was done to discourage this by the managers or by the unions. It reflected the community, a very ethnic community.

It was maybe the first five years that I was in the mill that they started moving blacks up on jobs. The people in the mill *knew* it was the right thing to do. They may have been racist, but they knew it was the right thing to do.

In the Open Hearth where I worked most of the time there were blacks in the pit (that's behind the furnace where they pour the steel). But on the floor where the first, second, and third helpers and the melters were, it was white until the early 1950s.

If you wanted to work on a furnace that meant you had to be able to take the heat. There were five doors on these furnaces. Let's say a black guy was going to go up there and try to learn that job, shoveling into the furnace. The first helper would pull the door all the way up when the black guy came near and the flame would shoot out twenty or thirty feet. We had some tough black guys who stayed, who could do their own job and the jobs of the guys on either side of them.

You had to pick away, pick away at these various practices. Most of the people in the labor pool were black because the coke plant, which was an almost wholly black department, was shut down. Willie Aikens, a black man who later became chairperson of the local's civil rights committee, was in the labor pool for a long time. So was I: the first twelve years I worked at Brier Hill I didn't have a full year's pay because of layoffs. He spent a lot of time on layoff and while he was on layoff white guys were hired off the street in some departments. That was a serious violation of seniority.

John Barbero and I supported the blacks to press the issue in the Open Hearth. We got an agreement with the superintendent that he would open up all jobs to people in the labor pool. But we're talking about half a dozen jobs at the most.

By the time the mill shut down, we had plantwide seniority because of the [settlement of a law suit known as the] 1974 Consent Decree. There were people that complained, "We've been here all these years and now these blacks are coming in! They don't know how to do this, and they don't know how to do that." But it was the foreman's responsibility to train a new worker. The company said, "He's got to have the *ability* to do the job." Well, who determines the ability? The company. And who's supposed to train them? The company. The company wouldn't train the black guys or wouldn't train them properly.

On the other hand, the company wanted production and didn't really care whether there was a black or a white guy. I had a friend named Archie

Nelson. He was a black guy in the conditioning yard. The conditioning yard worked as a gang. They scarfed the steel, burned the impurities off slabs: a hard, hot job. In those kinds of jobs you develop leadership. Archie was the leader of the blacks. He controlled that department. They knew how much they had to do. They did that much. They didn't work their heads off. All the supervisors were white. But if the blacks folded their arms there would have been nothing done. So they let Archie run the crew.

Many blacks had the feeling, "I've caught hell all these years. I've got a lot of seniority now. I'm going to go get Looey's job!" He could get Looey's job, but it had to be in a period when there was an increase in production and they opened up the bidding. Blacks would say, "Hey, how come I'm not getting that job?" There had to be an opening. If the black was entitled to the job, we fought to see that he got it. If he wasn't, you had to tell him straight out, "Look, you're not going to get that job until it's posted or until there's a vacancy or until they put on more turns."

The Consent Decree was a good idea assuming everything was booming, but we were losing jobs. So you were fighting over the few jobs that were left. In a growth-type time it would have been much better. We were in a dying plant in a dying industry and that was the unfairness of it.

Direct Action

I think we've got too much contract. You hate to be the guy who talks about the good old days, but I think the IWW had a darn good idea when they said, "Well, we'll settle these things as they arise."

I believe in direct action. Grievances were backlogged sometimes two and three years. You got to settle these things right at the point of production, and RIGHT NOW! Sure, we could say, "You guys can't strike. You better get back on the job and file a grievance." But that won't get the problem resolved. If workers don't sympathize, they won't engage in direct action. That's their own way of saying whether or not it's a good grievance.

Once a problem is put on paper and gets into the grievance procedure, you might as well kiss that paper goodbye. The corporations saw this when they started recognizing unions. They co-opted the unions with the grievance procedure and the dues checkoff. They quit dealing with the rank and file and started dealing with the people who wanted to be bosses like them, the union bosses.

We were the troublemakers. We'd have a wildcat strike. The international would say, "Either you get back to work or you're fired." It wasn't the company saying this. It was the union.

In a production department, say like the scarfing department where

Archie Nelson was, if they slowed down it affected production. Sometimes the stuff is needed at the next point of operations on a certain timetable. The further a piece of metal gets through the operation, the more costly it becomes. So the further down the line you make your move or take your action, the more costly it is to the company.

In the Open Hearth, we worked on a big furnace that held two hundred tons of molten metal. If you slowed down the operation, the furnace would melt. The people who could slow down the procedure were the people who put in the scrap and molten iron, the charging machine men and cranemen. They had some control over how the operation went. If your first helper wanted two boxes of raw lime and a box of ore in the furnace to make the steel up to specifications, the charging machine man could give them a little extra or not enough and screw up everything.

Once they were going to change the bonus system. They were going to give the first helper and the second helper an increase in bonus and cut the third helpers. In other words, they were just moving the money around. Third helpers refused to go on the job. Second helpers stuck with them. Then there was nobody there to help the first helpers so they agreed to go out with us. It was a wildcat.

We were out that night. The midnight turn gets there and discovers this. We are all sitting in the washroom. The superintendent shows up with the president of the local, Danny Thomas. "What's the problem here?" I'm sitting there. As spokesman for the group I said, "They're cutting our bonus. We don't want to hear it."

Danny Thomas says to the superintendent, "You get rid of that guy and your troubles are over." And the whole Open Hearth gang is sitting there. This doesn't hurt me at all politically. It got the guys hotter.

The superintendent was crying, "What am I going to do with this steel?" I said, "Tap it out on the ground. I don't care what you do with it." He said, "The blast furnace is ready to tap. We got to move that iron." "Dump it on the ground," I said. "We want our bonus." The company agreed not to cut our bonus.

We said, "Now who's going to get paid? Are we going to get paid for the time we've been docked here?" The superintendent said, "Oh, we can't do that. You guys didn't do any work." We said, "The furnace did the work. We want paid or we're going home right now." And it worked.

The wildcat over Tony's death was the first experience I had that showed that people really *can* be involved.[1] At the time I was Recording Secretary of the local, and John and I were both stewards in the Open Hearth. We filed a grievance with the superintendent about thirty-three

1. Drawing both on Ed Mann's account and on family memories, Robert Bruno describes the death of Tony Pervetich in *Steelworker Alley: How Class Works in Youngstown* (Ithaca: Cornell University Press, 1999), pp. 77–78. Tony Pervetich was an uncle of Robert Bruno's mother.

different safety violations. One of the items was we wanted vehicles to have back-up signals. They used big heavy trucks in the pit. There was a lot of noise. It was hard to hear. We wanted a warning horn on the back so when a truck was going to back up the people working there could hear it.

The company rejected the grievance out of hand. They weren't going to discuss any of the thirty-three demands. Shortly after the grievance was rejected, a man who was going to retire in about seven days was run over by one of these trucks. He was crushed. He was a well-liked person who had worked there a long time. This happened on day turn, about one o'clock in the afternoon.

I was working afternoon turn that day, three to eleven. I came out to work and somebody said, "Tony got killed." I asked, "How'd he get killed?" And I was told, "You remember that grievance you filed asking for back-up signals on the truck? The truck backed over him and crushed him."

So I got up on the bench in the washroom and I said to the guys coming to work, "What are we going to do about this? Are we going to work under these lousy conditions? Who's next? Who's going to get killed next? Don't we give a damn about Tony?"

Now some didn't want to go out. I said, "What's the matter with you guys? Here you are. A union brother murdered. We had a grievance in and it was rejected. Are you going to let the company pull this shit?" We actually had to drag some people out because we had all kinds of people. They said, "That's not my problem. I don't work down there. I run a crane." We said, "Let's get out! Let's go!"

We went up to the union hall. We were the afternoon turn. Day turn has finished by now, they've tapped the heats out, and they come up to the union hall. We've got two turns there. We tell them the situation. They agree, "Shut her down!" The guys called their buddies on the midnight turn from the union hall. They said, "Don't come out to work tonight."

They were looking to me for leadership. I said, "Here's what we'll do. Rather than get the stewards fired, let's appoint a committee for each area and let's start listing our demands on safety," bypassing the union structure. It worked. Every area—pit, cranes, floor—was represented.

Lefty DeLarco, the departmental chairman of the Open Hearth, was working day turn. He calls over to the union hall on the company phone and says, "Hey Ed, what's going on? Why aren't these guys coming to work?" I'm sure the phone is bugged. I could have been fired for leading the strike. I say, "Why don't you come up here, Lefty, and find out?"

We didn't just say, "Goddamn it, Tony got killed and we're shutting it down." We said, "This and this and this is what we want. Get a meeting with the company. We'll meet at any time they want."

They set up a meeting for that night, about nine o'clock. They had to get the plant manager from wherever he was. The company said, "We're only going to deal with the departmental chairman." I said, "Then you're not going to deal with anybody because this is the committee." I said, "The only reason you want to deal with Lefty is that you want to fire him," which wasn't the case but it got Lefty off the hook. He wouldn't have to tell the people to go back to work.

We refused even to have the superintendent in the office because it was he who had rejected the grievance. We said, "We're not going to deal with him. We want to talk with somebody that has more authority." They brought in the division manager. We met late in the night and all the next day. They agreed to everything. They wanted this committee to meet with the company on a regular basis about safety conditions, by-passing the union safety committee because this was an immediate issue. (The union safety committee worked on things month by month: a meeting this month to say that this light bulb had burned out, next month they come back and say, we didn't have any light bulbs.)

So next day we have a meeting at the union hall to explain what we gained. We're discussing whether we're going back to work or not and I'm saying to the guys, "Look, if there's anything else you want, let's hear it."

Then the Youngstown newspaper comes out. It reports the accident and the strike and it says, "Tony got killed because of his own negligence." The company sent out that statement. The guys got furious: "We want that statement retracted in tomorrow's paper." Not just a phone call or a letter. They wanted it in the paper, retracted. The paper doesn't come out for another twenty-four hours. The guys stayed out another day. And in the next day's paper the company retracted that statement and then the guys went back to work.

They reprimanded everybody in the Open Hearth that went out and they gave me three days off. We said, "Wait a minute, take the reprimands away." And they did take them off everybody else. I said, "Hey, I don't care. You guys go back to work."

Other departments didn't go out on strike in sympathy, but there was just no work for them, because we made the steel. That's a feeling of power. And it isn't something you're doing as an individual. You're doing it as a group.

If you're not going to *do* something, then you're not going to be a leader, are you? It wasn't prepared timing. It fell into place. You've got to recognize those situations. Be there when there are credible steps to take.

Being a Radical

When we integrated the better jobs in the Open Hearth, it wasn't a popular position to take. It was a correct position but not a popular position.

To be anti-Vietnam War, anti-Kent State,[2] wasn't a popular position. I was Red-baited. But I found that the people didn't really care what my politics were as long as I won grievances, did my job as a union officer. Their question was, does he produce as a union representative?

In a steel mill the type of work we were involved in was gang-type work. You couldn't do the job yourself. You had to help the guy in the next furnace. He helped you. You didn't have to like him but you knew that to get the job done and not die, you had to help each other.

So then you start talking. "How's the kids?" "What kind of car do you got?" Everyday stuff. And before you know it, "Come on over and have a beer. We're going to have a party. Why don't you bring your wife?" Before you know it you're friends.

You go to the union meetings and speak your piece. Somebody says, "Hey, I don't know him but that's the way I feel." So you go over and say, "Hey, I'm Ed and I work in the Open Hearth." If you're going to be a socialist, you got to be sociable.

We were communicative. We would talk to people. We could express ourselves. We weren't afraid of the boss. You got a job, you did it. You didn't do any extra. You helped your fellow worker. Over the years you develop a certain credibility.

For me to have gone out to the gate and pass out the Socialist Workers Party newspaper, and not know anybody there, and expect to recruit thirty people by the end of the month, would have been insane! You got to put down roots if you want to change anything.

President of Local 1462

It was always a part of our strategy to run people for local union office because we figured you had to have a base.

In 1970, I ran for president against Augie Naples and lost by about 100 votes. It was an honest election. Steward elections were held a month later and I was elected steward in the department. In 1973, I ran for president and defeated Augie Naples. I ran two more times after that and won. The last time I ran unopposed.

You got 10 percent of the folks in the union that are company and 10 percent that are real union folks. The rest pay their dues and go home. People only come to union meetings when *they* have a problem. It's contract time? OK. Are we going out on strike? Everybody's there and wants to know. Or in one department, something may happen that brings every-

2. Ed Mann refers to the events of May 4, 1970, when National Guardsmen killed four students at Kent State University. The university is less than an hour's drive from Youngstown and one of the students killed was from a Youngstown suburb. To be "anti-Kent State" was to oppose what the National Guardsmen did.

body together. But no continuity. People aren't die-hard dedicated. People have other interests.

We knew we couldn't get them all to a union meeting, so we mailed a newspaper to every member. If a guy didn't want to come to union meetings he was still entitled to information, and his wife could read about it too. We'd all contribute articles. We put articles in from anybody who wanted to submit them. It was controversial as hell.

The international filed charges against us for what we printed. And we'd print those charges, so the members could see. Then we'd have a local union meeting and say, "What do you want to do about it?" They'd say, "Just keep doing what you're doing. It's the members' paper." We told the international that we'd give them equal time if they wanted it.

We gave them democracy in the local. Once we had elected stewards for a couple of years you couldn't appoint a steward, because the guys would jump all over your ass. "We don't want that son of a bitch. Here's the guy we want." That made it easier for me as president, too. I didn't have to accept the heat for somebody I'd appointed. I could say, "You guys elected him. If he's no good, get him the hell out of here."

Guys who didn't get elected could be appointed to committees. We had committees on workers' comp, unemployment, pensions, hospitalization, that did their jobs. We had one guy who wasn't a good union steward. We made him head of the Blood Bank. It was a non-controversial job. He loved it. It gave him a role in the local.

We Are The Union

We had assumed the mill would always be there. In October 1978 we learned otherwise. The Brier Hill Works were going to be shut down as the result of a merger between the Lykes conglomerate, owner of the Youngstown Sheet & Tube Company, and the Ling Temco Vought (LTV) conglomerate, owner of Jones & Laughlin (J&L) Steel. The first notice to the local union was in a prospectus concerning the proposed merger that Lykes and LTV mailed to their stockholders. The prospectus described phasing out Brier Hill as one of the "anticipated benefits" of the merger.

We organized a picket line at the mill. About 200 steelworkers carried signs reading "Keep Brier Hill Open," "People First, Profits Second," "Impeach Griffin Bell" (a reference to Attorney General Bell's approval of the Lykes-LTV merger), "Youngstown Victim of Corporate Rape," and "Save Our Valley." This was the first direct action taken by steelworkers in response to the Youngstown shutdowns.

On January 22, 1979, Local 1462 held a meeting at the union hall. By coincidence, Gordon Allen, Sheet & Tube's superintendent, was speaking that same evening at the Mahoning Country Club not far away. At the meeting I mentioned the fact that Allen was speaking nearby. I said that I still had the signs from the picket line in the back of my pickup truck. People began moving toward the door. We drove to the Country Club and set up a picket line outside the front door. Ken Doran moved up and down the line. He kept saying, "Let's go inside." Finally, Doran opened the door and Barbero led the group through. In the lobby we set up a chant, "Where's Gordon Allen?" It was a way of saying, Will we ever get to talk to somebody who can make a decision to save our plant?[3]

The management of the Country Club called the Girard police. The police arranged themselves inconspicuously and made no attempt to interfere.

Roger Slater, J&L's Youngstown district manager, and Gary Wuslich, superintendent of industrial relations, pleaded with me to keep the demonstrators outside. After a heated discussion, I agreed to hold people in the lobby until Allen came out.

We waited ten or fifteen minutes. When Allen finally approached he paused and said to me, "Now Ed, you know we are handling this through the union." I and several others responded in one voice, "We *are* the union!"

We made the best fight we could. I think John Barbero and I had different attitudes. John thought we should fight to the end to keep the mill open. I felt that was unrealistic. You had to cut the best deal you could in the real situation that existed. We had people who were close to retirement, people who had very little seniority, and people in the middle group. I figured I was elected to represent everyone.

We bargained for Trade Readjustment Allowance. The company said, If you promise not to destroy the mill (they were paranoid as hell), we'll agree that we are shutting down because of foreign imports (which was a lie). I said, "I guarantee you the guys won't tear the mills down." It was a sure bet. The agreement included Campbell, Brier Hill, Rod and Wire, everybody from the plant manager down. It came to about $15,000 per employee.

"I'm Going Down That Hill"

In November 1979, U.S. Steel announced that it was closing all its mills in the Youngstown area. Another 3500 workers would lose their jobs. Later that month about 300 Youngstown steelworkers together with Pittsburgh

3. *The Brier Hill Unionist*, v. 6, no. 4 (Feb. 1979), published a photo of members of Local 1462 with their picket signs inside the Mahoning Country Club confronting Gordon Allen. The video *Shout Youngstown* includes narration of the encounter by eyewitness Gerald Dickey, Local 1462 Recording Secretary.

supporters occupied the first two floors of U.S. Steel's national headquarters in Pittsburgh. The occupation lasted several hours.

Then on January 28, 1980, there was a rally at the hall of Local 1330, USWA, in Youngstown. The hall was just up a hill from U.S. Steel's Youngstown administration building. The politicians came and made their speeches. They didn't say anything. I think the crowd thought they were there to get votes.

I began my speech by saying, "You know, we've heard a lot about benefits this morning but I thought we were here to save jobs." I went on:

I think we've got a job to do today. And that job is to let U.S. Steel know that this is the end of the line. No more jobs are going to be shut down in Youngstown. You've got men here, you've got women here, you've got children here and we're here for one purpose. Not to be talked to about what's going to happen in Congress two years from now. What's going to happen in Youngstown today?

There's a building two blocks from here. That's the U.S. Steel headquarters. You know the whole country is looking at the voters, the citizens. What are you going to do? Are you going to make an action, or are you going to sit and be talked to?

The action is today. We're going down that hill, and we're going to let the politicians know, we're going to let U.S. Steel know, we're going to let the whole country know that steelworkers in Youngstown got guts and we want to fight for our jobs. We're not going to fight for welfare! [Cheers.]

In 1919 the fight was on for the 8-hour day and they lost that struggle and they burned down East Youngstown, which is Campbell. Now I'm not saying burn anything down but you got the 8-hour day.

In 1937 you wanted a union and people got shot in Youngstown because they wanted a union. And everything hasn't been that great since you got a union. Every day you put your life on the line when you went into that iron house. Every day you sucked up the dirt and took a chance on breaking your legs or breaking your back. And anyone who's worked in there knows what I'm talking about.

Now, I don't like to read to people but in 1857 Frederick Douglass said something that I think you ought to listen to:

"Those who profess to favor freedom and yet discourage agitation are men who want crops without plowing up the ground. They want rain without thunder and lightning. They want the ocean without the awful roar of its waters. This struggle may be a moral one (and you've heard a lot about that) or it may be a physical one (and you're going to hear about that) but it must be a struggle. Power concedes nothing without a demand. It never did and it never will. Find out what people will submit to and you will find out the exact measure of injustice and wrong which will be imposed upon them. And these will be continued until they are resisted in either words or blows or with both. The limits of tyrants are prescribed by the endurance of those they oppress."

This was said in 1857 and things haven't changed. U.S. Steel is going to see how much they can put on you. And when I say you I mean Youngstown, you know. We've got lists. We've got an obituary of plants that were shut down in the last twenty years. When are we going to make a stand?

Now, I'm going down that hill and I'm going into that building. And anyone that doesn't want to come along doesn't have to but I'm sure there are those who'll want to.

People liked the idea! At least 700 people were involved. When we got to the U.S. Steel building we told the property protection people to step aside, and they did. We took over the building.

On the top floor we found an executive game room no one ever knew about. My daughter Beth changed her baby's diaper on the executives' pool table. At the end of the afternoon Bob Vasquez, president of Local 1330, decided to end the occupation. But if we had it to do again, I know that he, and I, and everyone I know who was there, would have stayed in that building for as long as it took.

"I Think There's a Better Way"

I retired in 1980. In 1981 the Workers Solidarity Club of Youngstown was organized. It's a pretty free-wheeling organization. We don't have membership lists. We don't have dues. I think the makeup of the Club is exciting: people from different unions, unemployed folks, retirees, people from all walks of life. We do a lot of support work for people on strike. We make an effort to organize the unorganized.

I joined the Industrial Workers of the World (IWW) about 1984. And in 1986, after LTV filed for bankruptcy, I became active in an organization of LTV retirees called Solidarity USA.

The IWW is a lot like the Solidarity Club. Whoever wants to do their thing at the moment, does it. If you want to participate, you participate, and if you don't, you don't.

I like the Wobblies'[4] history: the Bill Haywood stuff, the Ludlow mine, the Sacco-Vanzetti thing. I like their music. I like the things they were active in.

These folks believed that workers should exercise power, instead of handing it over to bureaucrats they elect, and letting the bureaucrats make the decisions. The people have to live with the decisions. If you make a decision that's bad, and you have to live with it, you can't blame somebody else. But what happens when a bureaucrat makes a decision and you have to live with it?

4. IWW members were pejoratively called "Wobblies."

A lot of our folks belong to established unions and they don't want to attack the AFL-CIO because they feel that by doing that you're attacking the union movement. I don't sense that there's any movement there at all. We have people who are sensitive about attacking the AFL-CIO for not doing its job. But it's not going to do its job. It's not structured to do its job.

I don't regard the AFL-CIO as "the union." I think the union's in the people. Don't forget, there are only 13 million workers organized in the AFL-CIO, but there are probably 100 million workers. As long as people work they are going to have grievances. Now, who is going to handle those grievances? Some kind of organization, that is, people together. Bureaucrats aren't going to solve our problems.

It's very unpredictable. If we read our history, we know that back in Eugene Debs' time the railroads were one of the biggest industries in the country. They had a lot of shops: people worked as blacksmiths, machinists, whatever. The company cut their pay so much a day. They didn't do anything about it. Six months later the company cut their pay again, quite a bit. Then the company came up with a pay cut that was infinitesimal. That was enough! The whole country went down. It was like a general strike. They burned the railroad yards in Pittsburgh and in many other places. Who knows what is going to make the workers say, "This is enough!" But the point is, somebody has to be there when they say, "This is enough!"

Maybe the AFL–CIO has run its course. Maybe there will be unions but they won't be structured as we see them today.

The companies say they want workers to participate in the work process, in management. But they're not giving away any decision-making. The company's rights are very clear-cut and defined. You may be able to discuss how many parking places there will be in the parking lot, or what kind of pop will be in the pop machine. But when it comes to hiring, firing, disciplining, the rules of production and so on, you're not involved. They talk about "work teams." This is garbage. A work team tends to say, Hey, this guy isn't keeping up, let's get rid of him.

The Wobblies say, Do away with the wage system. For a lot of people that's pretty hard to take. What the Wobblies mean is, You'll have what you need. The wage system has destroyed us. If I work hard I'll get ahead, but if I'm stronger than Jim over here, maybe I'll get the better job and Jim will be sweeping floors. But maybe Jim has four kids. The wage system is a very divisive thing. It's the only thing we have now, but it's very divisive.

Maybe I'm just dreaming but I think there's a better way.

James Trevathan

"This society has declared war on black males"

James Trevathan is an African American from Youngstown, Ohio. Like his father, he sought employment in the basic steel industry. In 1974, a suit filed by two black steelworkers in Alabama against both the steel companies and the union resulted in a Consent Decree that made it possible for Trevathan to move from the Mason Department to the Machine Shop. A few years later the mills in Youngstown shut down.

Trevathan developed second and third careers, as a painter, and as counselor on employment problems for the local NAACP and Urban League. Trevathan has not found unions very helpful in addressing the problems of minority workers.

This conversation took place at the Lynds' kitchen table in November 1998.

I was born in Youngstown, Ohio in July 1925 in a wooden apartment house they called a "flat."

I don't remember the exact year, but I was about eight, nine, ten years old when my father used to get up every morning about 4:30, 5 o'clock, and go down to Republic Steel on Poland Avenue. They had this system. There would be fifty, sixty men. One of the foremen or supervisors would come out, and he would pick who he wanted, and how many he wanted. The others had to go back home.

My father did that five, six days a week. Some weeks he was fortunate. He might get picked three days that week. Sometimes it was four days, and a whole lot of times, none.

So my father developed a little side skill to support his family. He was a painter and a paper hanger. That went on until we moved from a street right up the hill from Poland Avenue to the South Side. Then he went full-time as a painter and an interior decorator with my grandfather.

He used to do a lot of work on the North Side of Youngstown for people who could afford it. He used to do, say, a $900 interior painting job and get paid maybe $350–400. At one time, when he didn't have transportation, I remember seeing my father carrying a paper-hanging board, a table that folded up, and a stepladder, and walk eight, ten, twelve blocks to get to the job.

As we started getting a little older—I must have been, oh, twelve, thirteen—he began to take us with him, and teach us. We would start off painting garages, cellar windows. As we got older he taught us how to hang paper. That's how, later on, I got involved in it myself.

Segregation in 1945

I've had a good life, wife and children and things. For a black man, it's been OK. But I've had nasty experiences with people that caused me to be the way I am. And it hurts; it hurts.

I went in the Service in 1942. In 1945 my mother was living on West Federal Street and she had a massive heart attack. The Red Cross interceded for me to get a leave to come home. They gave me fourteen days.

So I came home on the trains. When I got here, she was in South Side hospital. After I had been here six or seven days, they released her from the hospital. She came home. And when my fourteen days were up, she was home, and my oldest brother was there. I said, "I'm going to go to the train station by myself, Momma."

The B & O railway station was on the near West Side. Now, I had on my uniform. I was in the 82nd Airborne. I was a paratrooper. I had my jump ribbons on. I had a couple of little combat ribbons. So I went to the train station and they said I had about an hour and a half to wait.

Right across the street was a little bar. I had never been in a bar in my life before. But I did drink a little bit. So I went across the street and sat there at the counter. I was going to have me maybe a shot of whiskey and a couple of beers, waiting on the train.

There was a white lady behind the bar. After I sat there for about five minutes she came up and said, "May I help you?" I said, "Yes. I'd like to have a double shot of Calvert's and a bottle of beer." She said, "I'm sorry, we don't serve colored."

Now this was in 1945. I'd been over there. I'd been shot at. I had gone through the training at Fort Bragg, North Carolina, I had jumped out of airplanes and was scared to death. I had done all of this and I hadn't bothered anybody. I did it because the white man said, "Do it: sign here, go here, and do this." Why did I have to go through all this mess?

I got up to leave. And this shows you that there are some good white people in the world. There were two white guys (I didn't know they were truck drivers) sitting at a table. One of them got up and came over. He said, "What did you say to this soldier? Did I hear you say you don't serve colored?" "Well yes, that's our policy." He started cussing her. His buddy came up to try to stop him. They started talking about how they were going to turn the place completely out. I said, "No, no. Come on. This might get back on me because I'm in uniform. Please, don't, come on."

We went outside. The one truck driver almost had tears in his eyes. He said, "Come here, soldier." They took me over to the tractor parked over on the side. It didn't have a trailer, just a cab. He reached up under the seat and he had a brand new quart of Johnny Walker Red Label Scotch. He said, "Here. Take it with you. Keep it." Gave me the whole bottle, sure did.

I don't understand it. All because of this [tapping the skin on his forearm].

Take Your Hand Off My Wife

When I first came out of the Service, I went to Youngstown State University for a semester and a half on the GI bill. Then I fell in love and got married. My uncle got me a job at Valley Mould and Iron. I was working out there in 1949, 1950.

One pay day I had asked my wife to meet me downtown. There was a bar called The Rainbow Bar which used to cash pay checks. This particular morning I was working 11 to 7, and I was going to give my wife my money and go fishing with my buddy.

When we pulled up in front of the bar, I looked up the street at the new furniture store, Haber's. My wife was standing there and a police officer was holding her by the arm. So I got out of the car, and I walked up there, and I said, "Hello. Hey, what's going on?"

He said, "Who are you?"

I said, "Well, that's my wife."

He said, "We've been getting reports about women hanging out down here on pay days. We watched her standing here fifteen or twenty minutes."

I said, "I told her to meet me here. I'm going to give her some of my pay check." I showed him my pay check.

He said, "How do we know that this is your wife? You got any papers?"

I said, "No, I don't carry no wedding papers with me. That's my wife, and you take your hand off her."

My first wife was a small, short lady. The cop was about six feet. He must have tightened up on her arm, hurting her, so she started to cry.

Then I used some profanity and told him to take his hand off my wife.

When I said that, he turned her loose and took a step back. Now, I don't know for sure, and I doubt I'll ever know, but something inside of me said he was going to pull his gun and shoot me. I didn't have anything. I just ran and grabbed him, and picked him up, and threw him through the plate glass window of the furniture store.

They told me later in court that it wouldn't have been so bad, but I picked up a big piece of the glass. I intended to kill him. But his buddy got out of the car, and ran over and started beating me across my shoulders with his stick. I dropped the glass, and they were able to subdue me and arrest me.

That was in the morning. About ten or eleven o'clock that night, they came and got me out of the cell, and took me downstairs in the basement. They bent me over the back of a chair, and used wet towels, and beat me in the kidneys. The towels don't leave a mark, that's why they do that. But you can't control your water for a couple of weeks.

After my father got to see me, they were able to get me some pills, and it was all right. There was no permanent damage. I guess I had to be taught a lesson for assaulting a police officer.

My father was a Mason, and Mr. Oates, who was a barber, was a Mason, and an attorney we knew was a Mason. They decided that if I was indicted by a grand jury, I would go on trial in the county. They would surely send me away, because the jury would all be white.

So they used their Masonic connections and got me out of jail. But I had to leave Youngstown. They knew that the police would be picking me up every weekend, harassing me, and they told me to get out. I left Youngstown and went to Chicago.

I got a job as a bus driver up there. But the cost of living was so high, with a wife and two kids, I had to come back to Youngstown.

Bus Driver

Then I got to be the second black man to drive a city bus in Youngstown. The company was called the Youngstown Municipal Railway Company. It was privately-owned, and there was no union.

I could understand that the city had never seen black bus drivers. People got on the bus, and some were all right, and some would roll their eyes at you.

One day I was working the Elm Street bus line. At that time there were a lot of black women who went up and down that part of town, doing housework. A white lady got on the bus. She threw her fare on the floor. There were fifteen or twenty people on the bus, mostly black women.

I told her, "Missus, you have to put your money in the fare box." She looked at me and said, "If you want it in there, you black son of a bitch, put it in there yourself," and went back and sat down.

I didn't move. I just sat there. In our training we were taught not to curse anybody out, not to argue, but to get to a telephone and call a supervisor. So I sat there for about five minutes. The bus was not moving. The women got mad, and started to call this lady all kinds of names, because they had to go to work. They talked about throwing her through the window. Finally she got up, and ran off the bus, leaving the money laying there on the floor.

The pay was so low! One day a friend of mine was riding the bus. I was taking him to work down in Struthers and telling him that I needed a better-paying job, so he told me to put in an application at the steel mill.

Youngstown Sheet & Tube

I went into the Rod and Wire Mill in Struthers in 1952. You had to join the union at the company employment office. When you signed your W-2 forms, you signed a card to be in the union. Union dues were deducted from payroll.

In the Wire Mill, it was about fifty-fifty black and white. You started as what they called a wire drawer helper. They had great big machines called bull frames. They took a wire coil about three inches in diameter and ran it through the machine and brought it down to a smaller size, stretched it out. You started off with a big spool of rod on the floor. You pulled the rod up to what they called a pointer machine, stuck it in, and put a point on it. Then you took it out and took it over to the die box on the bull frame, and stuck it in there. Then the wire drawer operator ran the machine.

They had one department there called "the die room," where they made all the dies. They worked in nice warm conditions, shirt sleeves in the winter time, clean, and good money. There were never any blacks in there.

Machine Shop

After the Rod and Wire Mill shut down, I was transferred to the Mason Department at the Campbell Works. I was a bricklayer helper for a while.

Then I got to be a labor foreman, what they called a "pusher." It wasn't really a foreman because the foreman were on salary. It was a crew leader.

I used to see the way the big bosses would talk to the foremen, the guys on salary. They weren't in the union. They couldn't say anything. I knew I couldn't handle that. As a crew leader, if they cussed me out, I could cuss them back and just go back to the gang and start loading bricks again.

After the Consent Decree came in, I went up to the employment office and took an aptitude test. I passed it. Then they gave you a list to select which trade you wanted to go into. They had bricklayer, welder, carpenter, millwright, pipe fitter, machinist.

Well, when I had first gone to work in the Mason Department, we used to go over to the Machine Shop where they had a pop machine. When you went in there, the Machine Shop was a great big nice, warm building, the machines just a running, the guys in the wintertime, in January with little short sleeved shirts on, clean. We used to go there and stand by the machines while we drank our pop. We couldn't hang out too long, or the foreman would come get us.

I thought it was a nice place to work. So when I passed the aptitude test, I marked "Machine Shop." The gentleman at the employment office said, "Oh, no. You don't want to go there." I said, "Why not?" He said, "Oh, it's hard." I said, "No, it ain't hard." He said, "Did you graduate?" I said, "Yes, I graduated from East High School." He said, "Well, you know, it's math, and it's been a while." He did everything he could to dissuade me from going into that Machine Shop. All that did was to make me more determined.

So I went in there. I had been out of high school for a lot of years. The math was hard. But I got my oldest daughter and my oldest son, and they would sit up with me at night, and we would go over Algebra 1, Algebra 2, trigonometry. They'd teach me.

And there was a black machinist in the mill, the first one in there, named Hubert Clardy. We would go to his house. And he would teach us. There were only six of us out of some 120-some machinists. Then in the shop he would teach us. You had to put so many hours in the shop, and so many hours at the Buckeye School.

You'd go in the shop in the morning, and the foreman would say, "Trevathan, you go over there and work with Blackie Naples." Blackie was a white machinist. I would go over there. He'd look at me and tell me, "OK. Have a seat over there." So I'd sit down. Twelve o'clock would come, and I'd be sitting there. The whistle would blow at three o'clock, I'd still be sitting there.

They weren't all like that, but a majority were. And the supervisors didn't seem to care. There were a couple who were different. There was one white fellow who was married to a blind lady. He was real nice. He would teach you.

One time a foreman was sick and the company made Hubert Clardy an acting foreman on afternoon turn. A lot of the machinists went home. The next day they came back to ring in for afternoon turn, because you worked the same turn the whole week. The superintendent, a big German fellow, was standing at the clock. As they were coming in the door, he was standing there with their time cards. He had taken them out of the racks.

They asked him where their cards were, and he said, "You're not working today. Go back home." He did it for three days. Work was starting to pile up, and it was going to cause a lot of confusion. Finally, from what I understand, the big bosses across the river, plus the union, stopped him. But thirty-five or forty men, almost the whole afternoon turn, lost three days' work. That superintendent was a fair man, and he didn't have any more problems out of them about working with us blacks.

After the company made Hubert Clardy a foreman, the men knew that they had to be more cooperative. After they saw that we were going to be there, most of them would help us.

The apprenticeship was four years. Then you took your final test and got your journeyman's card. If you worked a lot of overtime, you could do it in less than four years. We didn't get a lot of overtime.

In the test, you had to run the machines by yourself. There was a lathe machine, a planer, and a boring mill. Those were the three basic ones. They would give you a job. The foreman would come by at the clock and give you an order. It would have drawings on it. It could be a gear, or a rod, or a shaft. You would take that and go to whatever machine you needed. If it was a big shaft, you'd probably go to the lathe machines. If it was a big gear, you'd go to the boring mills. Then you would call a crane and go down in the back where they had all the material, metals, stocked up. You would measure what you needed, bring it up to the machine with the crane, and put it on the machine. Then you would get your tools and mark it and measure it, what you needed, which way you had to go. Diameter, length, circumference. Then you started up your machine.

We carried our plant-wide seniority into the Machine Shop. That was another contention in that shop. A couple of us that went in there, a couple of blacks, had more seniority than some of the white machinists. So when it came time for vacations, we would be able to pick the June, July, and August months, because we had more seniority. Then sometimes if things got slow, and there was a layoff, they had to go out before we did.

The Machine Shop was shut down in 1982. I had been there seven or eight years, making decent money. By that time I had thirty years' seniority and the age to qualify for the magic "rule of 80." So I took my retirement.

Looking back, the union helped only when it was backed into a corner. The union president at the Campbell Works was a piece of work. Some of the blacks in the mill had some very serious thoughts about doing some violent things to that president. The union did just what it had to do for us blacks. No more. That's all. The least possible. Sometimes they would reach out and make a couple of blacks shop stewards, or grievance people, but these blacks were well-chosen. They did what they were told. No, the union wasn't nothing to rave about.

I was a member of the union but I never wanted to be involved in it. I had no time for activism.

Painting

All the time I was in the mill I worked at two jobs, taking care of five children. I never stopped painting. When I was in the Wire Mill, the Mason Department, the Machine Shop, I would always try to trade shifts. You would be scheduled day turn for one week, 3 to 11 for one week, 11 to 7 next week. For eighteen years I almost always worked 11 to 7, so I could do my painting in the day time. It wasn't hard to get.

You got children running around, you've got to get shoes, and pants, you don't worry too much about sleep. You do what you have to do. I would take small jobs, living room, kitchen. Sometimes in the summer I would take outside jobs. I had a couple of guys that used to help me. We would paint together.

There were two brothers who founded the Haber's furniture store. (Yeah, the same place where I threw the cop through the window.) They had come here from New Castle, Pennsylvania. They gave me a contract to paint the whole downtown store. I rented some scaffolds and things. The union came down and stopped the job.

I had my cousin, Oscar Hill, and another friend, Harry Venable. There were going to be four of us. We were going to work evenings, after the store closed.

On the second or third night, the union started picketing in front of the store. Mr. Haber called me in the office the next morning. Mr. Haber told me, "Jim, I'm going to have to stop your job." I said, "Why?" He said, "You see those pickets out there. That's no good for my business. I don't know what to tell you."

So I went out and talked to one of the union guys who was picketing. He told me to go to the union hall on Rayen Avenue. I went up there, and asked if I could get in the union. I said I would be willing to pay my initiation fees, dues, whatever it took for the four of us to get into the union.

They told me that they weren't accepting new memberships at the time but I could form my own local. I didn't know how to form a union local! I said, "You need lawyers to do that, don't you? There are a lot of legal issues there. I don't know anything about it."

So I went back to Haber's, got my stuff, and we left. That's all we could do.

My Wife's Family

I married again in 1960. When I met my second wife, she was from Clinton, South Carolina, down near Spartanburg. You drove down the main highway, then you turned off to go to where her parents lived. I must have driven ten miles down this dark road to get to where they lived, back in a big clearing. There were a number of houses up on wooden poles.

She had a couple of elderly uncles. Her grandfather on her father's side was still living. One of her uncles had his own whiskey still, way back in the woods. They came up to the house one morning, about four of them, with their shotguns and hound dogs. You drove way down there to a beautiful creek. It was so clear you could count the bricks at the bottom. That's where they made the whiskey.

They would be drinking, and I would be right there with them, too, because that was some good whiskey. They told me some of the experiences that they had in the South. Things that people up here could never, never, never dream would happen.

They told me how one man, my wife's father, lived on the white man's land. He had four daughters and a son. They all worked. The girls and their mother worked in the big houses, the men worked in the fields.

A white man named Copeland had three sons. His sons used to come down to where my wife and her family lived, in the evenings, and ask for the two daughters. The father would be sitting on the porch. He'd say, "They're back there in the house doing dishes or baking pies." "Tell them we want to see them." He had to call his two daughters out, and they'd get in the car with these white boys, and they'd take them down into the woods, bring them back maybe an hour, two hours later, their hair all over their heads. And they'd go back in the house.

Now, the father had to sit there and see this happen. If he had raised his voice, they would have kicked his family off the land, they wouldn't have had anywhere to stay. Or he would have been a dead man.

I know that God teaches, "Don't hate. Don't hate. It's a sin to hate." He wants you to love this man just like he was your brother. But then when you see things with your own eyes, and hear things with your own ears, how can you do that? How?

It started to get to me. It may have had something to do with me getting involved with the NAACP or the Urban League.

Troubleshooting

In 1988 or 1989 I met Willie Oliver, the head of the NAACP. We used to sing in male choruses in churches. He sang with Friendship Baptist Church, and I sang with Mt. Zion.

He was always telling me that he needed somebody to be chairman of the Labor and Industry Committee. He kept bugging me, and bugging me, and I was starting to wind down my painting work, so I had some spare time. I said I would give it a shot.

The office was downtown, right across the street from the police station. I was there until about three years ago, when I left and came to the Urban League.

The NAACP didn't pay. It was all volunteer. After I was there for about a year, they voted to give me $50 a month for gas. But out of all the years I was there, I never got but about $300 or $400. They never had any money.

I learned how to get people to talk to me. I learned how to get the confidence of workers. I would listen. I would go to a meeting, just sit there and listen, and take notes. Basically, you just need to have common sense, "mother wit."

I learned that if a person came to me with a complaint, the first thing you have to do is to use your own judgment. You have to look at this person while they are talking, look into their eyes. You have to make sure that they are being 100 percent straight with you, because you don't ever want to go to a meeting where you start saying something, and people start pulling out papers, documents, showing you that you are way off base. That can be totally embarrassing. So you try to investigate any way you can: check it out.

I've had individual cases from Big John's car wash to a good job downtown working at the TV stations, how they discriminate against them, how they mistreat their black employees. Big John's car wash, on Belmont Avenue, makes all the tips go into one box, and claims to keep it to divide it up at Christmas time. Who's going to still be there at Christmas the way turnover is at a car wash? Then he would take the black employees and in winter time, put them out in front, drying off the cars with towels, where it's cold, while the whites are in the back, where they vacuum out the cars, with great big heaters; then in the summer time they reverse it.

You know about Denny's restaurant, McDonald's restaurant, Burger King. It doesn't matter where blacks go. Look at how they do with good-paying jobs at a plant like Packard Electric. We were trying to get blacks into the apprenticeship program. Blacks would pass the written test and then they would go to the interview. Interviewing a person is perception. They were flunking us out at the interviews.

Black and White

This society has declared war on black males. I'm the father of three boys, the grandfather of four grandsons, and the great–grandfather of four more boys. They have declared war on black males. They are building prisons today for my great–grandsons.

This is my belief: they are out to genocide the black race in this country. If you don't have seeds to plant grass, no grass is going to grow. If you incarcerate all the young black males between the ages of seventeen and twenty-five or thirty, and all that you don't incarcerate, you make sure that they have plenty of drugs to sell, and plenty of guns to kill each other with, slowly but surely you're going to kill off blacks in the United States.

The white man plans, fifty, sixty, a hundred years ahead. We don't do this. We are more reactive than proactive. Just as sure as God is in heaven, if nothing changes the way it is now, forty-five or fifty or sixty years from now the black race will be almost gone in this country.

As I said before, there are some beautiful white people in this world. Yes, I've met some. That one truck driver was ready to do something very upsetting. That big German supervisor at the Number One Machine Shop. He wasn't friendly or buddy-buddy, but he made sure everything was straight. He kept everything on an even keel. There was no mistreating. When he did find out about it, he stopped it the best he could. His hands were tied by the other workers and the union and the big shots across the river, so he had his limitations, too. Otherwise he wouldn't have had a job.

I keep going for two reasons. Number one, I can't sit still. I've been working all my blessed life and I'm too dumb to sit down and relax. Number two, maybe, just maybe, I may go out here tomorrow morning and I may help two little young black people keep their jobs. I can't do anything for these forty or fifty other ones. But I may help these two. And maybe, some of that will rub off on one out of the two, and maybe he'll go and help two more.

Charlie McCollester, Mike Stout,
and the TriState Conference on Steel

"We needed something more than
a labor-community-church alliance"

*The movement against the closing of steel mills in Youngstown and Pittsburgh,
1977–1986, was the most sustained struggle against disinvestment and downsiz-
ing anywhere in the United States.*

*The TriState Conference on Steel was a network of steelworkers, clergy, com-
munity residents, public officials, academics and lawyers. The organization
took its name from a one-day conference held in Pittsburgh on March 27, 1979.
The gathering brought together people from the three states of Ohio, Pennsylvania, and West Virginia. Participants were alarmed by the prospect of plant
closings in the steel industry and the devastating effect it would have on their
communities.*

*By the early 1980s the only ongoing branch of TriState was in Pittsburgh. Tri-
State organized the Steel Valley Authority (SVA), which sought to use government's eminent domain power to acquire plants that were being closed and then
to run the plants under employee-community ownership.*

*Mike Stout was chairman of the grievance committee at the U.S. Steel Home-
stead Works, where a rank-and-file caucus took over Steelworkers Local 1397 in
1979. The Homestead Works was closed department by department between
1982 and 1986. Charlie McCollester was chief steward at Union Switch and Signal in Swissvale, east of Pittsburgh, when the plant closed in 1986. Charlie Mc-
Collester and Mike Stout were central to all phases of TriState's saga.*

*This account is drawn from two occasions. On April 11, 1997, a number of
persons gathered at St. Ursula's Church in Pittsburgh to record a collective oral
history of "The Struggle for Community/Worker Ownership." On March 16,*

*1998, we interviewed Charlie McCollester and Mike Stout about the campaigns
to prevent the destruction of a U.S. Steel blast furnace in Duquesne known as
Dorothy Six, and to save the Switch and Signal plant. On both occasions, a time-
line prepared by Charlie McCollester helped in establishing exact dates.*

Founding the TriState Conference on Steel

CHARLIE: On March 27, 1979, the TriState Conference on the Impact of
Steel convened in Pittsburgh. I was working as a machinist at Union
Switch and Signal, second shift. I knew things were shutting down in
Youngstown. I went to the meeting.

That morning when I got to my car, I found an 18-inch piece of steel rail
from the Edgar Thomson Works sitting on my car seat. I had told a carpenter friend of mine I wanted to make an anvil. He cut it for me.

In the course of that conference, I heard the lawyer from U.S. Steel and
the president of the Steelworkers union, all these important people. Basically they told us that the closing of steel mills was inevitable, there was
nothing that could be done. Then, in the afternoon, John Barbero got up.[1]
He told a story about being in the first American contingent to enter Hi-
roshima, Japan. He had lived through that experience and married a Japanese woman. He said he was living through the experience a second time:
in Youngstown he was seeing families, friends, people he'd known, just
disappear. Their homes got dark. They left in the night, looking for places
to go to make a living. It was an awesome moment.

There was a coffee break after that, and I went out to the car and got
my steel rail. When we reconvened, the lawyer from U.S. Steel said, "I
don't see why we're talking about this at all because you have no right to
talk about it. This is a question of private property. The company will
make its decision according to the dictates of the market, and that's how
it's going to be."

I stood up and I threw this 18-inch piece of steel on the middle of the
floor. It went, bam! People thought I threw a bomb. And I said, the Constitution of the United States says that government should provide for the
common defense and promote the general welfare. That's what gives "we
the people" in this room a right to speak to this issue!

After that meeting an organization started to form which we called the
TriState Conference on Steel or "TriState."

---

1. See the preceding account by Ed Mann; the narrative of John Barbero, Ed Mann and
others, in *Rank and File*, 3d ed., pp. 259–278; and Staughton Lynd, *The Fight Against Shutdowns: Youngstown's Steel Mill Closings* (San Pedro: Singlejack Books, 1982).

TriState Starts in Pittsburgh

MIKE: The first time I talked to Charlie McCollester was at a "right to ratify" rally, December 6, 1979. And he kept saying, "We've got to get something going in Pittsburgh. They're going to do the same thing here." They
hadn't shut anything down yet in Pittsburgh.

The summer of 1980 I was laid off from the mill. Charlie had been laid
off at Switch and Signal. We met with Monsignor Charles Owen Rice at
St. Anne's. We told Monsignor Rice our idea: we needed a church-com-
munity-worker alliance; we were the workers, and we needed the church
people. Monsignor said, "I'm too old." We said, "All right, who are some
young nuns and priests?" He told us about Father Rich Zelik and Father
Gary Dorsey.

Our first meeting solely to form a Pittsburgh TriState chapter was December 14, 1980, at St. Stephen's Church in Hazelwood, Father Dorsey's
church.

CHARLIE: Jones & Laughlin (J&L) was closing its strip mill in Hazelwood. We approached Father Dorsey about holding a meeting at
his church. He said absolutely, and he invited a friend and parishioner,
Frank O'Brien. Frank was a former president of one of the local unions
at J&L.

Frank O'Brien had also served in the Pennsylvania state legislature.
There he noticed the frequent use of the eminent domain power to acquire
private property for public purposes. He also recalled that J&L had used
the eminent domain power to evict people from their homes in order to
expand its land around the mill. O'Brien suggested to TriState that the eminent domain power could be used in reverse: to acquire steel mills and put
them back into production.

MIKE: Between 1981 and the Dorothy Six struggle in 1984–1985, we
had a number of unsuccessful campaigns to save plants that were shutting
down. They included Mesta Machine in West Homestead and Crucible
Steel in Midland. We would try to get people to form a regional public development authority that could legally exercise the eminent domain
power. They were all scared of us. At one point in Midland, Monsignor
Rice even called them "chicken." He tried to embarrass them, and couldn't
get anybody to do anything. The West Homestead Borough Council actually voted in the Steel Valley Authority by a 4 to 3 margin in August 1982,
but the mayor vetoed it two weeks later.

We had our big meetings at the Local 1397 union hall, and our regular
meetings in St. Stephen's basement. We literally lived in Father Dorsey's
basement as our second home for about two years. He had a wonderful
Italian cook, who cooked for him, and cooked for us once a week.

Finally on October 29, 1983 we had a conference at Local 1397 and put a booklet together about forming a Steel Valley Authority that could carry out a "steel revitalization plan." This became our founding manifesto.

CHARLIE: Something needs to be added about the TriState culture, or style. I think a lot of tribute needs to be paid to Father Dorsey. He had the ability to allow very rambunctious, energetic people with very different visions to operate. He tried to make sure that those who weren't quite as forceful as others got a chance to speak, and that while people could differ, they could still come back in a kind of family way, and get things straightened out. And that worked pretty well for a lot of years without very many formal rules.

MIKE: During that period we were struggling for funding. We ran out of money several times. Looking back, I think we functioned well when we *didn't* have money, and started to fall apart when we got it. We came to have paid staff, and had to go by rules and regulations and contracts, and things started to get squabbly. The familial style was put on a back burner. Individual interests became more important than the common whole.

Dorothy Six: The First Phase

MIKE: In December 1983, U.S. Steel announced that it was going to close [a blast furnace at its Duquesne Works named] Dorothy Six. The Homestead Works were still limping along with the structural, and the slab and plate, divisions. It would be another year and a half before the 160 inch plate mill was shut down. During the whole period up to December 1983, U.S. Steel had not declared anything in the Valley to be permanently shut down, except for the open hearth at Homestead.

CHARLIE: The Duquesne Works made steel for pipe. There was a collapse of the pipe market.

MIKE: Duquesne was an integrated mill to some degree, but basically it supplied steel to the National Works across the river in McKeesport. In the latter years of its existence, National Works mainly rolled pipe. They were the premier pipe roller in the area. When the oil crisis came along, National went from working around the clock—three shifts, all the overtime you wanted—to almost a total shut down.

CHARLIE: Dorothy Six was technologically more sophisticated than anything else in the Valley. U.S. Steel, while leaving all its 1890s and 1910 blast furnaces intact, was going to blow up its best and most advanced blast furnace! People felt that was a slap in the face. There was genuine anger. Four times we blocked the destruction of the furnaces.

MIKE: The big meeting, the power broker meeting, was in Swissvale on

October 29, 1984. Two Congressmen showed up, along with several state senators and representatives, County Commissioners Forester and Flaherty, a number of borough officials, and representatives from the Steelworkers and the UE. It was the first time in TriState's history that politicians came and sat down at the table with us. They didn't say, "We have a plan. We have ideas." They said, "What do you want?" We laid out a whole program.

CHARLIE: I wrote out by hand a resolution that these guys all signed! [2]

MIKE: We had three points. One of the points was stopping the demolition. Two was a feasibility study to see whether Dorothy could be reopened as a slab producer. And three was to form the Steel Valley Authority, an entity through which the various municipalities in the Valley could exercise the power of eminent domain. They jumped on the first two, and gave lip service to the third. They had no idea that we could go out and organize the Steel Valley Authority.

Right after the Swissvale meeting, County Commissioner Forester called up David Roderick, chairman of the board of U.S. Steel, and said, "Don't tear this thing down. We've got some problems." On November 8, 1984, U.S. Steel announced that it was postponing the demolition of Dorothy Six.

CHARLIE: On December 19, 1984, the workers themselves went into the Duquesne mill with anti-freeze to winterize the furnaces and save them from freezing. TriState helped to organize the action. We shamed the Steelworkers union into paying for it. That was a very dramatic moment. The Dorothy Six campaign caught on with the media as a good will, positive, constructive alternative idea.

MIKE: At the same time, we approached the international union about funding a feasibility study. The international agreed, got Mike Locker to do it, and in the process took control away from us.

Organizing the Steel Valley Authority

MIKE: TriState and the Steelworkers met and divided up tasks. The political process to stop the demolition was going on behind the scenes. TriState couldn't do a whole lot about the feasibility study except to try to watch it and steer it wherever we could. So we decided to do the all-out, grassroots, mass organizing around the Steel Valley Authority.

2. The resolution read: "We the undersigned call upon the Allegheny Co. Commissioners to provide emergency funding necessary for an initial feasibility study of the steelmaking facilities of U.S. Steel's Mon Valley Works and other industrial facilities with first attention paid to the Duquesne Plant, as a means of developing a comprehensive plan for renewing the industrial base of the Mon and Turtle Creek valleys."

We got a big boost on January 19, 1985, when Jesse Jackson spoke in Duquesne. It was about five degrees above zero, and snowing. It seemed that the whole community was there. He declared that "Duquesne is the Selma of the plant closing struggle," and the papers carried it on the front page.

Then on January 28, 1985, 800 people attended a meeting at the Saints Peter and Paul Byzantine Church in Duquesne. Mike Locker presented his initial feasibility findings. He said that Dorothy could be a profitable enterprise.

CHARLIE: It was very important because it gave us the credibility of knowing enough about the business world to make an argument that this could work.

There followed an incredible organizing drive inside these towns to form the Steel Valley Authority. We had an office at St. Michael's Church in Homestead with big butcher paper all around the walls. We had each town mapped out, and who was responsible. Initially we got eight towns to vote for the Authority, and all together we put on fourteen different drives. It was exhaustive and exhausting.

MIKE: The period between October 1984 and May 1985 was the most significant grassroots effort in this area that I have seen. We went to steel towns on both sides of the Mon River to endorse the creation of a Steel Valley Authority. Tedious doesn't even describe it.

The towns I got were Munhall, Homestead, and McKeesport. I worked at the Homestead Works with some of the Munhall and Homestead council members. For example, I worked with Ronnie Watkins in the 160 inch mill.

Right after the Swissvale meeting I started talking with some of the Munhall people. The mayor and Ronnie Watkins, who was probably the most influential person on council, decided to give us an audience. At that private meeting Ronnie was the one who stood up and said, "Let's go for it! What have we got to lose?" On November 19, 1984, the Munhall borough council voted to join the Steel Valley Authority.

In Homestead, Betty Esper was on the council. She also worked with me in the 160 inch mill. She had over thirty years in.

Betty told me before the Homestead town meeting that the vote on council was nine to nothing against the Authority. I said, "Oh yeah? We'll see about that." We went to the meeting, and I brought just a smidgin—about fifteen—of Homestead steelworkers.

The meeting was at the MUSA (Methodist Union of Social Agencies) Center. We got up and did our presentation. The council members were acting as if they weren't going to do anything. So at one point I said, "Let's have a vote for the crowd here, so the community knows where you're at. Could you please stand up and say whether or not you're for the Authority?" There were about 150 people in attendance. One by one—I think

Betty Esper was the first—members of council stood up and said, "Well, I'm going to be for it. I don't care who else is." Sure enough, all nine supported the Authority!

CHARLIE: Mike took one side of the river, and I the other. I did Swissvale, East Pittsburgh, and Turtle Creek, tried Wilmerding and failed, and then got the City of Pittsburgh.

Dorothy Six: The End Game

MIKE: It was as if there was a war going on and there were little battles happening everywhere in the Valley at the same time. We were doing the Authority thing, and meanwhile Jim Benn was organizing at Dorothy Six in Duquesne.

Jim was a laidoff member of Local 1256, USWA, the local at the Duquesne mill. Jim worked with the Mon Valley Unemployed Committee in 1981–1982. The Unemployed Committee was doing mortgage foreclosures, unemployment benefits, and self-help. In 1984 he decided that he needed to leap into the plant closing battle.

The organizing in Duquesne consisted of winterizing and watching. They set up a shanty across from the mill, and watched the mill twenty-four hours a day to make sure that nothing moved out. At one point the company was going to move out some equipment, and I think Jim had about thirty guys there within a couple of hours to block the gate.

Things progressed very nicely up to May 1985. On May 18, 1985, we had the big parade and rally in Duquesne.

CHARLIE: The slogan was, "Save Dorothy! She can work!" There was a strong family and young people's hope for the Valley. There were families on both sides of the street, thanking us as we marched down the hill.

MIKE: We had a potential market. We identified about eight different slab purchasers who were either importing slabs, or had a severe shortage and needed them badly, and were willing to buy from this operation. But Wall Street was unwilling to finance it. Lazard Fréres, the people to whom the international union was looking for financial advice, told the union that there was no way. So the international decided that the Dorothy campaign was futile.

CHARLIE: There was also absolute hostility from the Pittsburgh ruling groups. It was total and unbroken during this period. We faced a freeze from the upper level. I don't know of any crack in the Pittsburgh corporate establishment. We could beat up on the politicians and make them move in our direction. But we never got anywhere with the money people.

MIKE: So in January 1986, Lefty Palm, the Steelworkers District Director, called us and said it was time to announce that this battle was over. We had been hearing rumors that the project was not going to fly, that the international union was not going to pursue it further. In essence the international came to us and said, "We've decided this won't work. We're abandoning it. We would like you to join us in a press conference and tell this to people."

Our problem was that we were so enmeshed in the battle to form the Steel Valley Authority. In this same period, from July 1985 to January 1986, eight or nine boroughs tentatively agreed to join, and we were dickering with their solicitors, going back into these endless meetings, crossing the t's and dotting the i's, saying, "Don't worry, your borough is not going to be sued, it's not going to go under, you're not going to lose your job as borough solicitor." We were being accused of dual boroughism, that we were eliminating the boroughs by forming the Authority.

This affected the ability of the TriState leadership to react to the situation at Duquesne. It was such a big . . .

CHARLIE: To take over a steel mill!

MIKE: And because of the positions different ones of us were in, we weren't ready to abandon everything, go sit down, and chain ourselves to the mill. I was embroiled in a huge conflict at Homestead. The 160 inch mill had just been shut down. A strike was looming. The structural mill was the last place going. I had no fight left for the Duquesne struggle. Charlie was into the Switch and Signal battle.

Union Switch and Signal

CHARLIE: In 1981–1982 there was a six and a half month strike at WABCO, including the Switch.[3]

The strike ended with a handshake agreement. The agreement included arbitration for twenty-odd members who had been fired for picket line activities. When the union leaders presented the handshake agreement to the stewards, they almost got lynched. The leadership came back to the company and said they could not get the agreement ratified. Almost certainly the next day, the company decided to move production at the Switch and Signal plant to Macon, Georgia. (We didn't know that for another three and a half years, however.)

3. Union Switch and Signal in Swissvale, and Westinghouse Air Brake in Wilmerding, were plants originally owned by Westinghouse with a long history in the Valley. They made brakes and related equipment for railroads and were collectively known as WABCO. In the 1980s, the two plants were owned by the American Standard company, and represented by local unions of the United Electrical, Radio and Machine Workers (UE).

It took us twenty-one more days to get back into the plant. Eventually the company let the union name the arbitrators and all the discharged workers returned. I got re-elected as second-shift machine shop steward in July.

Then in October 1982, I ran for chief steward and won almost two to one. It was in part a young person versus old person vote. Although I had been active in the union before the strike, and had three times been elected steward in the machine shop, it was the backlash against the leadership's role in the strike that caused me to be elected. The incumbent chief steward hadn't been on the picket lines very often. I clobbered him. The Local 610 business agent, who had dominated the local for thirty years, was beaten three to one by a guy who had never been a steward and rarely came to union meetings.

In the spring of 1985 we went through brutal negotiations. We were there ten hours a day, five days a week for nearly two months. They put more than forty concession demands on the table. We didn't dare call a strike vote, because we were worried whether we could win it.

Two days before the date on which the union was going to have to make a decision about authorizing a strike, the company withdrew all but seven of its concession demands. The remaining demands were nasty. They went right at the union but not so much at the pocket book. They hoped that the membership would run over us. We had long, all-night bargaining sessions. We were exhausted.

We went into the Sunday meeting with 1300 people who were scared, angry, and upset. What we had decided to recommend was a strategy that went right down the middle. We urged the members to reject the contract overwhelmingly, and go back to work the next morning! We said they should shake up the plant, slow down, and refuse any and all overtime. We were going to wait it out.

It worked brilliantly! The people were so grateful not to be called out on strike. Our stock went right through the roof. We union representatives went around the plant as if we were kings, because we had not put people on the street. And people had a wonderful time! Nobody worked overtime. Everybody read all the rules and acted accordingly. Production went at a crawl.

Before the union meeting the company had brought in cots and food, encouraging a strike psychology. People laughed at them as they were taking the cots out!

We finally called for a strike vote at Switch and Signal, and got 93 percent support. There was a great deal of trust in the leadership at that point.

Then on August 7, 1985, we got called down to the front office. We were told, "You've got six months. We're closing this plant."

The Fight for the Switch

CHARLIE: The mayor of Swissvale was Chuck Martoni. He became the central figure in our struggle to form a Steel Valley Authority and to save the Switch.

MIKE: There was a lot of tension between TriState and the UE leadership. They had decided, for their own reasons, to enter into a front with us. They said, "We have a little different take on this thing, but we're going in the same direction." Their take was that they could raise enough hell that maybe a "white knight" would come in and buy the place and keep it running, as in the Morse Cutting Tool battle in New Bedford, Massachusetts in 1983–84. We said employee ownership should also be considered as an option.

CHARLIE: Except for Ron Carver, who staffed the Morse Cutting Tool campaign, the UE international was ideologically opposed to employee ownership, and overtly hostile to any form of Employee Stock Ownership Plan. Their line was, "fight the boss." I kept thinking of the Bob Dylan line, "when. . . . negativity won't pull you through."

The UE international was also ambivalent toward labor-community alliances. My connection with Monsignor Rice made them extremely nervous.[4] And they were very suspicious of any direct contacts with lower-level management, who I believed to be critical to any successful plant closing struggle.

MIKE: We had almost everything we wanted in Swissvale. We had all of the churches. We had the local government. We had the politicians from the county and the state at least condoning what we were doing. And we had support in the local unions.

CHARLIE: Everybody in Pittsburgh knew Swissvale. It was a visible, media-accessible place, right off the parkway.

MIKE: But we had no money! There came a time when we went to court and said, "Hey, we want to take this plant under eminent domain." And the Judge said, "OK. Use your eminent domain power. But have you got the money to buy it? If you don't, get the hell out."

We had a meeting outside with several lawyers from the international union. It was crunch time. Some of us proposed, "Hey look, we have a mayor and a couple of people from council who are willing to bring in

4. As a young priest, Charles Owen Rice had directed a broad-based campaign against Communists in the CIO. His major impact was on the United Radio, Electrical and Machine Workers (UE). Rice later publicly revised his views and repented for certain of his actions. See *Fighter with a Heart: Writings of Charles Owen Rice, Pittsburgh Labor Priest*, ed. Charles J. McCollester (Pittsburgh: University of Pittsburgh Press, 1996), pp. 64–70, 76–108.

bulldozers and tear up the road in front of the plant, and stop them from moving equipment out. We have some nuns and priests and some community people and local union people who want to chain themselves to the gate, to get arrested." The UE lawyers told us, "No, don't do it." We said, "Why?" And the lawyers said, "Because we have people who have grievances for severance pay and benefits, and we don't want those grievances to be affected."

We learned from the Switch and Signal battle that we needed something more than a labor-community-church alliance, with everybody in the world supporting us. We needed radical action to call the question.

CHARLIE: The company had laid off all the militant stewards. We did three plant gate rallies at lunch time. Had we been able to move to nonviolent resistance, we would have had the support of Wilmerding and the local union leadership at Air Brake, the other WABCO plant. We were not able to get the international union to commit at that point, and the Swissvale local was deeply split.

TriState debated going it alone and we decided we just didn't have the forces. That was the last chance. My deepest regret is that we didn't just go ahead, and that I didn't take the lead, because the union would have followed. The people's hearts were with us.

MIKE: I think it was the lesson taken up by Jeff Swoggert, the president of the local union at Sharpsville, when the foundry there was going to be shut down. This was long after our stuff was over.

He had a smaller situation than we did, of course. But his attitude was, "I'm not ever going to take No for an answer. And we're not going to leave this plant until we get a buyer. If I have to sit in here for the rest of my life, then that's what I'm going to do." I think his determination and vision ignited people in the community to take up that cause.

It's that kind of determination that you have to have. There come critical junctures when you can't walk away. You've just got to stay. If there's a world chorus out there telling you No, you've got to say Yes, no matter. You've got to keep going.

CHARLIE: Yes, that's what has come down to me for the last ten years. It is the point I regret the most deeply.

When you're in a situation like that, it's so hard to know whether this really is the moment. There was such division inside the union. There was a constant barrage of criticism. If I had taken the lead in nonviolent civil disobedience, against the will of the international and much of the local union, some would have seen it as egotistical, self-serving.

But looking back, what I think would have been critical was to force the issue in a nonviolent way, either by chaining ourselves to the front, or going on a hunger strike, or combining the two. Somehow to have made time absolutely of the essence. Just to have sat there in front of the plant on that April 1st and to have said, "We ain't leaving until American Standard reverses itself and says that they are going to stay in Swissvale, or sells the plant to someone who will."

I think if we had done that at that point, even a handful of us, even if I was the only one from the plant, there would probably have been a couple of stewards who would have joined initially, and after a while there might have been hundreds.

The tinder was there. A spark was needed. I consider it a great failing in myself. I was in a position to make that decision, and I didn't do it. It really might have caught on.

MIKE: We'll never know.[5]

CHARLIE: What I saw as the great tragedy of Union Switch and Signal was all this intelligence, all this knowledge of building complex machinery, going to waste. Our people knew how to fit, finish, and file, to calibrate, how to make switch machines that would run for fifty years! They were pulling off Union Switch and Signal relays that were eighty years old, and sending them back. We would refurbish, refit, file a little here, replace a couple of pieces, and send them back for thirty or forty more years. I admired it.

I gave many speeches about inventorying the whole Valley, looking at which buildings are still good, looking at equipment and machinery, sorting out the good from the bad, then assembling what we had that was good and looking at the possibilities. Many good structures were razed to the ground. That great old building at Switch and Signal was built like the pyramids, an unbelievably powerful building. They tore it down.

I had a vision for the Switch. I wanted to put a dome on that wonderful old building. The company argued that you couldn't run a modern industrial facility in a multi-level building. I thought that was horse shit. That building was 400,000 square feet, five stories in the shape of a double H. The center was an ugly, open space, but it interconnected everybody. I wanted to cap the center and make it a place for the cafeteria and for all the social and educational functions.

Then all the production would have surrounded the center. You could have driven loaded semi-trailers on the fifth floor of that building. They had had presses and punch presses on the third and fourth floors. Those floors were two feet thick. They had columns that were bigger than at the temple of Karnack, in Egypt. I've been to Karnack. The basement of the Switch and Signal looked like Karnack. I had a vision of what that place could become.

5. A successful plant occupation of the kind Mike Stout and Charlie McCollester envisioned took place at the Coca Cola plant in Guatemala City in 1984–1985. See Deborah Levenson-Estrada, *Trade Unionists Against Terror: Guatemala City 1984–1985* (Chapel Hill: University of North Carolina Press, 1994).

Tony Budak

"One for one—Job security for the next generation"

Tony Budak hired in at the Packard Electric Division of General Motors (now Delphi Packard Electric) in Warren, Ohio, north of Youngstown, in 1963. The company makes electric harnesses for vehicles. Since 1973, Packard Electric has been shifting production away from its unionized facilities in Ohio to lower-wage plants in Mississippi, and, especially, to Mexico.

As of 1999 there were approximately 40,000 Packard Electric employees in Mexico and less than 10,000 in Ohio. Tony Budak proposes as a response the concept of "one for one": for each worker that retires or quits, the company must hire a new one.

Budak's diverse experiences in the plant include periods as a "group leader" and foreman; a stretch of years during which he drove a tow motor, often distributing leaflets or newsletters en route; and since 1997, work as a full-time "sub chair" and member of the bargaining committee of Local 717, International Union of Electrical Workers (IUE). Along the way he earned a Master's Degree at an alternative college in New England (while continuing to work full-time at the plant). He also used vacation time to visit the worker-owned factory complex in Mondragon, Spain.

This account is drawn from testimony at an "alternative Reich Commission hearing" held in Youngstown on August 21, 1993; from interviews on February 12, 1994, May 16, 1997, and October 8, 1997; and from The Disappearance of Local 717: An Underground History of Packard Electric *(1994), a collective oral history compiled by Benjamin Sachs.*

My Father

My father was a Croatian nationalist. He had a third grade education in Croatia. When he came here, he worked for a few years in a steel mill and he quit. He said, "That's too dangerous! I'm not working there!"

So he made his living as a racketeer. He was in charge of all the numbers rackets in Steubenville, Lowellville, Campbell and Struthers, in the 1940s and 1950s in this Valley. He frequently got in trouble with the law, and it was in the papers. I would see it when I was growing up: "Budak—racketeer—Youngstown gambler." Kids at school would pick on me about that.

My dad was forty-three when I was born. He had a European accent and a European, peasant view. He would talk to me in parables. He would say, "If you want to be a bum, be a good bum! I don't want to be ashamed of you as a bum."

At the same time, my dad never hurt a soul. He was very gentle. He was weird politically, but he gave me good values. My father was a criminal in the eyes of the newspaper and of the world, and yet to me he was a God-fearing, gracious, good guy. He would not let his children play with cards or dice.

Also, because my dad was from Croatia, I became interested in Yugoslavia, of which Croatia was then a part. In 1953, Yugoslavia under Tito instituted a national experiment in workplace democracy, such that every worker in every firm had the vote. There came a time when I wondered, "How come those guys over there are voting for their plant managers? Over here we have collective bargaining."

Management

I went to work for Packard in 1963. I did not expect to stay there. In those days parents wanted their kids to be doctors and engineers. But my dad couldn't support sending me to school full-time. So my dad said, "You gotta go to school. You're going to work there for the summer, but I want you to be educated." I went to school part-time, and I did poorly.

At Packard I worked real hard and had a good work ethic. I kept busy on my production job. The foreman saw that I was conscientious and asked if I wanted to be an assistant group leader. I became a group leader, and then a foreman. I was in supervision for ten years.

A letter appeared in the factory mail from the Dana Street administration building of Packard, addressed to all the foremen. It said that if a person was absent for a third time, you gave a written warning; if he or she was absent a fourth time, you gave a written reprimand; and for a fifth time, four hours off or the balance of the shift. The letter said in no uncertain terms that you would go by these numbers.

I had been working with people as a supervisor. I knew that this would be a tough thing for me to implement, and that if I did it in my conscientious way, it would backfire, because people would not put up with it. People have lives outside of work that don't go by numbers. They have babies, they have families, they have sickness.

I talked with some other foremen and said, "We need to let the labor relations people downtown know that they're crazy if they think we're going to live up to this policy. I've got some of the most dedicated Packard people in the world but if I treat them like this, they're going to be outside looking in for a job. And they're good workers!"

I got a couple of foremen to kick it around at the coffee machine. Next thing I knew the phone on my desk was ringing. The plant manager said, "Budak, come up to the office." I went up there. He said, "What are you doing, trying to organize a union of foremen?" I said, "What are you talking about?" He said, "The word is out that you're trying to unionize." I said, "I don't know what a union is! I've been working here for twelve years. My dad wasn't in a union. I don't know the first thing about it." We talked for three hours. Finally he said, "OK, go back to work."

His name was John. A month later John gets transferred. There's a new plant manager. He calls me in. And when I walked in the door he says, "I know what you're doing. Friday's your last day. You're going back on the floor." I had hardly walked into the office. I didn't even know this guy. And I didn't get a fair hearing.

I didn't know what to say, except to talk in one of my dad's famous parables. I said, "I want to tell you one thing. See those swinging doors out there? They swing both ways. I'm going out." I had two chips on each shoulder. I was angry!

From the following month on, I've missed maybe one union meeting.

The Warehouse

A few months before I was demoted, my grandmother died. I went to the funeral, left my mom and dad there, and went back to work. I got a phone call. They said my dad was in the hospital. When I got to the hospital my dad had died. After that I got put back on hourly. And a few months later, my wife filed for divorce.

After the divorce I started smoking pot, and began to go into a deep depression. I had discussions with some of my friends, and tried to think about what was important, and who I was, and what I wanted to be.

I started reading ferociously. I got a job in the warehouse as a tow motor driver. I started taking books in to work. When I would be waiting for a lift, I'd be reading.

The guys in the warehouse had it made. They'd work an hour, and then they didn't do anything for an hour. When the supervisor handed out what they called the "puts"—here's how many lifts you got to put into the warehouse, and here's how many lifts you've got to pull out—they'd go, "Nah, I'm not doing all that." This went on for an hour every day at the beginning of the shift. There were only going to be four hours of output per shift. They knew what they could do in four hours, and that's all they would accept.

These older fellows literally ran that warehouse. If they wanted to work Saturdays, they'd slow down on Wednesdays. If they wanted to work Sundays, they'd slow down on Tuesdays. They knew every trick in the book about safety, about delaying production. Management had nothing to say about the way the warehouse was run.

We'd have outside carriers come in. A truck driver would wait three hours for two lifts. They were amazed. They'd say, "What kind of a place is this?"

Here's an example of the culture of that warehouse. My shift ended at 12:30. One time the foreman said at 11 o'clock, "Start unloading that truck." Well, the norm in that department was that you'd quit at 11 o'clock, even though you didn't ring out till 12:30. So I started talking. "Why do I have to do this truck?" On and on for half an hour. Finally he put me on notice.

The next day I came in. The foreman said, "You're still on notice. Go to the office while we decide what we're going to do with you." I sat in there the whole shift. This went on for two days.

On the third day, instead of going to the office I went around to everybody in the department. I said, "Look, I'm sick of sitting in that office. I want you to go slow. Instead of taking three stacks on a lift, take two. Make twelve trips. Let's slow down."

They had real solidarity. I had never seen anything like it. It's not happened to me since. Everybody has to have that experience once in a lifetime. It was a *magical* day.

A few years later, the company built another warehouse. They laid out the floor plan in a new way, and in doing so destroyed the workers' sense of timing, of how much they could do. They changed all the rules and standards. The men knew there was going to be a real battle. A lot of the key organizers opted to go elsewhere. Leadership in the workers was gone.

When the new building opened up, we began to work eight for eight. Eventually, if they don't change the personnel too much, the people will get control of the floor again, and solidarity can come back.

I left the warehouse in 1992. I was there about eighteen years.

Jointness

Our contracts contain flowery words and expectations, but there are no action deadlines. There are no doable things that you can measure. When

I was young, I thought that the flowery words meant that those things were actually going to occur. They were nothing but false expectations. There was nothing like, "You're going to have the vote to overturn a management decision."

In the late 1970s, the company began to promote joint union-management programs.[1] I volunteered to facilitate weekly joint meetings. Managers and foremen would sit there. Workers would make proposals, and nothing would be done. This went on for two or three months. During that time the foremen began to come less and less.

I tried to keep the group together, even without the foremen. We carried on meetings without management for two and a half years. I was trying to get back that old warehouse kind of solidarity. It was a struggle. Now I know why. Even though we had the time to talk together, we still weren't going to get anywhere. The constraints against it were outside of the room, were in the legal system, were in the culture and ideology of what was going on. We needed a real self-interest, a common bond. Only ideas of that kind could have travelled through the group and brought about solidarity.

The company and the union said that they were developing better ways of working together to increase efficiency. For example, the company claimed that the union could help the company to be more "flexible" by eliminating (or merging) job classifications. But while such flexibility might make sense if your goal is to increase profit, this is exactly the wrong thing to do if your goal is job security. Job classifications ensure that there is employment for as many people as possible. Efforts to merge job classifications are efforts to decrease the number of workers needed to complete a job.

When the company began to move jobs south, they said there would be "no more bricks and mortar in Warren, Ohio." After the jointness programs began they started to open small branch plants in the Warren area. When the plants were being built, the company said that "harness component work requires more floor space." This sounded like a benefit for workers. But componentry work required more floor space because new machines were brought in to do work previously done by workers at the main plant on North River Road. Total floor space increased, but only to

1. According to *The Disappearance of Local 717*, pp. 11–12, 14–16, the first joint program was a combined effort to raise money for the United Way. Tony Budak describes this as a "way to break the ice" because "who could argue with giving money to charity." In 1977, the union and company conducted a joint survey, asking workers, "Should the union and management work more closely together to provide job security?" In 1982, a two-tier wage system known as the Progressive Hiring Plan (PHP) became part of the contract. According to the PHP, new hires would be brought in at 55 percent of the base wage rate and given a 5 percent raise every year. Later a third-tier plan (the CHP) was adopted. Despite being paid at half the rate of senior employees, new hires under the PHP and CHP plans pay the same monthly union dues as everyone else.

make room for the new machines, not to create new jobs. The union and management tried to make it seem that they were creating more jobs, when the hidden agenda was creating more automation which would actually put people out of work.

When you're "participating" with management, you may think you're making inroads, but you're not making any real gains. Management sets the agenda. You're participating about the color of yellow lines on the plant floor. So when job classifications get changed, you don't pay attention. When machinery and jobs are moving out the back door, you don't pay attention. You lose your sense of what's important. By participating, you forget how to fight. When it comes to talking about things that really matter to the union, all you have is group meetings that don't have any power at all.

Labor and Capital

If I were an artist and made a statue, or built a bird house, you'd all say that's my bird house. I can sell it for what I want to or I can keep that bird house. But when I'm twenty-one years old, and I go to work, and I ring in a clock card, I have no say-so about the income from selling these bird houses, or cars, or electric harnesses.

Why? Why am I treated less when I ring in a time card than I am when I work in my own garage?

When a neighbor kid comes to me and says, "I want to cut grass. I want to rent your lawn mower," I say, "Let's make a deal." I say, "I'll rent you the lawn mower for a dollar a day. Give me five dollars on Friday." He can take that lawn mower, manage it, cut as many lawns as he wants, set the rate, sell his labor or his product—which is cut lawns—for whatever price he can get. He pays me five dollars and he pockets the rest.

He's twelve years old. We're treating him with dignity. He's self-determined, self-managed. He's a whole person. He's making all kinds of decisions. When I walk into the plant and ring a clock card, I can't get treated like a twelve year old.

We make the firm's profit. But we lose it because we signed away any input over how the firm's income should be spent. We're happy to have wages, and to hell with it if they build plants in Mexico. We don't want to be responsible for the location of plants. Paragraph 7 in the GM contract says, in effect, "Management has the sacred right to determine the location of plants and the means to manufacture." Workers don't have any say-so about where the plants go.

Those issues were negotiated years ago in some key, model contracts, with immigrant, non-Americanized workers like my grandfather. Those contractual clauses are old and out of date. Pope John Paul II in his encyclical, "On Human Labor," says that labor is the primary cause of production and services, while capital is a mere instrument. I think it would be nice if we had an amendment to the United States Constitution that would establish this principle of the priority of labor over capital.

We also need a law that establishes the principle of solidarity in income by requiring United States firms to observe an income differential ratio. What I'm saying is that presently income earners at the top receive 150 times what I do, or 250 times what I do, and they say we're on the same team! We need a solidarity ratio. When the floor sweeper gets a raise, then the boss gets a raise. We need not only equality of opportunity, but equality of treatment and condition. In a new firm, a start-up, the ratio of lowest to highest incomes should be 1 to 4. There is such a law in Sweden. Every business must work toward solidarity in wages.

If you want to make a cooperative, then you have to design a cooperative organizational structure. You can't paste cooperation on to a system that's inherently skewed, and biased, and unfair.

Workers should elect their managers as well as their union representatives. If that were the design, then those who ran for management positions could debate the policy of the firm. Given the assets of the firm, how does the membership want to use those assets? Debate this publicly. Debate it at the union hall. Debate it in forums at the workplace.

People look at you weirdly if you say, "The workers should control their factories." You're some kind of a Marxist nut.

But the model in Russia failed. The model there was that you went through a third party, the central government in Moscow, which controlled everything. I don't want Washington telling me. And I'm sick of Detroit telling me. As I say, if I made this bird house, it belongs to me.

I'm against all teams and cooperatives under the present structure. But a workers' cooperative would be a true team. The rules would be fair. The rules are not fair at General Motors and Packard.

How My Awareness Evolved

Meantime, I was driving the tow motor and reading history books. I read about Mondragon, and workplace democracy, and cooperative organizations. Mondragon is in northern Spain, in the Basque country. There is a strong anarchist tradition. I read about Proudhon. I read about the anarchists who fought in the Spanish Civil War in the 1930s. It was the anarchists in northern Spain fighting against the royalists in southern Spain.

I said to myself, "These anarchists, these people living up in the mountains of northern Spain, what in hell were they talking about?" That connected to the workers in Yugoslavia, who had the vote. The workers at the Ulgor cooperative at Mondragon have the vote.

When I say I'm an "aspiring anarchist," it doesn't mean that I'm against all rules. There are going to be some rules. Rather than saying that the government sets the rules, anarchism says that we're going to go by another set of rules. Small-scale, human-scale societies of people will decide what the rules are, rather than the large state deciding. The best rules are rules that people can understand, and that respect a lot of diversity, and ecology, and gender, and class.

What's at the bottom is rules made by the people. In the union hall, the membership votes and ratifies the contract. That kind of law an anarchist isn't opposed to. Because if I want freedom, my freedom's going to hinge on your freedom. We're going to go by consensus or majority rule or some kind of collective decision.

You begin to see that you're up against a whole system. The only way to be is to say that you are against it. I say, "I'm an aspiring anarchist." That makes me have to come out of the closet and be what I am capable of being.

Organizing

Let me give some examples. I'm driving the tow motor. I see Sarah talking to Jack, people I've known for years. I know that when Sarah is talking to Jack there's some hot politics going on. I put the brakes on, and say, "What's up?"

Sarah says, "My committeeman won't fight my safety grievance." Jack says, "Give her the OSHA number." I say, "I don't have it. It's in the phone book."

Freire has a theory that a lot of facilitators and coordinators talk about, which is that there is no leader and that you talk to people, and get them to take responsibility. You organize organizers. But you don't lead the charge.

So I don't call the number. Next time I see Sarah I say, "Did you call the number?" And she says, "Yeah. They told me that I had to have a good reason. And they wanted to give me a form."

The struggle against the twelve-hour day was such a struggle.[2] The same thing that happened with Sarah happened with the guys at Plant 10.

During the winter of 1995–1996 I heard a rumor that the ten- or

---

2. The collective bargaining agreement at Packard Electric calls for time and a half pay for any hours over eight worked in a shift. The bylaws of Local 717, IUE require a membership vote to ratify any collective bargaining agreement *and* any memorandum of agreement changing a collective bargaining agreement. In 1995–1996, the company and the local union signed a memorandum of agreement under which workers in Plants 3, 4, and 10 would work twelve-hour shifts at straight pay. The agreement was not submitted to the members for ratification before it was put into effect. Tony Budak and other discontented workers filed a federal law suit. The judge ruled that Local 717 must hold a ratification vote.

twelve-hour day was coming. There was an executive board meeting on a Friday and a general membership meeting the following Sunday. At the meeting there was a handout that said, "We're not going to vote on this." The union administration didn't go to the membership to ratify. They were fearful that the membership would vote against the twelve-hour day.

Then at break, in the plant, I hear that Plant 10 workers are going to work twelve hours. The guy says to me, "How can they? We didn't vote on this." I said, "I know. I don't understand it either." He said, "What kind of union do we have that we don't get to vote on it?"

I'm driving my tow motor and a carpenter comes by. He says, "Gee, we didn't vote on this." I said, "What are you guys going to do about this? If you don't do anything about it, nothing's going to get done." I told them, "I'm a French general. You start the charge and I'll get in next to you."

So they went to the next union meeting with a petition. They pulled it off. I had no knowledge of that coming up. I was way out of the loop, way out of the culture.

I just let it cook. It's like cooking on a stove. You put the right things together, and you get wonderful veal parmigiana, or law suits, depending on which you're looking for. You put together the right people, and the right issues, and the right lawyer.

I relate to them that way. They need to decide what their common bond is going to be. They need to decide what brings them together. If I tell them, it's a lost cause.

One for One

I see the company's demands for continuous run schedules and the creation of new, multi-skill classifications as employment policies. An individual member may say, "I'd like to learn two skills," like machinist and electrician. I tell them to look at how what they want would affect everyone.

What I found coming out of the twelve-hour day struggle was that giving individuals freedom of choice can impact on long-range policy decisions of the organization. Today I am torn about allowing individuals in Local 717 to decide whether they want to go on twelve-hour days. I keep telling people, "You're not deciding only for yourself, you're deciding for your union. You're putting your union in a situation where that decision is for everybody, and not everybody wants to make that decision. Not only that, you're deciding for this Valley, for where there are no unions and where there are small unions that cannot live with that decision. You shouldn't make that decision without recognizing that you're making a class policy decision as to what the hell we're about. We've got women, we've got people with families who are not going to be bound by your individual decision to work a twelve-hour day whenever you want to. That's not our policy."

We need to find a way to go on the offensive. In my place, that may be the issue of "one for one." We have contract language which says that for every three persons who retire or quit, one must be hired. That language permits the total work force at the plant to go down steadily, from 7000 to 6000 and 5000. We have lifetime *income* security for those presently employed. We don't have *job* security, in the sense of a guaranteed number of jobs: a guaranteed work force of a certain size.

"One for one"—that is, a new hire for every person who retires or quits—would address job security for the union as a whole. It would be job security for the next generation.

The 1997 Strike

In the spring of 1997, I got elected to the bargaining committee of my local. I had 34 years in. My election was based on a rank-and-file campaign for the right to vote on contract changes.

Going into bargaining we felt like we had seven different unions. Everyone had different demands. There were the old people. There were the young people. There were the Plant 10 people, concerned about the length of the work day. There were the skilled trades. How in the world were we to get everyone on the same wave length?

The company asked me to keep corporate proprietary information confidential. I said I couldn't do that. I said that I felt that I had to evaluate everything on a case-by-case basis. If I thought I had to tell my bosses, the people in the plant, then I would. I said, "You tell your boss what goes on in these meetings. But you don't want me to tell my boss, the people who elected me."

Because the proposed new contract had been rejected, the old contract was about to expire. At that point we had gotten all our demands except that the company was short on the job security issue.

At 11:40 P.M., twenty minutes before the contract would terminate, the company checked and raised. They told the union representatives that they wanted the unilateral right to move equipment and machinery out of the plant.

For the union, it was the beginning of solidarity. It brought the union back together. We went out for one day, and got a much better contract as a result.

One of the things we got with that one day strike in 1997 was a commitment of 120 million dollars as a down payment on 60 new molding machines. During the course of bargaining in the following year it was mentioned, "Well, you know, we can't put these machines in an old site. Let's put them in a new site." That sounded good. The next thing management said was, "We've got 220 machines in the old site, maybe we can up the number of machines in the new site from 60 to 120 or maybe 200."

The bargainers start biting on this. All we have in black and white is 60. The next thing I know we have a proposal on the table that says, "We're going to renovate two sites. They will have new molding machines." It doesn't say how many.

On sub-committees we're talking with management about the manning of these sites, the number of people and the classifications. Once again, as an expression of the new union ideology, the bargainers are saying, "Let's eliminate these classifications. Instead of an operator running ten machines he ought to run sixteen machines." The plant manager and superintendent are just sitting there. And the union guys, strategically, are speeding up production, eliminating manpower, eliminating classifications: taking away the members' right to deal with this from the bottom up because they're preempting and deciding ahead of time.

So I get in a cat fight internally. And this internal discussion becomes the shop floor debate. The leadership in effect is saying, "We ought to downsize. We ought to buy into this pig in a poke." And I'm publicly opposing what the leadership recommends just like I used to when I drove a tow motor. Nothing changes.

If there was a weakness of our one-day strike in 1997, it was that we didn't have the time to build cross-craft, cross-industrial, cross-union solidarity. We haven't tested our muscles for a regional mobilization. The weakness in the Valley is that people are not used to class mobilization.

That's why it was so important that we struck for something important to everyone: job security for the next generation.

III

ANYWHERE BENEATH THE SUN

Manuela Aju Tambriz

Manuela's father

Manuela Aju Tambriz

"Necio para seguir adelante" (stubborn to keep moving forward)

Globalization often forces small farmers to sell their own land and to go to work as wage laborers for large landowners who produce cash crops for an international market. This interview describes Mayan women in the Guatemalan highlands who are resisting that destiny by forming weaving cooperatives. Many of the women speak only indigenous languages.

Manuela Aju Tambriz organized a weaving cooperative in the village of Sololá called Ayúdemenos ("We Help Each Other"). Before she began to work with indigenous weavers Manuela Aju Tambriz was employed by Christian Children, which collected money from godparents in the United States and bought needed articles for Guatemalan children; and by a Mayan writers' organization for which she took oral histories from older people, wrote down recipes and children's stories, and produced pamphlets to teach literacy.

We conducted this interview in Sololá, Guatemala, in November 1997. Martha Lynd translated from Manuela's spoken Spanish to English, and then, when an English transcript was ready, translated it back into Spanish so that Manuela might make corrections.

My Father Worked on the Coast

In times past, many people from this region went to the coast to cut coffee and sugar cane, and to plant coffee. They also planted corn. They would rent land, plant corn, and bring the money back here. On the coast there are two harvests of corn a year, whereas here in the highlands, a colder area, there is only one harvest.

My father worked a lot on the coast. He was hardly ever here. He made money from the two corn harvests, and with it he bought land here in Sololá. When he had enough land here to grow enough corn to feed the family, he quit going to the coast.

My father and others would tell stories about what it was like to live on the "fincas." There, people were given only a little bit of beans and a counted number of tortillas. My father said he didn't want anybody else from the family to go. He said, "Why go there to suffer?" He said that it was not good there. He wouldn't let anybody from the family go to work on the coast. Fewer people go to the coast now because their families were able to get together enough money to buy land here.

At the time he stopped going to the coast, my father met a man who knew how to do upright weaving on a European-style loom. Previously, it was very rare for men to do that around here. But my father learned how to weave and dedicated himself to growing corn and being a weaver. Many people bought from him.

Learning to Weave

I learned how to weave when I was eight years old. I learned how to do the intricate designs that we call "bordados." A young woman who lived with us for a long time taught me how to weave. I didn't find it that hard.

I remember the time when I was eight years old because there were birds called "chocoyos" that would go into the corn fields. My father used to make another young girl and myself go out there and scare the birds away. There were a lot of peach trees in the fields. We would attach to these peach trees the ropes that we use to do the backstrap weaving. We would weave under the peach trees.

Working for the UN

I was the first woman in my village to graduate from high school. I met a man who told me about a position with the United Nations (UN), working around weavings. He said the salary was 800 quetzales a month.[1] The Mayan writers' association for which I was working paid only 300 quetzales a month. I said I was interested and filled in the paper work to apply for the position. I got the job.

As part of the UN project we gave workshops to improve the quality of weaving. The women who participated in these workshops were all

---

1. At the time of this interview, one United States dollar exchanged for about 6.15 quetzales.

weavers. They knew how to weave, but I realized that as well as making their traditional shirts (the "huipiles") and belts, they could improve the quality, and that this was important in order to sell the work in the international market.

I was learning and teaching at the same time. The UN project gave workshops to sixty different groups all over Guatemala. They would drop me off in a community for two or three weeks. During that time I would help them develop weaving samples and give a workshop on quality control.

I did this all over the country for two years. When I began, my son was one month old. I took him with me. During the day, I didn't have time to do reports because I was busy. I would write up the reports at night to tell them what I was doing.

It was hard, because my son would cry, and I would have to breast–feed him. A friend of mine at work who was trying to encourage me said, "Well, that's the life of a woman! You have to work, and you have to feed your baby. You have to keep on going."

From the sixty different groups, the UN chose seventeen for further intensive work. Some of them were co-ops, some were associations. Each one had its own character. I went back to those seventeen communities and did more workshops, mostly on improving quality, and also on improving design. They used traditional designs but they had to adapt colors for the international market. I helped them to develop samples that were sent to many different countries.

After that, we put a store together in Antigua and began to get a lot of orders. I went to work there for one year. There I was able to see the quality of products coming in, and I was able to say, "This is good." "This is bad."

When there was an order for one of the seventeen communities, I would take it there. We would develop new samples. If the women needed to come to a meeting I would tell them about the meeting. I would pick up the product they had made and bring it to Antigua to sell. Also I would pay people, either for what they had already made or for new samples. I was happy when the UN chose just seventeen communities. I was exhausted!

"La Violencia"

In 1992 there was still a lot of fighting going on between the Army and the guerrillas. One day we were going to a region called Nebaj where there was still a lot of fighting. We had brought a good deal of money with us to pay the people from whom we were picking up weavings. I was nervous, because we were in a pickup truck that was only 15 days old and looked new.

There was a driver and there was myself. We went to the communities where we had to pay for products, and we picked up many weavings. Then we went to an organization called "PRODERE," a project for children of refugees. At the PRODERE office somebody told us, "Be careful, there are a lot of guerrillas around here right now. They are bothering people." I thought it was untrue. I said to the driver, "Come on, let's go."

We went ahead with our pickup full of weavings. About five kilometers from the town of Nebaj there was a curve, and we could not see the long line of cars that were stopped just around the curve. When the driver saw them he said, "Oh no! The guerrillas!" I said, "That's just a bunch of lies." I couldn't see very well because it was raining.

All of a sudden a man dressed in olive green stopped the vehicle, came up to the window, and said, "Keys to the truck, please." The driver gave him the keys because at PRODERE we were told, "If they ask you for anything, just do it. Don't risk your life." I was beginning to tremble. I stuck what was left of the money in my huipile. Then another guerrilla came to my window and asked for my "cedula," which is your identification card. If you are Guatemalan, you have to have one. I said, "I didn't bring it."

He looked at me and said, "Do you know me?" I said, "No." I had a stack of documents about four inches high on all the groups we had visited. The guy started questioning me about what we were doing, and asked where we had gone, and why we were here. I said, "We only went to pick up the weaving products." I also said we had gone to PRODERE. I had a terrible cold feeling.

The guerrillas told us to get out of the truck. We began to beg God that nothing would happen to us. There were bus drivers who had also been told to get out of their vehicles. They told us, "If the Army comes, we are dead."

The guerrillas ordered us to put all the cars in a line. They gave us this order because the Army was coming. The Army was two kilometers away. The driver of the pickup said, "How can I put this truck in the line if I don't have the keys?" The keys were returned. The guerrillas said, "If the Army asks you, tell them you didn't see anything." We started driving away.

Then we saw the Army. The Army stopped us and questioned us, asking what we had seen. We said, "Nothing." They said, "Then why are you so scared?"

Somehow we got through it. The Army let us go. We didn't die. The driver dropped me off in Sololá about eight o'clock that night. I asked him to tell my boss in Xela (Quetzeltenango) that I was taking the next day off. It was frightening, because the guerrillas had burned many vehicles belonging to PRODERE and the UN.

During this time many people rejected the kind of work I was doing. It requires a lot of patience and a lot of desire. Many people just won't do it, but I like it.

My son, Eduardo, came with me everywhere until he was two years old. After that, there was a woman from near my village who took care of him in Sololá. This woman, Isabel, became a member of the weaving cooperative.

A Sololá Weaving Group

During my work for the UN over the course of the four years 1989 to 1993, I came to realize that the idea of selling weavings had validity. I said to the director, "What about my community?" I began to organize a group here in Sololá. This group in Sololá was not only one of the original sixty groups but was chosen as one of the seventeen grassroots weaving groups ("grupos de base").

After that, an association of women in the seventeen groups was formed called Trama ("weft"). The forty-three groups that were not chosen remained involved as support groups, "grupos de apoyo." If a huge order came for pillow cases of this region, Sololá would be the principal group that would receive the order, but if they couldn't produce it all, then there would be a backup group from the same region with which the order could be shared.

Our group started with ten women. It was very difficult. I had to go house to house, talking with them about why it was important to join the group. It was hard to get even ten women together. I trained those ten women in the quality that would be expected. I oriented them as to what products to make. Little by little, more people joined when they saw the ten weaving and heard that there were orders.

Around 1994 the group had gotten up to fifty-six people. There was a period of time when the UN project kept many people busy making samples to send all over the world. There was a lot of work at that time. But from those samples the groups received orders for only a limited quantity of items. There wasn't enough work from the orders to employ fifty-six people. We would get orders for twenty-four or twenty-five pieces, which wouldn't even be one per woman. So the group shrunk as the women became disenchanted. About a year ago (November 1996) it had shrunk to as few as fifteen people.

Now there is a fair amount of work weaving huipiles for dolls for export. There are now twenty-eight women in the group. If there is a period of time when we don't get orders, say for three months, the women despair and look for work wherever they can. They end up weaving huipiles and belts for sale in the local market, where they don't get as good a price.

The group wants to do weaving with a lot of different designs, to have a repertoire we can show people. But why make a mountain of weavings if you lack a market and don't know where to sell what you make?

Problems

We are thinking about becoming a legally recognized organization, which would mean having bylaws, and raising a certain amount of money. A number of international organizations that make donations to groups will only do that if the groups have legal status.

Legally, there are two different kinds of organization. One is called an "association," the other is a "cooperative." The way that they differ is that in an association each member makes an initial payment, but you only have to pay once, whereas in a cooperative there is a quota that all the members have to pay periodically.

Cooperatives also make loans, and when they do, each member must give a certain percentage. Let's say that a cooperative buys something on credit. Each member has to pay a percentage of the total loan. Thus in a cooperative there are continued costs. I think an association is better because you only have to pay one time.

Another difference is that in a cooperative you have what's called a "general assembly." When any decision is made every single member has to be there, and has a voice and a vote. The board of directors ("junta directiva") can't make a decision.

When an order comes in that won't provide work for all the women, we call together the whole group and have a meeting. We ask, "Who already has something in progress that they are going to sell?" Those women who are already weaving don't get the order. It goes to the women who don't have anything. Of course, if there's enough for everyone we give work to all.

With regard to rules for the Sololá group, we've written them down, but we can't find the paper on which they were written! We gave it to the secretary. Who knows what the secretary did with it?

So our rules are not very clear. We have some of them in our heads, but we realize this is something that we need to work on. I've tried to call meetings where we would draft the rules, but the women don't come. When I try to explain to them the importance of having rules, they say, "Yeah, yeah, yeah," "It's important," "OK, we'll do it." But at the time when they are actually supposed to sit down and write up the rules, they don't come.

The way that we actually function is that when there are decisions to be made we call a meeting. Everybody comes. We tell the women everything that's going on.

I organized a board of directors, and we have our responsibilities. For example, whenever there are visits the whole group meets and decides what activities should be planned, whether or not they are going to make food, and so on. But there are also certain courses offered to members of boards of directors on subjects such as "administration." Or if papers are sent to the group, they go first to the board of directors. Sometimes student groups visit. I always speak to them because I'm almost the only member who speaks Spanish well. Then I translate for the other women, who don't feel very comfortable speaking in Spanish.

When we elect new members to the board of directors, everyone has to be present. We will write names on the board. Then each one has to vote.

There's a problem with the elections, however. No one wants to be the president, or the secretary, or the treasurer. Why? Because they can't speak Spanish. The people on the board of directors have to travel a lot, and they have to communicate with people who speak only Spanish. On the one hand, I understand that. It's true that the trainings are usually done in Spanish, and the person won't understand anything. On the other hand, if someone was really motivated, they could go to a training and look for a translator or look for a way to be heard.

How then do I motivate the women to participate? The women are afraid to express themselves in the presence of a foreigner, that is, someone from outside of Sololá, even if that person speaks K'iche. But when we have a meeting here, just among ourselves, the women will speak up, even to the extent of telling somebody that she's not doing her job properly.

So when a new member joins I talk to her and say, "You know, you have to do a lot of thinking. I want you to give your opinion." Or sometimes I'll make a joke and say, "What happens if I die? You guys are going to say, 'Let's ask Manuela.' But I'll be in my grave, and then what will you do?"

Working with all these different groups, I've realized a lot about groups. There are women who want to make something of their lives, to get on with it (as we say, "seguir adelante"). These women say what they feel. With women who speak Kakchiquel, when I arrive I joke with them, I hug them, and when I sit down with them they'll talk. For some reason those people don't seem to have a lot of fear. And there's a group from Xela who speak Mam, and even though there's a language barrier and they have to speak in Spanish, they'll still talk to me.

But then there are other groups who don't talk at all, and you ask yourself, Why? I believe the violence ("la violencia"), when people were pulled out of their homes and killed, has left a big mark on people. There's a group of women from the little mountain in front of the volcano on Lake Atitlan who don't talk. I asked one of their husbands, who was translating, why it is. He said, "Because of the violence." They are particularly hesitant to talk with someone they don't know.

Globalization

Women's groups are very affected by globalization. There's a lot of competition. There is competition in prices, and also with respect to the quality of items: the design, the quality of the thread, the finishing, all of those things.

Also there is the question of dyes. In Europe, and most of all in Germany, laws have been passed that have very particular requirements about the dyes. There is a dye that causes an allergy to the skin. If we use this dye, our products won't be accepted in countries that have those requirements. The association for the export of non-traditional products ("gremio de exportadores") wishes to unify all the cooperatives and associations of artisans who do exporting, so as to start a factory where we would make our own thread, meeting the requirements of the European nations.

What's more, the association also wants to standardize prices for similar products of similar quality. The idea is that for such-and-such a product, so-and-so many hours of work, it should cost such-and-such. With back-strap weavers you can't calculate their work by the day. It needs to be calculated by the hour. For example, a woman will get up in the morning, and she has to cook breakfast, so she doesn't get to sit down to weave until nine, and then she can weave till eleven or eleven-thirty, and then she has to make lunch.

I attended a workshop at which the teacher said that each woman weaver needs to keep a little log for each product she makes, in which she writes down the hours. I already talked to the group about this and we're going to do it. We're going to take some samples, and calculate the hours, and then add on a percentage for what each woman wants to earn, and come up with a standard percentage above cost that will be pure profit.

All artisan groups should do this. We should come up with an accurate number of hours, to be fair to the customer, and then the customer should pay fairly to us, based on the number of hours that we've worked.

When I talked to the women, at first they didn't agree. They thought they should earn five quetzales a day. But I don't agree that it is accurate to account by the day. If you charge by the day you don't know if you are making or losing money. I have attended two trainings at which it was suggested that it is fair to charge one quetzal [about 16 cents in United States currency] for an hour of work.

I'll give you the example of a place mat. For a place mat twelve by eighteen inches we calculate that the thread costs five quetzales. Then the time to measure out the thread for the weaving takes an hour, so that's one quetzal. Setting up the loom takes another hour. That's another quetzal. It takes six hours to weave something this size, so that's six quetzales more. Then we add 20 percent that would cover, say, if you broke a shed stick of the loom and there would need to be an allowance for repairs, or it could turn into profit. That adds up to 16 quetzales for a place mat.

"Necio Para Seguir Adelante"

Women or men, if they're in groups they act the same way. Men may fight more. Women, we cry, we blame each other. But basically it's the same.

What's the solution? I believe people have to think very carefully before they join a group. They have to think about themselves, their own attitudes, so that when they join a group they don't provoke problems, and if a problem arises they're going to have the attitude of trying to solve it.

They have to think about making decisions together. Whenever decisions are going to be made you have to have the whole group present. If everyone has a chance to give his or her opinion, then once they've made a decision if somebody comes back later and complains, I say, "Well, you were there in the meeting, why didn't you speak up?" That is the way you can back yourself up.

You've got to keep going forward. Even if problems come up, you have to keep working on them. You have to grit your teeth and do it even if you don't feel like it. What the people here say about persons like that is that they are "necio" ("stubborn"). Somebody will say, "Ah, forget it. Let's not do it." Then somebody else will say, "No, we've got to keep on."

You have to be "necio para seguir adelante" ("stubborn to keep moving forward").

The Hebron Union of Workers and General Service Personnel

"The worst that they can do is to put me in prison"

Hebron is a city in the so-called West Bank of Palestine which was occupied by Israel in 1967. The union described here includes Palestinian men and women from different trades and factories. In that respect it resembles "mixed locals" formed by the Industrial Workers of the World in the United States in the first years of the twentieth century.

This interview took place in August 1992 at a union hall in Hebron. Sam Bahour translated. The three men who spoke have been given fictitious names for security reasons.

YAKUB: When I was young I used to hear that there were unions. When I went to work, I came to recognize that a worker can't progress without a union behind him.

HASAN: I was actually recruited to the union by people who gave a workshop on the rights of workers and the right to organize. To be honest with you, before then I spent my energy on how I could be sure I would get paid at the end of the month, so I could pay my bills. After the workshop, I began to care about more than my personal rights. I attended some union events to see what they did, how many people they had. But I registered for the union with a lot of hesitation, because I didn't exactly know what I was getting into.

I don't know quite how it happened, but after two years I was elected General Secretary. And that's what my work is now.

BASHAR: I'm from a village. I became interested in the union through a sports event when I was young. When I became a worker, I went back to that union to which I had already been introduced.

I was in Hebron in 1985, when our union was established. The goal was to organize workers in both factories and offices. An executive committee was elected to run the day-to-day operations.

It became clear that the task of organizing workers would have to be two-fold. First, we faced class oppression. Second, we faced the oppression of the Israeli Occupation. The national Palestinian question was going to play a role in the development of our union. It was natural for the nationalist movement to draw workers into the larger struggle.

The seeds of organization were very hard to plant. We found that it wasn't just a matter of registering workers with the union. Rather, the initial stage had to be education in the importance of being organized. Twenty-four workers joined together. They were the preparatory committee, or founding members of the union.

Today there are 1,092 registered union members. Women are a majority of those who work in offices. So it was a priority to make sure that women became members of the union and of the union executive committee. There is also a women's committee within the union, which met earlier today and had an internal discussion of their projects with one of the women on the executive committee.

We are now the third largest union in Hebron. And in the opinion of those who oversee union work in the entire West Bank, we are one of the most active.

There is no law that totally oversees the needs of workers. Therefore there is a vacuum that the union is obligated to fill. The Palestinian worker in Hebron is part of the working class in Gaza and the West Bank, and of the working class internationally. His or her needs are similar to the needs of workers everywhere. The problems begin in the morning when the worker leaves home, and continue until nightfall.

Palestinian Workers and Israeli Employers

BASHAR: Of our 1,092 members, approximately 60 percent work within Israel, 40 percent in the West Bank.

Palestinian workers specialize in construction and agriculture. This work is very difficult. You have to know what you are doing. Israeli society needs the Palestinian worker to carry on this type of activity within the borders of Israel, because the Israeli worker, first, does not have the experience, and second, does not have the will to do this hard, dirty work.

Even though the Palestinian work force is so critical to Israel, we receive about half the wages of the Israeli worker, and we receive no health benefits or other fringe benefits. Also, Israeli society takes advantage of the

Palestinian worker in his time of need, at strike time, at curfew time, at times when there is illness in the worker's family, and puts him on the street. They know that the market place is full of more Palestinian workers who are willing to take these jobs.

The international standard says that a worker should work eight hours a day. However, Palestinian workers must leave home very early in the morning due to harassment at the checkpoints for getting in and out of Israel, and must travel very dangerous roads, causing them many times to be late. When they are late, their special circumstances are not considered but they are viewed as Israeli workers, and their pay is cut for the hours they are not present. Likewise, when they leave work, the Israeli worker may be home in one hour, but the Palestinian worker will not get home until seven or eight o'clock at night. As a result the Palestinian who works in Israel puts in a 12- to 15-hour day.

Another obstacle is this: If I were to work 32 days a month I could barely make ends meet for food in the home. What happens when my village or town is under curfew and I cannot get to work for five or ten days? Economically this becomes very stressful.

There is also the problem of inflation faced by those who work within Israel. The official inflation rate within Israel has reached 200 percent. The wages of the Israeli worker are buffered to take account of changes in the cost of living, but the wages of Palestinian workers are not tied in this way to the Israeli economy.

Further, a work permit is required to go to work in Israel. This permit can only come from the civil administration. If there is a curfew, how do I get to the civil administration to obtain this card so I may continue my work? If you are caught in Israel without a work permit you are faced with a 350 shekel fine,[1] and probation for one year (during which you are not allowed to go to work in Israel). Also, if you are arrested and put in prison, you are forever forbidden to have a permit. Eighty percent of the Palestinian work force has been in prison and are therefore not allowed to go to work in Israel.

Finally there are obstacles that arise from the general political situation. For instance, if there is a military operation within Israel, that area will be closed to any Palestinian less than 28 years old. So those closed military zones become non-workplaces for Palestinians for a period of time. It's equivalent to a curfew in the West Bank.

If you have a permit, if there is no curfew, if you get a ride, if, if, if . . . you're able to go to work. Your boss will designate a meeting place where he will pick you up. The authorities take no responsibility to safeguard the waiting places. On Black Sunday several years ago seven workers were killed at such a location when a "deranged" soldier opened fire on them.

---

1. At the time of this interview, one United States dollar exchanged for about 3.3 shekels.

There are many incidents of which you do not hear when workers are harassed and provoked at these places. The settlers know the Palestinians will be there, they know they are workers, they know that any violation will cause their permission to work to be revoked: the workers are very easy targets.

Stressful situations arise on this side of the border, too.

I can go right now and get a job, work the day or work a week, and then at the end of the pay period have the boss threaten me gun in hand and tell me to leave without pay. At that point I must decide between two options. One is to leave my rights, leave my pay, leave everything behind in order to ensure that I will find work the following day. The other is to return, to make an issue out of it and try to get my pay. The bad thing about this second choice is that it is so simple for the boss to call the security forces and say that I came back to threaten him, and I can be put in jail. I have to make a decision based on what I want to do tomorrow, not how I feel today.

HASAN: Let me give you an example. A friend of mine in the union lays tile. He tiled the whole floor at a settler's home. It was supposed to be for 500 shekels. When he finished the job, the settler told him right then and there, "If you come back, I will report you to the authorities. Not only that, I don't want to see you in this settlement again, or you'll be reported." The worker was never paid.

YAKUB: The larger Israeli companies do the same thing. To show you the racism we face, a company that lays tiles told a union member to do two rooms in a settlement home. If he did them well, they would hire him on a long-term basis. He completed the two rooms. The company looked over the rooms and said, "You did a good job. We want to hire you." The Palestinian worker asked for a contract so he could have some kind of guarantee that the work he did would be paid for. The company manager told him, "Look. I have one thousand workers around me. None of them have contracts. Why do you specifically need a contract?" He said, "Because I have a large family and I need the security that I will be paid." The manager said, "You don't have an Arab mind. The Arab mind is that of a slave laborer. If you don't work for us without a contract, you're not going to be paid for the two rooms that you did."

The man got a lawyer through the union, and the company gave a check to the lawyer for 15 percent of what he should have received.

BASHAR: Within Israel the only union is Histadrut. Any organizing that we do must be done here, in the West Bank. If you mention within the State of Israel that you are a member of a union in the West Bank, you can be arrested.

If the union believes that there is enough evidence to support a worker's claim, the union will hire a lawyer to represent the worker in the Israeli courts. The only role the union can play in Israel is behind the scenes. And even if the lawyer is successful, there is no mechanism to implement the decision. Someone can win a case but still not get the money.

The Union in the West Bank

BASHAR: In the West Bank, union organizing is very rudimentary. This [showing his union dues record] is initiation fee plus union dues for one year: five shekels [about $1.50 U.S.]. Yes, it's not much. We understand the conditions under which people are working. But the goal of the union dues is not to finance the union's work. Five shekels allows the individual to feel that he or she is part of a larger body, it gives the individual some sense of responsibility to the union.

When you register, the union provides several things. It provides a by-laws booklet that tells what the union is all about. And it provides a registration booklet. The registration booklet has a picture of the worker, taken by the union. It lists the worker's children and the goals of the union. It shows the different months in which the worker paid dues. Also when you register, you get this card which lists most of the good doctors in town, and the percentage discount that each will give to a union member.

HASAN: There are two sub-committees named by members of the executive committee. One is for women, the other for men. Each sub-committee has a chairperson who is a member of the executive committee.

The role of these committees is to visit the workplaces weekly. After each visit the committee members report on the conditions they found, and on what discussions they had with the employers of the different factories. This is an ongoing thing.

All committee members are volunteers. Some expenses—for publications, transportation, and so on—are paid from the treasurer's office of the union.

The union's income comes from union dues, a market stall at the time of the holidays, a yearly calendar, and donations from the community at different activities.

BASHAR: Let me explain how we manage to work for the union.

I do floors. My work is not continuous. I work perhaps three days a week. I fill in the schedule that I can be here the other days.

Another member has a chicken farm. He goes in the morning to clean and to feed. Then he leaves, and does not return until the evening. Three hours each afternoon he can be here.

HASAN: In Palestine we have four or five specializations among construction workers. We have hotel workers, we have other kinds of service workers. Ideally there would be a union in every city for each of the professions. Currently we don't have that. Currently our union consists of a number of different trades.

Also, we can't separate our union and our political work. Because of the Israeli Occupation, they become mixed and overlap. There is a General Federation of Workers for the West Bank as a whole. We have differences as to how that body should oversee the work of local unions.

Our union does not belong to any political entity. As individuals we are political, but we try to keep the organization itself worker-oriented, not politically-oriented. We are against the view that the various political tendencies should designate the members of a local union executive committee, with each tendency naming a certain percentage of the leadership. We believe that every local union must hold elections to choose its leaders.

We never organize with finances as our organizing tool, because we would never be able to do anything that way. Some of us, as people interested in the union, have brought our personal funds to carry the union through some difficult times. We cannot allow our funds to define our work, or we would not have been able to get this far.

The right way is that funds should come from the General Federation, too, but because of the crisis that they are in we haven't seen one agora (less than half a penny) for two and a half years. So we are really on our own right now.

The executive committee meets weekly, and every six months there is a general union meeting. Every Saturday the committees in the villages surrounding Hebron are supposed to meet. This friend [pointing] is a representative of one of those village committees. He says they meet every week or two. He is here today to report on their activities.

On May Day we have a field trip. We pass out plaques, like this one on the wall behind me, to the workers who did the best volunteer work. The person for whom this plaque is intended was arrested, and couldn't go on the field trip, so it's waiting for him when he comes back.

The union will sponsor a sports event for all union people five days from now. The membership has been divided into teams, and they'll play each other.

Once again I have to say: Funds are important, but believe me, funds or no funds, this union will go on.

Collective Bargaining

HASAN: Our members on the West Bank mostly work for Palestinian employers. In Israel, we may build a campaign against the Israeli employer. We can't do that with Arab employers because we understand that there is a common bond between the worker and the employer. Both are under occupation.

But that doesn't mean that we surrender the basic rights of workers in Arab factories. If there is a problem with an Arab owner, the law that oversees us is Jordanian labor law. We believe that this law is not sufficient. However, this is where the discussion must start, because this is what we have.

The overall situation does not permit stable long-term relationships. We negotiate for that particular job, that particular market, that particular year.

BASHAR: In a given factory, we seldom have members of more than one union. We handle it case-by-case. As I said in the beginning, although we are the third largest union in Hebron numerically, we are also the most active.

In each factory the union deals with the owner not by someone from here going to discuss for them, but by a committee of the workers themselves. A committee of three workers carries on the negotiations. So if, for some reason, there is more than one union it will be represented on that workers' committee. One time a majority of workers was from the second union in town. What we did, we gave that union authority to negotiate a contract for all the workers in the shop. The contract that they created we adopted for our members.

So let's look at one of our contracts. The first thing it says is: "The minimum wage for workers should be 180 Jordanian dinars and those dinars should be paid at an exchange rate of four Israeli shekels per dinar." Then it continues:

> Every employee has a right to 21 days of vacation yearly, or to compensation for that time if he cannot take the vacation.
>
> Friday is a paid holiday every week. Religious and national holidays should be paid. National holidays are May Day and the day on which Palestinian independence was declared, November 15.
>
> On the ninth day of each month, there is a general strike against the Occupation. If on that day the worker cannot come to work or is late coming to work, nothing will be subtracted from his pay.
>
> If a curfew does not permit the worker to go to work, the owner should pay for half the time the worker can't be there.
>
> The length of the work day should be eight hours.
>
> Health conditions must be upheld (meaning first aid and the ability to call an ambulance must be there, as well as protective gear if the job requires it). If a certified physician says that an injury was the result of work, the owner must pay the medical bills. The employer is required to have insurance that will pay some or all of the worker's lost wages.

As to sickness or accident that is not related to work, that is dealt with on a humanitarian basis. If a worker has a heart attack, or his wife dies, we as a union will get together and sponsor something. We will take him food, take his son a present. The employer will do the same in a different way. He'll say, "you have a job when you come back." Returning to this contract:

Transportation to and from the workplace must be paid by the employer.

If a person does not show up for work for reasons other than what has been stated in this contract, the owner has a right to take legal steps. If some emergency prevented the worker from attending that must be dealt with case-by-case. In any event, there must be three warnings, then the employer can decide to fire you.

There must be a 5 percent raise yearly.

All machinery and tools used must be in quality condition. Hand tools are provided by the worker.

The employer has a right to set production schedules so long as they do not exploit the worker. Production goals must be achievable by normal labor.

This agreement is considered final and comprehensive from the date it is signed, and cannot be changed unless those that have signed it, amend it.

The contract is signed by three workers from the shop, the owner of the company, and the union.

The company that entered into this contract makes sponges. No women work there, so there is no provision in the contract for maternity leave.

The union is now trying to negotiate city-wide contracts for similar factories, like all the sponge factories, or all the cement factories. This takes a lot of time, a lot of resources and energy. We haven't accomplished it yet, but this is the next stage. We want similar factories to have one contract, even if different unions represent the workers in those factories.

We have the problem that sometimes the employer doesn't carry out his contract. The first people who try to solve the problem are the elected shop stewards in that particular workplace. They are the members who, first of all, are affected by the employer's non-compliance, and secondly, have detailed knowledge of conditions in that shop. That committee of workers goes to great extremes, and tries its best to solve the problem. If it cannot be solved, it comes to the union, and there is discussion between the union and the employer. To date, we have not had to go beyond that point.

Why do we wait so long before we take a problem from the workers' committee in the workplace? There are two reasons. Number one, we feel that this approach creates cadres within the working environment. And number two, we don't want them to become dependent on having someone above them solving their problems.

The Future

HASAN: The Intifada [uprising that began in 1987] has helped us and made us stronger. It created an atmosphere of solidarity that allowed us, for instance, to make the ninth day of every month, or curfews, part of the contract. Before the Intifada the employer could say that the situation was not widespread: "You have troublemakers in your town, I shouldn't be paying the price for that." But now, because it is widespread, because the whole community is involved, we're able to make these days paid holidays.

There is a committee of eleven persons to build some kind of relationship between this union in Hebron and the General Federation. Some members of the committee are from here, some are from the Federation.

We need a new labor law.[2] I was part of a committee before the Intifada to suggest to the General Federation matters that need to be addressed on a large-scale basis. After the Intifada began, relations with Jordan were officially broken. That created a vacuum which the General Federation should have quickly filled with a Palestinian labor law. They didn't do it. The proposals we made are still in Ramallah, in Arabic.

We have not been expressly recognized as a union by the Israeli authorities. We applied more than three years ago for recognition. We have not received a reply, and the law says that if you don't get a reply, after three years you can assume it's permitted to continue. So we consider ourselves officially recognized.

BASHAR: After time passes, you don't ask any more. You do your work. If they find you, you go to Ansar for six months.[3]

HASAN: We face continual harassment. When we applied for recognition, we had to give the names of the members of our preparatory committee. These persons became targets for harassment. I was the general secretary of a union in Ramallah. I saw our files confiscated monthly, yet that union was officially registered! Sometimes we got the files back, sometimes not.

Another form of harassment is that most of our members are in prison. We hardly ever have a full executive committee. For instance, I was in prison three times, he [pointing] was in prison for four years, and he also [pointing] was in prison.

The problem is not that we're in prison, because we can continue our studies and our work there. The problem is that once you are released from prison, you are given a green ID card which restricts your activities.

BASHAR: I was in prison. I can't get a work permit. I have a green ID card, but how do I work?

I made a decision: the worst that they can do is to put me in prison. I was in prison. I know I can take it. So I take the chance. I go to work un-

2. On September 13, 1993, the Declaration of Principles on Interim Self-Government was signed in Washington D.C. between the Palestine Liberation Organization and the Israeli government. This opened the way for the creation of the Palestinian National Authority in parts of the West Bank and Gaza Strip. Thereafter, the first Palestinian Legislative Council was established and as of May 1998 was working on enacting a unified Palestinian Labor Law to be applied in both the West Bank and Gaza Strip.

3. Ansar is an Israeli detention camp in the Negev desert.

til I'm caught. When I'm caught, I'll be in prison for a couple of months, and then I'm going to do the same thing. I have no alternative.

HASAN: The issue of identity papers should not be taken lightly, especially for us as union organizers. If we are to rejuvenate the General Federation, we as union people in the different towns need to have democratic discussion amongst us. We cannot wait for the General Federation to come together and then see how well it did.

If I want to meet with my union brothers in Nablus, I need a visa or a travel permit to go through Jerusalem. I'm always going to be scared that if I don't have such a paper then I'm going to get a 48-hour detention and a fine of 350 shekels, which I can't afford. It makes union organizing almost impossible.

Mauricio Vallejos

"We're not meant to be desk leaders"

This interview was conducted in August 1988 at the Metasa steel mill in Tipitapa, just north of Managua, Nicaragua. The translator was Marta Parajón. In 1998, Father Joe Mulligan, S.J., located Mauricio Vallejos and reviewed the transcript of the interview with him.

Metasa (Metales y Estructuras, S.A.) was founded in 1958 by United States Steel. By the late 1980s it had become a public enterprise and was Nicaragua's only steel mill. About 700 workers were employed in a complex of four plants. Semi-finished steel imported from abroad was fabricated into pipes, reinforcing bars for concrete construction, tanks to hold water and petroleum, bridges, and corrugated roofing. Technology and equipment at Metasa were antiquated from the beginning, and in 1988 the tube mill had been down for months because the United States embargo made it impossible to obtain needed parts.

As he explains, Mauricio Vallejos began to work at Metasa before the Sandinista insurrection that overthrew Anastasio Somoza in 1979. His position in the local union was similar to that of a shop chairman or chairman of the grievance committee in the United States.

Two years after this interview, having become dissatisfied with favoritism, big salaries and benefits for plant administrators, and pressure on workers to participate in political demonstrations, Mauricio Vallejos organized a second union at Metasa. Both unions went out of existence in 1993 when Metasa was privatized. Workers bought 25 percent of the shares in exchange for their severance pay and benefits. As of 1998 workers had received no dividends. At that time there were 70 worker/partners, 110 temporary workers, no union, and the average wage was only about three-fourths of the basic cost of living for a family.

Before 1979, there was no freedom for union organization. Very few unions existed because it was prohibited by the government. As we approached 1979 there were more organizations, and after 1979, even more.

There was a struggle in the workplace before 1979, but we didn't have a real collective bargaining agreement. A contract of sorts existed since the early 1970s. In reality, however, even though everything was written up and the agreement was recognized by the Ministry of Labor, there was no way to enforce it because we were not free to protest. If we protested, they would send out the National Guard. If we ever dared to ask for anything, like uniforms or boots, immediately we were arrested. It was almost a joke to negotiate any kind of bargain because it wasn't worth anything.

There were also spies in the workplace. Whenever we had a meeting, they would inform on us and we would be arrested, either here in the workplace or at our home that night. For that reason, very few agreed to be leaders of the union.

Before I came here I had been active at other companies. At one place, they wanted to pay us what they felt like paying, and didn't want to pay us overtime. I was kicked out along with twenty-four others for trying to start a strike. I was arrested and spent two and a half months in jail. That was in 1971.

In every workplace there are always people who fight for their rights. I've always had the spirit of struggling for a better way of life for us workers, and to prevent management from putting its foot on people. When management wanted to make fun of a worker, or blackmail him, I would speak out for the worker even though I wasn't a union leader at the time.

Before the revolution we had to organize ourselves undercover. None of the organizations could be public. One time when we were protesting they sent two military trucks, one full of soldiers to force us into the other truck, which was empty, and take us away.[1] They told us we had no rights, so we shouldn't be protesting about anything.

Since 1979 there has been freedom to organize labor unions and an open relationship between the plant administration and this union. Even though there's a military invasion of our country and an economic crisis, a collective bargaining agreement can be negotiated freely.

Chairperson of the Grievance Committee

When you give management your hand, they always grab up to the elbow. Since I became a leader in this union I've always been the secretary for grievances. The workers say I'm very dedicated to my work.

---

1. According to other workers, after the earthquake of 1972 the cost of living rose sharply, and workers at Metasa and elsewhere went on strike. It was during this three-month

The Labor Code was written in Somoza's time. It was not easy for us then to study the provisions of the law. They put whatever they thought was convenient for them into the Labor Code. Since no one could protest, they drafted the Labor Code as they wished. We have analyzed the Labor Code and asked for a revision. It's very rigid and harsh. For the most part, the first seventeen articles consist of prohibitions directed against the worker.

Article 4 says that workers are subject to the provisions of the collective bargaining agreement. Article 5 directs them to follow hygiene and safety provisions. If the worker does not wear the proper safety equipment, he can be fired. It is also prohibited for the employer to force the employee to work somewhere where he is not covered by the contract.[2]

Article 16 of the Labor Code specifies that workers must obey management orders. There are exceptions. The boss may not ask employees to buy or make things for the personal use of the boss. The boss may not prevent workers from joining a union, or any other organization, and the boss may not interfere with the union's internal affairs.

Article 17 requires the worker to take care of the working equipment, and everything that is assigned to him, and return it to the employer in the same state that he received it.

When a fellow worker is going to be fired, we form a bipartite commission consisting of two union members and two representatives of management. If the worker is right we defend him, but if he or she is wrong, we don't try to make up excuses. For example, there was a nurse in the clinic who took medicines for her personal use and also committed immoral acts in the clinic. We told her that we would not defend her, because we didn't consider that she was right. We said that she was free to find her own lawyer and to appeal to the Ministry of Labor, but that we wouldn't be there.

The most common reason for discharge is petty theft. If the worker has been here eight or ten years, and steals, say, ten pounds of welding material, then the worker will usually be discharged but also paid all his accrued benefits. It's negotiable. The Code also says that if a worker misses three days of work in a month, he will be fired.

In some cases a worker is fired for a personal reason, because the supervisor doesn't get along with him. We're not in agreement with this. We've had a couple of managers who wanted to fire a worker because the worker did not understand some instruction or order. They tried either to fire the

strike that strikers were loaded on trucks and taken to the Masaya area, where they were dumped on the street.

2. Metasa workers are sometimes assigned to work in locations far away from the mill. During the years following 1979 they built the Roberto Clemente hospital in Masaya, petroleum tanks in Guatemala, and the Aurora hotel in Costa Rica.

worker or pressure him into quitting. Such a worker will come to this department of the union, so that it's not only he that is struggling against the supervisor, but the whole department.

The union representatives on the bipartite commission are myself and the union secretary general. The worker and the person with whom he is in conflict are also present. We talk about the problem, and analyze it. We determine whether the boss or the worker is right. There must be concrete proof, real facts. If the worker doesn't wish to remain in employment because he feels the problem will continue, he can choose to quit.

We have some cases of indirect discharge. If I'm a structural worker, and I'm sent to work in the mechanical department, we view this as an indirect firing. Since my boss doesn't want to pay me the benefits that I would have if he fired me, he tries to get me to resign.

There have been a few cases where the administration or the immediate supervisor has wanted to fire a worker for being disrespectful to the boss or to a member of his family. This offense is contemplated in the Labor Code. Sometimes the worker will say the disrespect was not directed at the boss, but at someone else. We meet and decide whether there was a misunderstanding.

All in all, it's difficult for the employer to fire a worker for no reason at all. If the bipartite commission cannot reach agreement within forty-eight hours, the problem goes to the Ministry of Labor.

Struggling with Corrupt and Arbitrary Managers

On paper, we as leaders of the union don't have the same authority over management that we do over the workers. But the workers demand that we apply the law equally. We feel a great responsibility about all the effort that the workers put into this enterprise. We know that the labor of those who work here is responsible for the investment that the enterprise makes in new machinery and raw materials.

In a specific case, the workers came and told me what was going on. This manager was very agile. But one day he fell into a trap. I personally found him building a water tower for himself, using the machinery, raw material, and workers of the mill. He didn't have permission from his immediate boss or from the board of directors.

I immediately called the general director. We sat down at a table in his home, and discussed the case, and I and the other compañeros asked that this manager be removed. The general director doubted what we were saying. However, we presented the paperwork that the manager had drawn up for the job. The manager was ordered off the premises and warned not to come back again. The workers shook our hands, and congratulated us for applying the law equally to managers and workers.

We had a similar conflict with a general director.[3] In 1983, Freddy Sandoval became director at Metasa. Sandoval was kicked out by the workers at two other enterprises before coming here. He had been a combatant in the insurrection but he did not communicate well with us, nor did he show respect for our union. Once he ejected the union executive committee from his office. He also violated the contract and fired supervisors whom the union wanted to keep.

A problem developed in contract negotiations. Sandoval and the Ministry of Labor wanted to do away with a provision that we won in 1973, which required the company to pay fifteen days' pay for each year of service at the time of a worker's separation. This provision affected 110 older workers.

The argument of the authorities was that this clause of the contract was obtained during the Somoza regime to counteract problems of that time, but was no longer productive. They pointed to the economic hardships caused by the war with the Contras and said that the government could no longer be as generous as it was right after 1979. The authorities wanted this provision to be removed from the collective bargaining agreement.

The union's position was, if this clause was going to disappear the workers should first be paid the benefits accumulated up to that time.

After four months of negotiations, the Ministry of Labor refused to accept a contract containing the disputed clause. We went on strike. We locked the gate and occupied the plant. This was an unlawful strike because the State of Emergency, forbidding strikes, was in effect.

The strike attracted a great deal of publicity. After five days, the Ministry of Labor agreed that benefits accumulated under the 1973 contract should be paid. We went back to work. These sums were finally paid in 1985. Also, a more limited form of severance pay based on years of service was continued in the new contract.

Conflict with Sandoval continued. The union met with the Minister of Labor, the regional FSLN (Frente Sandinista de Liberación Nacional, or Sandinista National Liberation Front), and the director of the metal-mechanical industry. After three months of negotiating, the union went to the Ministry and said that Sandoval had to be gone in eight days or we would do the job ourselves. Sandoval was removed.

The Oath of a Union Representative

Before I came to Metasa, the boss in the company where I worked offered me money to keep my mouth shut. But I considered that if I accepted, I

---

3. The narrative of the following incident is drawn from interviews with other workers as well as Mauricio Vallejos.

would no longer have any moral authority among the other workers. The workers believed in me. Had I accepted money from management, how could I have stood up to them? There were others, including one man who had been in jail with me, who took money from the company. And I noticed afterwards that in a meeting, he defended management's position instead of defending his own class. We didn't embarrass him in the meeting, but later, when we went out for a couple of drinks with him, he finally admitted that he had been bought off. This man was immediately removed from union office.

When we take a position in the union as leaders, we vow to defend the workers and the workers' interests only. We agree that we will never be bought off by the administration, and that if this occurs, we should be removed from office. We make a commitment to the workers, and if we can't keep this, then the workers will not be interested in electing us. We have to be prepared for anything: we must accept criticism from workers, jail, whatever may come.

The same problem has presented itself here at Metasa. Some union leaders mix personal problems with their labor work. All workers should have the same rights here, even if they are not Sandinistas or not in favor of the revolution. They may belong to another political party, but as workers, they should have the same rights. Some union leaders say, "Well, he's a member of another party, let that party solve his problems." I feel that if he is a worker and has a problem, I have a duty to help him resolve it.

A worker may say, "My son is sick, or my wife is sick, or my mother is sick. I need a loan to buy medicines." Some union leaders respond, "Go see the finance director of the enterprise, maybe he can help." I try to put away whatever I have to do and say, "Come with me, I'll go with you."

To be honest, I'm not a member of the Sandinista party. But I'm in agreement with the policies of the government. About two years ago, the secretary general of the union here was a member of another political party. He wasn't in agreement with the policies of the government. He would make propaganda for his political perspective. The workers saw that he was paying no attention to their problems. They threw him out.

We're not meant to be desk leaders. We should be out where the workers are. Workers have told me that this is the kind of leader whom they like: a person who solves problems quickly, who isn't a bureaucrat, who doesn't tell lies. The workers can immediately tell whether a person senses the interest of the working class, or not.

Virginia Roman
and Mayra Guillen

"The power of the people
is not just a slogan"

*In revolutionary Nicaragua, FETSALUD was the Nicaraguan Health Workers'
Federation. The following interview took place in August 1986 at the Ministry of
Health in Managua. At the time of the interview, Virginia Roman was a member
of the union executive committee and union general secretary, and Mayra Guillen
was a sectional representative of epidemiological workers. Amy Bank translated.
In 1998, Father Joe Mulligan, S.J., located Virginia Roman and reviewed the transcript of the interview with her. By then she was not active in union matters, the
union was very weak, and workers could no longer participate in administrative
decisions.*

VIRGINIA: I was never a member of the union before the revolution. My
whole union experience is very new, during the past three or four years,
and always in a revolutionary context.

Anyone who works at the Ministry of Health and is not an administrator can join FETSALUD. Nothing is required relating to religion, political
belief or ideology, color, sex, age, or work function. The only requirement
is the willingness of the worker to join the union.

As we are the national complex of the Ministry of Health, we do not
give direct services to people. We are a bureaucratic institution. As a result, union members take a much more passive attitude than in other kinds
of work. They are stuck behind desks with mountains of paper and usually don't get to see the results of their work. It is not the same as somebody working in a shoe factory or a coffee factory or even a nurse who is
caring for somebody in a bed.

So we don't have as much participation as we would like. It has been hard to get the base moving. Our hope is that people will begin to realize that when we talk about the power of the people it is not just a slogan, it is a reality, and they will feel it.

A workers' union is always the same: to make requests and demands on the part of the workers.

We have a collective bargaining agreement. The union collects the concerns of the workers—uniforms, shoes, transportation, etc.—and then proposes them to the administration and negotiates a contract.

Realistically, I would have to say that a lot of times our demands are denied. Sometimes it's because of limitation of resources. Sometimes it's lack of consciousness. And sometimes it's just bureaucracy: to be generous, I would say that unconsciously the administration often thinks that the union is an obstacle to developing the administrative work of the complex. We have the full and complete and open right to make demands, but the reality is that we often get a rejection.

When we make wage demands, we always seek to lessen the gap between the better-paid workers and those who are paid the least.

Similarly, in the union we look for representivity. One finds cleaning people as well as biologists on the union executive committee ("junta directiva"). There is an accountant, a doctor who represents the doctors' section, and a person who works with statistics as Mayra does. I happen to be a professional and a specialist. But that's not what concerns us. What is important to us is a person's representation, not his or her academic level. What we don't want is to have management people in the executive committee, because that would be a conflict of interest.

It would be good to clarify the structure of the union. The Ministry has seven directors who serve under the Minister of Health. Corresponding to each management director is a union representative on the union executive committee, which therefore numbers seven persons. Each member of the executive committee is democratically elected by the workers in that department.

In addition, each member of the union executive committee takes on a responsibility as secretary of organization, finances, propaganda, and so on. There is a general assembly of all the workers in which the workers vote for who is going to have each position. In this general assembly they first vote for secretary general. Whoever gets the most votes becomes the secretary general. Then, one by one, they fill each of the other secretaryships in what they consider their order of importance. There are six votes, and the seventh person takes the last position.

I happen to have been elected to the executive committee by the department of Hygiene and Epidemiology, and then elected general secretary by the general assembly. Within our department there are five sections, and Mayra represents one of them.

MAYRA: I am what in the United States you would call a shop steward. Within the section that I am a member of, there is a general election in which I am elected. I am the union representative who is closest to the rank-and-file worker. I am the intermediary between the union executive committee and the worker.

One of the ways it works is that the general secretary tells me what the union activities are, and I transmit this information to the workers at the base. Also, the workers come to me with their concerns and I resolve those that I can. For instance, if there is going to be a sale of shoes, people want to know when it is arriving. Or if somebody needs a letter signed by the union in order to make some kind of request to Personnel, I can get the letter done.

But if there is a complaint by more than one worker about one of the seven hospital directors, and I ask for a meeting with the director and he says he does not have time, and the problem escalates and becomes more complicated, because it is unclear whether he doesn't have time or doesn't want to have a meeting, and the other workers are demanding this, that, and the other thing, I can't resolve that myself and I go to a higher level. [Laughing] Whatever I can't resolve, I bring to Virginia!

VIRGINIA: Because we have a structure that goes from the base up, if what Mayra describes were to happen in a section like Mayra's section, she goes to the higher level of the union and we go to the head of the Ministry who is the director's boss, and put pressure on the director to oblige him to have the meeting with the workers.

Let me give you an example. When I began to get involved with the union in 1982, one of the first things that happened was a big assembly attended by more than half the workers here to try to remove two directors of the Ministry, the personnel director and one of the financial directors. The workers came in and said, "We don't want any more justifications. The fact is that they have been screwing us up. We are not going to work here until we get rid of those guys."

The Minister of Health at the time was protecting these two guys. The Minister said, "Let's discuss something else." The workers said, "We are not going to discuss anything else. These guys have got to get out in 72 hours or we stop working."

I was presiding over the assembly in a big high school. The workers were here until dawn discussing this. The workers were saying, "Forget it, no more justifications!" I said, "I don't think I need to reinforce what the workers are saying, it is very clear these people have got to get out in 72 hours." And they left before the 72 hours were up. They were gone. I think we were able to make our power felt pretty well.

In another case Mayra had in Epidemiology, the workers were demanding to see the work plan. They said to the director, "Why can't you even get a work plan together?" And he said, "What does the union have to say about my work plan? Why don't you deal with shoes and uniforms and transportation to work and stuff like that?" And they said, "Because it is important to us to know what work you are planning. For you to say that you have completed the work plan when we haven't even seen what the work plan says is a lie, and you shouldn't be able to get away with it."

They care what the work plan is and try to force an evaluation meeting on the work plan because they are aware of the priorities of the Ministry of Health. For example, if the Ministry says that our number one priority is diarrhea, because diarrhea is the main cause of infant mortality, the workers want to know what is being done to develop that program and if not, why it wasn't developed. We don't care about a piece of paper saying that we completed our work plan 100 percent. What we care about is dealing with the problem because that is what's affecting the population. So questions on the administrative level are of great importance to us.

This director was one of the least bad. He cares about the work. His problem is abusing his hiring power. He hires people without guaranteeing them work, and transfers people, and this, that and the other thing.

We in the executive committee of the union want to strengthen the sections. We think that problems should be resolved at the base. Some union representatives who are newly-elected are still somewhat timid in dealing with these problems. We don't have any set scheme as to what kind of problems the sections can deal with, and what kind of problems should go to the executive committee. The section has the absolute authority to deal with any problem it can. They should deal with it up to the point that they feel unable to resolve it.

MAYRA: I don't understand how Virginia can be general secretary and also fulfill her job as a biologist in one of the laboratories.

VIRGINIA: It's true, you have to do both. To be a union leader you also have to be an example in the work. This is not to say that we can complete either of these tasks 100 percent, but we try.

There is no such thing as a paid union person. You do it in addition to your job in the Ministry. Even though there are more than a thousand workers in this complex, you know when you take on union duties that you are going to be working overtime. That's going to be part of it. You have to be willing to make that sacrifice.

It's a lot of work. Nobody is doing it for material gain.

You don't enter into this for profit, or even to get appreciation. You know that you are not going to get very much appreciation, because the workers are demanding from below, and the administration is repressing from above, and so you get squashed into a sandwich. A lot of times people say, "Well, when we elected her we thought she was so good and now she's not concerned, she is not completing the things she said she was

Workers for Ford in Mexico

"It was a bogus election"

What follows are excerpts from a presentation by two Mexican auto workers at the Ed Mann Labor School in Youngstown, Ohio, in October 1993. Jim Converse provided the translation. This material appeared previously in Impact, December *1993, and is reprinted with permission.*

RAYMUNDO: I am unemployed. I had worked almost sixteen years for the Ford Motor Company in Mexico before I was fired. I was fired by Ford three months ago in Cuautitlán, which is in the northern part of Mexico. There is a big Ford Motor Company plant there.

I was fired along with six other workers who jointly set up a committee to defend workers' rights within the company. The committee, including myself, were elected in democratic elections a year ago.

JOSE: I am a union activist who has fought for workers' rights in various places. Until 1990 I worked for the Ford Motor Company. I also have worked in the textile industry and in the metallurgical industry.

RAYMUNDO: Our plant is the best paid of the Ford plants in Mexico. The wages are $1.40 an hour minimum up to $2.40 an hour, except that electrical people and mechanics get $2.80.

There is a government system of credit in place. We can buy stoves and refrigerators through the government, and make a weekly payment out of our paycheck.

We can never afford to buy the kind of cars that we produce. The best thing is to get a very used, very old car. There is no way we can go on vacation with our families, either. The payment we get does not leave enough beyond the basic necessities to save up anything.

In the *maquiladora* factories, along the border, 55 cents an hour is fairly common. The big worry about NAFTA is that it will produce a stratum of 55-cent labor.

JOSE: During the 1960s and 1970s, the Mexican economy moved away from nationally-based industry to international companies directly establishing their control over production in factories in Mexico.

Higher technology displaces workers. The shifting over to multi-national production meant dramatic cuts in the number of jobs. And the labor strategies that the multi-national corporations followed was to reduce and limit sharply the role of the unions within the production process.

The Ford plant at Hermosillo has very high technology. It includes technology once used in Ford plants in the United States. At Cuautitlán, on the other hand, there is a somewhat lower level of technology than most U.S. plants employ. They've introduced a little bit of just-in-time delivery. They've tried to bring in quality circles. The workers on the assembly line directly opposed them, saying, "No, we just aren't going to do it." And it didn't work. They haven't made anywhere like the inroads into the Cuautitlán plant that they have at other plants.

Most of the opposition in Mexico took the form of isolated individual events. There were thousands of spontaneous work stoppages. We were unable to tie these together into a coordinated opposition. Protest was often met by repression from the government or plant owners. There never got to be a consolidated, union-based opposition to this internationalization of production in Mexico.

At the Ford plant where Raymundo and I worked, we made just two basic demands. One was for a wage raise. The second was for our union to have normal union protection and to operate freely.

The company's response was to hire goons who came into the plant and crushed the efforts there. One person was shot, nine were wounded. About 200 people were beaten and about 1000 fired. The CTM [Confederation of Mexican Workers], the federation of government-sponsored unions, took part in the process. The Ford Motor Company also rescinded the existing collective bargaining contract, which resulted in a 50 percent cut in wages.

RAYMUNDO: Until the late 1980s we had one of the best contracts in Mexico. That was abrogated. The three consequences were: the 50 percent cut in wages; cuts in other benefits; and a lot more day-to-day pressure by supervision.

In 1990, as Jose related, there was a struggle in the plant in which many people were injured. In 1992, the workers got tired of all this repression. They stopped the production lines. The CTM has a committee that oversees the three different Ford operations in Mexico. The workers removed the local committee at our plant, because it was indirectly tied to management. They held new elections. Five separate slates proposed candidates. Seven of us won 73 percent of the votes.

With the new local committee in place, the workers began to see improvements. One of the things we did was to hold a general assembly to sit down and talk about issues. It had been six years since the previous union leadership had held a general assembly. We began to listen to suggestions about what the workers wanted.

There were a variety of different problems in the plant, especially safety problems because of the speed of the line. In one section, there were spot welders hanging on steel cables from the ceiling of the shop. One of these came loose, fell, and hurt a worker very badly. He went to the medical care unit. The doctor gave him a few pills and sent him back to the production line.

I went there as the representative of the union committee to see what was going on. The worker was up against the wall, very pale, scared, visibly shaken, unable to work. He was waiting for them to hang his welder up again so he could go back to work. They expected him to do that.

I intervened and called the doctor back in. I told the doctor that this person was really in some pain and in bad shape. The doctor agreed to give him a pass to go to the Social Security institute. He went there and they found he had a fractured collar bone. It was two months before he could come back to work.

This is just one example of how things work inside the plant. Workers have to come to work or they'll be fired. If a worker shows up with a high fever, they give him a shot and send him out to work. The food we are served often seems to be intended for animals rather than people. The meat is sometimes cooked so tough that it feels like shoe leather, and has no flavor at all.

Our committee was able to pressure the company to give us a 21 percent wage increase, at a time when the government had limited wage increases to 9 percent. This is how the lowest paid workers came to receive $1.40 an hour and the highest paid workers $2.80 an hour.

The company got more and more irritated with us. They made it very clear that they weren't happy with this kind of pressure. The CTM, too, considered what we were doing to be out of line.

In response, the CTM brought together 700 temporary workers in order to flood the union. The CTM stacked the meeting with temporary workers. The company hired these 700 workers for one day and paid them one day's wages only so that they could be seated in the general assembly and give the CTM a 51 percent majority.

When we were voted out of office in this way, the Ford Motor Company gave us a paper ordering us to go back to work as regular workers. We refused to vacate our committee positions. We asked the government labor judge to give us a hearing. It's been three months and no response.

There is a Mexican law which says that while there is an appeal pending, it is illegal to hold an election. The CTM called for an election. Because it was a bogus election 90 percent of the workers refused to vote. The CTM used 10 percent of the people, about 300 votes, to declare that an election had been held.

JOSE: A "despedida" is a going-away party, but a "despedido" is one who has been fired. The despedidos from Ford have begun to make contact with people fired from GM plants, and some of the Nissan people also. But it is pretty difficult. People really don't want to have that as their career. It is more like a problem to get away from so they can get hired somewhere else. I'm talking about the black list: the labor situation is very tight, very controlled.

So there have not been a lot of people trying to do much organizing. Even those who want to do so face really uphill problems, because the plants are very spread around. They are not in a ring around Mexico City. It's forty-eight hours by bus up to the plant in Zamora. Once you're fired, you don't have the money to ride buses. Nobody is supporting you financially. The idea is there. Some of the people are there. But it's not ready to take off any time soon.

JOSE: Another thing that has to be very clear is that Ford workers in Mexico are not in any way hostile to Ford workers in the United States, even though workers in the States get paid much better. Workers for Ford in Mexico see themselves as participating in a similar system and set of problems as the Ford workers in the United States. They would be concerned about hurting Ford workers anywhere. The goal is to change the Ford Company policy.

The Frente Auténtico del Trabajo (FAT)

"Women would make a beginning and then their husbands could join"

The Frente Auténtico del Trabajo (FAT, rhymes with "hot"), or Authentic Work-ers' Front, is a network of Mexican unions independent of the government (in contrast to the confederation of government-sponsored unions). In this interview, a woman describes how she became an organizer for FAT and how she works with women in the community, approaching maquiladora *workers through their wives and mothers. The interview took place in July 1997 and was translated by Claudio Fabiola Cabrera Vasquez. It appeared in* Impact, September 1997, *and is reprinted with permission.*

I was born in Charkas in 1955. I am the second of nine children. My fa-ther is a campesino, and my family was one of the poorest in the village. We had very little food and very little clothing. My father thought that women lack the capability to work. These are the three things I remember: no food, no clothes, and my father's ideas.

My childhood was among the poor. What we had was what the poorest people had. I started working when I was nine years old in order to bring money to my family. I did domestic work, cleaning houses. I worked in the homes of the more well-to-do in the same community. I was able to finish elementary school because my teachers gave me all the materials necessary for studying. But I was obliged to quit after sixth grade because my father felt he had to choose whether to give education to me or to one of my brothers. This began a period of my life when I was unable to go to school.

I was so angry with my father's decision that I left home. When I finished elementary school I moved to another state, Guanajuato. I moved in with relatives there. These relatives were better off than my own family, and by living with them I could give my brothers and sisters more chance to study. I also decided to earn money and send this money to my brothers and sisters.

I had a specific goal. It was to help my family move out of the community, and bring them to the city. I couldn't do it at that time. First, I was too young, only twelve years old. And another thing against me was the culture of my family. They felt that the roots of the family belonged to a particular piece of earth, to that place, to that municipality. It was the idea, "We were born here. We will die here."

So I returned to my *ejido* [agricultural land owned in common by the community] in the state of San Luis Potosi, where I was born. I stayed only three months. I decided to move again.

This time I moved to the city of Santillo in the northern part of the Republic. It made me feel brave to do so. I decided to work harder, as hard as I could. I had two jobs at the same time, one in the morning, one in the afternoon, cleaning houses. With the money I earned I bought a plot of land in the city. I invited my father to look over the land that I had bought. He became so motivated that my family decided to move. This was the first time I achieved a social objective, which was to move my family. It was my first fight: with my family, with my culture, with the ideas of my family. At the moment of leaving, my family was crying just as if some relative had died.

But when my family moved they were able to raise their class level.

Working for the Government

After my family moved I had to work for three reasons. The first was to bring money to the economy of the family. The second was to help my family to feel comfortable in the city, in their new life style. And the third was to buy the necessary things for a home: furniture, dishes, and all the other things.

Fortunately, one of my employers was a teacher, who motivated me to continue studying. I was nineteen when I went back to school. I finished secondary school when I was twenty-two. After that I studied social work. I was thirty-two when I completed my studies. My brothers and sisters did likewise. And some of them went on to professional careers, becoming teachers and, in the case of one brother, an engineer. As a result of education almost all my family have a middle-class level of life. The contradiction is that, because of my help to my brothers and sisters, I am the one with the lowest income!

Most social work jobs require you to work for institutions connected with the government. You have to confine your activity within what is allowed politically. You have to adapt to this politics, even when you are not in agreement. If you express disagreement then you get fired.

That's what happened to me. I tried to implement programs based on the idea of social service: to educate, to give people the facility to adapt to reality. But the programs I tried to establish were rejected by my superiors. It was frustrating. I decided to quit, and to look for another place where I could use everything I knew, and everything I wanted to do and to give.

I agree with the idea that human beings have the necessity of support in a material way. But I think they also have the ability to achieve whatever they want. I looked for institutions that had open systems, open programs, where I could have more autonomy from the government. Then I realized that official institutions never are going to have a politics of openness. I also realized that the only way to go was through independent institutions.

Frente Auténtico del Trabajo

I got into FAT in 1984. I met the person who became my husband, who was a member of FAT. When I came to know the experience they had, when I understood the objectives, the programs, the strategies, the lines of action that FAT had, I knew this was the place I was looking for. It seemed to me there was a chance to get into this organization and fulfill my own expectations.

FAT is an organization of workers, with a national presence. It started in 1960. The organization joins together unions, cooperatives, worker-owned factories, campesinos, and women. It is independent of political parties and of the government. It has at least 60,000 members [about 35,000 of whom are paid-up in dues]. The main objective is to defend workers' rights and to improve workers' lives. My specific job with FAT is to organize the "integral formation" of women.

I want to explain why I decided to work with housewives. I have to refer to the context of the city of Santillo in which I live. This will explain why I started with housewives and not with workers, and why I see this as the first step in building a union.

Santillo is a border community. The population of Santillo is growing rapidly, because of its industrial activity. Several suburbs have been added to the central city. On the other hand, the state of Coahuila in which Santillo is located is very dry and sowing is only possible during part of the year. So a number of rural *ejidos* have become "ghost towns." Immigration from these communities to the city has created many social problems.

The Santillo region contains about sixty factories. These *maquiladoras* make goods for export. Among other things they make electrical parts for automobiles. Most of the workers in these *maquiladoras* are women.

Some of the *maquiladoras* were established a long time ago. The Santillo Industrial Group, with fourteen factories, dates from the 19th century. The capital comes entirely from Mexican citizens. These factories employ 15,800 workers. There are also newer *maquiladoras* created by American investment. One of the most important is General Motors, with 6000 workers, almost all of them women. The second most important factory is Chrysler, with 4500 workers.

All these enterprises have an old-fashioned labor mentality and do not allow the organization of their workers. If they see any sign of worker organization, they try to destroy it. They have a blacklist. They fire a lot of people. This means that FAT cannot organize an open union.

In 1970 Santillo workers organized a general strike, with national repercussions. The consequence was that the corporations, together with the official CTM [Confederation of Mexican Workers] union, imposed new controls. After winning the strike, the secretary general of the union sold himself to the company. The mechanisms of control are stronger when the corporation is joined to the CTM, the official union. These corporations reject any idea of agreement with FAT. If a worker is seen near the FAT offices, he or she is fired.

Another Way?

In this reality, we have to look for new approaches to organizing. So we have started to spread the idea at the base. We have started with individuals. We have to do it with great care and great professionalism. We must not push the workers to the point that they get fired from their jobs. We have to give help to these people in such a way that the people receive benefits, not become unemployed.

The way to get into an organizational program proved to be, women first. Women are related to husbands who are workers, and to daughters or sons who are workers. Women are worried about their daughters who work in *maquiladoras*. First, they worry that the wages are so low. Second, they worry that young women are often encouraged to go to work before the legal minimum age of 16. And third, they worry about the one-hour bus ride to the factories in Monterey during which their daughters are not covered by liability insurance. If the women are educated, they give that education to their families. This is a long-term strategy.

The organizers start by making a diagnosis of the community. They base their work on the necessities of the community.

The second step is for the women themselves to decide what they want to do. Of course the organizers want to educate these women, so that they can see the reality of the factories where their husbands and children work. But to the women it seems that they started the organization, and they should decide the things they want to do.

I went to the women whose husbands and children worked for these corporations. FAT wanted to know what are the actual conditions of work inside the Santillo factories. But at first it was difficult to ask this kind of question, so my approach was to begin by encouraging the women to do whatever they wished.

The women wanted to take courses in "self-esteem." These courses lasted more than a year.

Next I began to seek personal interviews with the women, for of course by this time we were friends. I asked them about the working conditions for their family members. I got the information I wanted. And the women began to invite their husbands, because the workers saw that their wives were taking courses and they began to ask me to give them courses of another kind, for example, on the reform of social security and on AFORES, the new retirement plan.

As a consequence, men as well as women are now involved in the program. But the males in the group don't know that the program is part of FAT! In general, workers know about FAT and respect FAT. Some of them love FAT. Still they don't want to become part of FAT as an organization, because they are afraid of losing their jobs.

Self-Management ("Autogestión")

We have another form of organization, cooperatives. This is a way to put self-management ("autogestión") into practice.

Women started the credit and saving cooperative in 1986. They were wives of FAT members. They belong to the cooperative sector of FAT. The husbands couldn't make an organization work inside the places where they were employed, because of the controls, so the wives started this organization on the outside. It was an open organization to which other people could belong. Once again the idea was that women would make a beginning and then their husbands could join. The cooperative makes it possible for women to buy things like furniture or clothing for cash, rather than on credit, or to buy school supplies for their children.

They try to implement democracy also. The cooperative is directed by the people who belong to it. FAT provides only the education and orientation. This is a long process, too. We have a lot of apathetic persons. It is one of the problems we have to face. At the same time, the women can see that the membership is growing. The credit union now has 200 members.

We offer courses on women's rights, and the rights of organizations. So we have a chance to give ideas. There are also other groups, for example to do sewing, or to cut hair. There are problems in this economic work because of lack of money. We would like to expand to another area near Santillo. We need a location to do our sewing work. We need salaries for the organizers. We keep waiting for the right institution to give us money. I participate in all the groups. They all are groups of women.

If you belong to one of these groups, that doesn't mean that you belong to FAT. Joining FAT is a voluntary action. We want a non-corporatist system to which people do not have to belong. FAT has programs to help people organize themselves but that doesn't mean you have to be part of FAT.

Why I Do It

FAT doesn't have the resources to give a salary to everyone who works for it. I receive a minimum salary and money for expenses. My husband and I are separated, and I do not receive any money from him.

What keeps me going? I am proud of helping women to change their lives.

I think we must make a change in the distribution of wealth. I don't like it that a few people have a lot of money and a lot of people have none.

I know this is a long process. But I remember the Olympic torch: you carry it, and then you give it to someone else, and to someone else, and to someone else.

Maybe I can't do very much. I know that the little change of one woman doesn't have a lot of impact on the whole society. But at least in that woman, in that family, there's been a change.

Margaret Keith and Jim Brophy

"Your health is not for sale"

Margaret Keith became aware of occupational disease when her former husband was exposed to diesel exhaust in a salt mine. Jim Brophy worked in a Chrysler engine plant where he was exposed to machining fluids.

In 1979, Margaret Keith and Jim Brophy helped to found the Windsor Occupational Health Information Service (WOHIS), which Margaret now directs. Jim directs the Occupational Health Clinics for Ontario Workers (OHCOW). WOHIS is one of the most effective grassroots occupational safety and health coalitions in North America. Its publications include Workplace Roulette: Gambling With Cancer *(Toronto, Canada: Between the Lines, 1997).*

This interview was conducted at the WOHIS office in November 1997.

Margaret

MARGARET: My father was a physician and my mother a nurse; a retired nurse, because my father didn't want her to work. Dinner conversation was always about appendectomies and such. My father was a doctor in the years before we had socialized medicine. When he died three years ago, one of my sisters reminded us that about a third of the cases he did were not paid. She remembers people coming to the house and paying five dollars at a time, two dollars at a time.

My first job was helping out in my father's office, which was just a little den in our house. I did some record-keeping and billing. I was pretty familiar with medical terminology. I always wanted to go into some sort of medical something. But instead, I married when I was seventeen years old and pregnant, and eventually had four children.

I went back to school at night and took Communications Studies, learning how to make videos. One of the first jobs I had when Jim and I later got together was to produce slide shows on health and safety. I've always preferred to have other people do the speaking. I like to get the message together, and have other voices say what it is that I'm feeling. I help people get their message out.

I became involved in health and safety through my former marriage to a miner, Bob McArthur, who was battling diesel exhaust in the salt mines. He would come home and start coughing up all this black sputum. He was a safety rep too.

I took a tour of the mine once and was shocked to see that the walls were as black as in a coal mine. When you went into a new area, the walls were beautiful: veins of white salt in the rock, very clean. When you went into an old area the walls were covered with soot. My husband was in the maintenance department, so he wasn't out in the new areas as much as he was in the older sections. The whole environment was filled with diesel exhaust. All the trucks and heavy equipment were diesel-powered. They had very poor ventilation.

For years and years workers were down there with no protection at all. Then they fought for and won special helmets, which sit on your head with a clear shield that comes down in front. There is an air supply that pushes air up into your breathing zone, through a filter. It's not a self-contained breathing apparatus. It has a blower and a filter. That was a big win. But at the end of the day the workers would take the white fibre filters out of these things; they now looked like charcoal.

JIM: One time Bob McArthur ran a helmet outside the mine, at different points in the city, while running a second helmet for the same six and a half hours at various locations in the mine.[1] The filter running outside the mine remained completely white. The filter in the mine turned black. These filters were taken into Parliament and shown.

MARGARET: The workers at the mine belonged to an amalgamated union which included other workplaces. Eventually the salt miners decided to withdraw from the amalgamated local because they believed they were not getting enough support. They felt the amalgamated local was gun shy when it came to health and safety. The local includes many auto feeder plants that can pick up and leave just like that. They have lost many members through plant closure.

But the salt miners had a vein of salt that couldn't move! They held wildcat strikes over health and safety issues. They were very noisy about

1. Bob McArthur describes this homemade comparative experiment on the videotape, *Excerpts [from] WOSH History*, produced in 1991. He says that neither he nor the other workers can remember how they got the idea to do this.

it. The mining corporation was embarrassed, and eventually was pressured to make improvements. In fact, the Ministry of Labour finally came in and sided with the miners. It always seems that the government won't move unless there's enough of a ruckus made. They finally decided that just to keep peace they'd come in, and enforce the law that they should have been enforcing anyway.

Jim

JIM: I grew up in Rochester, New York. My parents' parents were blue-collar workers. One of my grandfathers was an electrician, the other one a painter. Although my father was a salesperson, I grew up in a strong union scene. I remember my grandfather breaking his hip when he was in his sixties or seventies, and fell from a painter's scaffold. He eventually died with lead poisoning. He was buried at the union hall, the oldest member of the union.

My first experience as a union member was in Elmira one summer, working in a Westinghouse plant six days a week. It was a horrible place. People got hurt there. The guy that was my set-up man got completely covered by acid, and was very badly burned. This was a place that made vacuum tubes for TV sets. All night long you would hear "Bang! Bang!" as the tubes exploded. Often the workers would have them in their hands, and they would explode. We got a little more than $2 an hour. I remember going to a union meeting and being told that in Georgia they were getting $1.35 for doing the job we were doing. We were members of the IUE [International Union of Electrical Workers].

I went to an all-boys Catholic high school. When I graduated from high school, I started looking around as to where I could go to college. The Basilian Fathers had universities in Ontario, in Windsor and Toronto. It was cheaper for me to go to Canada. I came to Windsor in 1965.

Chrysler Engine Plant

JIM: After college, I ran a book store in Windsor. To keep the book store going I got a job at the Chrysler engine plant, where I worked from 1972 to 1976. Back then it was easy to get a job.

In an engine plant, you have machining, and make lots of heads, and cranks, and rods, and pistons. They have to be ground, and holes are put into them, and they're carved out and polished. When you have metal on metal it generates tremendous heat and friction. So that the parts will not explode, oil is sprayed on them. The oil is a lubricant, but it also heats up and emits mist. You get mist, along with metal chips, and particles, and solvents, and whatever else is used in machining. When I worked in those departments, in the summer time you could not see the length of the department because of the oil mist.[2]

The other thing that goes on is an assembly process. You take all the different parts, and at the end of the line you get a finished engine, which is shipped to an assembly plant. I worked in cranks, and in blocks, and I did time on the assembly line.

At the time I went into Chrysler I was very influenced by what had gone on in Italy. To the best of my knowledge, risk mapping was developed in the Italian Fiat plants in the 1960s. We now use "risk mapping" in our work. You draw the floor plan of your workplace and then you indicate what the hazards are, who works there, who has gotten sick. Friends of mine had translated documents from "Lotta Continua" and "Poder Operaia" ("Continuous Struggle" and "Workers' Power"). They took a position of "no delegation." Everything had to be settled in a workers' assembly. They would stop the plant and have big meetings, so that all the workers could participate.

I found that there was a coalition of workers in the Chrysler engine plant, connected with people on the outside, who had been agitating about what was going on there. In fact, they had taken over the leadership of the union engine plant committee. And then there was a falling out, because as these guys got the positions they started becoming less militant. I started working with some of the rank-and-file folks who had been part of the opposition.

The president of the local union was an old CPer. He had played a very significant role in the Chrysler workers getting health care. The company had wanted us to agree to a bargained-for health plan. He wouldn't agree to that, because he thought it would take pressure off the government to create universal health care.

We put together a group that started doing leaflets. One of them had a gun pointing *toward* the reader and the words, "Armed With Your Contract!," because that's what they always used to tell us. The leaflets were written by the workers themselves. I helped them. I probably cranked out more mimeographed fliers than anyone in the world, or at least I thought I did. Looking at these leaflets today, I'm struck by the fact that almost all of them were on health and safety issues.

After four years, we had exhausted ourselves politically. It was not that people were particularly against us. People knew we were from inside the plant; it wasn't like some external group. People would take our leaflets and talk about them. But it was clear that workers were not about to abandon the union structure for some nebulous proposal about depart-

2. The work WOHIS has done to demonstrate the link between machining fluids (also known as cutting fluids) and cancer among auto workers is described in *Workplace Roulette*, pp. 50–55.

mental councils. (To this day, over twenty years later, I'm still not trusted by certain members of the union because of these leaflets.)

Almost the last issue was whether members of our group should run for local union office. I was against it. One guy I was very close to had been there ten years. He decided to run without really talking it over with the group. He and I had a big argument. Looking back, we probably should have run for office. Our failure to do that allowed the incumbent leadership to marginalize us completely. I left Chrysler's in 1976.

I decided I had had enough exposure to metalworking fluids. I thought I would go to the post office, where there is a very militant union. But instead, I wound up with the OPIRG [Ontario Public Interest Research Group].

Bendix

JIM: I didn't know anything about asbestos, but the woman I replaced had gone off to assist the union at a Johns Manville plant in Scarborough to help them write a booklet about asbestos. Newspaper stories began to come out. I called her up and said, "Look, I think we're on to something here at the Bendix plant in Windsor." The Bendix plant made brake shoes out of asbestos. We decided to hold a public meeting to discuss the potential health hazards associated with asbestos exposure.

MARGARET: The asbestos meeting was July 17, 1979. The asbestos issue was front and center. But after the discussion about the hazards of asbestos a number of people put up their hands and started talking about other issues, including diesel exhaust in the salt mines.

After that meeting there seemed to be the possibility of forming a coalition around health and safety. A few days later, there was a meeting at my house around the kitchen table and we started talking about the idea of a COSH group.[3]

That was the beginning of what we have now: first the COSH group, and then the information service that was eventually funded by United Way, and now the clinic.

I didn't start working, officially, until the following summer. I had begun to see how huge this problem was, that it was not just the salt mine, or a single company. That summer I found out for the first time that there were actually people who were totally committed to social change. I hadn't known anyone like that. Here were human beings thinking about other people before themselves, who had decided to devote their entire lives. It was heady. I knew that if there were people like that, I could be one of them.

3. COSH (Committee for Occupational Safety and Health) groups had been formed in a number of cities in the United States in the mid-1970s.

Had I been asked when I was eighteen what social justice issue I wanted to get into, it wouldn't have been health and safety. I was more into environmental issues, women's issues. But having had the opportunity that summer to work in health and safety, I decided to make that my issue.

We didn't have much money. We managed to keep going with little make-work grants from the government. The university students had a referendum, and threw out OPIRG. They were more interested in non-union issues. Health and safety seemed to them a worker's issue.

That's when CUPE (Canadian Union of Public Employees) took us under their wing and gave us some office space. Public employees like sewage workers and health workers had health and safety problems. The national director of health and safety for CUPE was a former miner. Clifton Grant, for whom our annual award is named, was a public school carpenter who died of mesothelioma after exposure to asbestos. It was more difficult with the UAW, which represented the Bendix workers.[4]

JIM: What happened at Bendix was this. In 1977 the UAW, responding to Occupational Safety and Health legislation in the United States, started to demand health and safety reps in their collective agreements. The Bendix workers put that on the bargaining table. The company was not going to give them one, and it became a strike issue. They ended up with a safety rep named Jack McCann. He was allowed four hours a day to work on health and safety issues.

So he was reading the newspaper and he read about a worker in Sudbury, Aimee Bertrand, who had been compensated for cancer of the larynx because of exposure to asbestos. The man had been a steamfitter, and when he worked on boilers he had to strip off all the asbestos.

Jack thought to himself, "You know, we work with asbestos. And we've had all these cancers of the larynx. I wonder if there's a connection?" UAW Local 195 had regular meetings with the WCB [Workers' Compensation Board]. They had a meeting for which the union prepared a brief on behalf of three widows whose husbands had died of laryngeal cancer. At the end of the meeting they gave the brief to the WCB representative, and said they were concerned that there might be an asbestos problem. So the Board said to the union, "We've been watching this problem for a long time. We were wondering if something might happen." The union said, "What do you mean?" And the Board handed them written orders going back to 1966. Thirteen years later the union saw these government orders for the first time! At that time neither the government nor the employer had an obligation to give the information to the union.

MARGARET: It turned out that for years at Bendix, the government had come in and issued orders that were not followed. The orders directed the company to end dry-sweeping of asbestos, to put in proper ventilation, to

4. The Bendix story is told in *Workplace Roulette*, pp. 42–45.

make sure that people were wearing their breathing apparatus. The government would come back in years later and write the same orders.

JIM: In addition, we found out that they had done X-rays in the mid-1970s. At least one worker had a spot on his lung and they didn't tell him. He went back into the exposure.

In 1978, the company hygienist was seen standing in the parking lot, watching clouds of asbestos float over the nearby residential area. Asbestos is microscopic. When you're talking about seeing clouds of it, you're talking very heavy concentrations. We know that there was at least one woman who lived in the vicinity of the plant who died of mesothelioma, although she had no exposure at work. There was an elementary school next to the Bendix plant!

MARGARET: We encouraged the workers to make public their concerns and to file compensation claims. The union was terribly embarrassed by this. When the plant closed, the union accused us and said that if we had been quiet about it, the shutdown could have been avoided.

But we felt we had to do something. People were getting sick, and there was an incredible lack of enforcement. There was collusion between the employer and the government to hide the health and safety problems.

JIM: In the middle of all this, Tommy Dunn, to whom our book is dedicated, died of mesothelioma. It was one thing if older workers, in their sixties and seventies, were dying. Tommy Dunn was thirty-four. Now all of a sudden the issue was out of the union leadership's control. The newspapers were no longer going to the local union president, they were going to Jack McCann, the safety rep, or Bob McArthur, or other rank-and-file health and safety reps. They were circumventing normal labor relations. This was not a matter of, "We'll trade you five grievances for that issue." These reps were saying, "If it's unsafe, it's down. If it can kill us, it's out. We're not negotiating that."

A new Ontario occupational safety and health law had come into effect in 1978. It gave workers the right to refuse unsafe work. In the months after Dunn's illness became public, two workers in the brake shoe department refused to work. The union split. The younger workers identified with Tommy Dunn, a popular guy, a steward in the plant. They felt that the union hadn't done enough. The older workers, who wound up losing their jobs when the plant closed, felt that the union had overreacted and had gone too far.

Independence and Support

JIM: We work with the unions now more than I did at Chrysler's. But we have always insisted on our autonomy. That has been a big struggle. We've been accepted enough by the union leadership that they're not about to try to do us in; in fact they've been fighting to help us keep our clinic open. CUPE, the biggest union in the country, supports us strongly. But at the same time, we have enough independence and enough grassroots support that we can do pretty much as we see fit.

The Canadian Auto Workers (CAW) have also been very supportive. Bud Jimmerfield was a health and safety activist who developed cancer of the esophagus after being exposed to metalworking fluids for almost thirty years. He died at the age of 49, leaving behind seven children and his wife Diana. His illness triggered a national cancer prevention campaign among the Canadian Auto Workers. They negotiated a five-fold lowering of the metalworking fluid standard in the Big Three because of what happened to Bud.

We have established his claim in front of the Workers' Compensation Board, so his award, along with another one we won for an auto worker with cancer of the larynx, constitutes a precedent in our fight for cancer prevention at work.

MARGARET: The Bendix plant closed in 1980. It made a rocky start for us. We had had a serious setback. Soon after that, the UAW and its Canadian representative blacklisted us, saying, "We don't want any of our members to go see these people."

JIM: We became the scapegoats. I remember we had a meeting at UAW Local 195 with fifty people, all safety reps. The leadership of the local sent two guys into our meeting, one of whom has since died of cancer. They were drunk and threatened to beat everybody up. About half the workers there were women and they were completely blown away by this. Most of them we never saw again.

MARGARET: We did a mailing to most of the union locals in the city that were members of the central labor body. I got a phone call from the treasurer of the council who threatened me, saying, "We've got you now. You got ahold of our mailing list. You had no right to it. You're washed up." We had a perfect right to the list. It had been given to us.

The mailing was for a conference on cancer in 1983. UAW members were told not to attend. They came anyway.

How did we manage to pull that off? I think it's because we were the only people who were really listening to these folks, giving them a voice, taking their concerns seriously. They were very frustrated with the local union. It would have been so simple for the union to say, "Here's a problem we haven't been paying enough attention to. Here's a place where we can improve." But no, the local said, "We're doing a good job. It's those outsiders who are causing the problems." So, despite the official boycott, we carried on.

Reflections on Nicaragua

JIM: Also in 1983 Margaret and I went to Nicaragua. I was sent by the Canadian equivalent of the Peace Corps. CUPE gave us money to go. When we came back, the local paper gave us a whole page in which we wrote about our experiences.

The trip had a powerful emotional effect on Margaret and myself. As much as I thought of myself as knowledgeable about the living conditions of the Third World, within a day of being in Nicaragua it was clear how completely unaware of the reality I had been. When you think of what people have to do to survive on a day-to-day basis, and compare that to our situation, the difference is unbelievable.

So Nicaragua completely changed our sense of the world, and of the role of American multinationals. It anchored a global perspective.

We had already been into "popular education" not knowing that that was what it was. In Nicaragua we were walking around with bags of material about their literacy program, stuff on polio and malaria, basic hygiene. When we got back we did an asbestos slide show using cartoons, as they did in Nicaragua.

MARGARET: I remember riding on the bus to Matagalpa and looking up at the sky, and thinking, "That's the same sky that we have sitting over Canada and the United States. We are all people, all part of the same world. Why should there be such incredible differences in living standards?" It seemed terribly unfair.

I came back with a sense that you can do more than you think you can do, you can be a lot stronger than you had ever imagined. I was so impressed with how the people there continued to fight, and continued to speak out, and continued to sacrifice. When I came home I felt, "If they can do it, I can do it." Although it was so out of character for me to talk in front of a group of people, this pushed me to do what I have never been comfortable doing. I came home and went around with slides and talked about Nicaragua.

In the Third World there is a sense of danger everywhere. Here we are lulled into thinking we are safe. We have laws. The government is taking care of us. We have health and safety reps in our unions. We don't have anything to worry about. But we are not really safe and we are not protected. That's why so many workers get sick and die from workplace hazards.

JIM: That's exactly what happened in the United States with benzene. OSHA demanded an immediate emergency standard of one part benzene per million parts of air. The industry argued that while that standard would reduce the risk of leukemia and lymphatic cancer, the cost would be prohibitive, and that therefore the standard should be ten parts per million. And they were successful.

MARGARET: The largest trash incinerator in the world is located in downtown Detroit. They did a risk assessment and projected that there would be a certain excess of cancers, but that was acceptable because all the wealthy white folks have gone to the suburbs.

Casino

MARGARET: An example of the work we do now is the research project we undertook with the Canadian Auto Workers at the Windsor casino. It opened three years ago. About 3500 people work at the Windsor casino. It will be up to 5000 within the year. The CAW organized the casino around issues like wages and job security.

People started coming in to see us. We had people who were sick, who had repetitive strain injuries from standing there dealing all day, who had respiratory problems from second-hand smoke. We had people who weren't sick but who were having to clean up blood spills, and body fluid spills, in the bathrooms, and were having to deal with hypodermic needles. The workers call Saturday night "fight night."

We got started in May 1997. We had a series of focus groups to find out what the main problems were. Union people ran these sessions. All I did was observe.

We held thirteen sessions in Windsor with an average of five or six people in each group. The casino workers put dots on a diagram of the body to show where they hurt. This gave each one a chance to see that he or she was not the only one with shoulder problems, or wrist problems, or headache. Then we would ask what the dots represented.

They drew a map of their workplace, and identified the hazards. This is a "hazard map" or a "risk map."

Finally, we had a map we called "your world." There is a figure in the middle with a box around it. We asked, "How are you affected by your work when you're away from work? How is your life?" This was the most amazing of all. At the casino there are constant lights and noises geared to keeping the customers excited, awake, spending money, and the workers are run off their feet responding to customers who are agitated, and may be drunk. The workers started talking about how when they get home from the casino, they don't want to talk to anybody. They talked about how it affected their relationships with spouses, with their children. They often have to work on weekends and holidays, so their social life is affected.

Afterward we all got together, and looked at the results, and talked about what was going to happen next. We determined what would be the top three or four issues. Emotional stress was number one. Second-hand smoke was next, along with ergonomic issues. They're never allowed to sit down. Some of them are working twelve-hour shifts, constantly on their feet.

A lot of the stress is caused by understaffing. Patron harassment is a problem. The workers say that as long as customers are losing money, the casino will not throw them out.

The research results were made public and provided the union with ammunition for negotiated improvements. They've won hepatitis B shots, a universal precaution for people exposed to body fluids. They've won much improved ventilation. Sound baffles have been installed around certain very noisy machines. They've had the weight of coin buckets lessened, so that they're not getting back injuries from lifting. They've gotten the uniforms changed. Before, women had to wear low-cut blouses, miniskirts, and high heels. They can now wear pants.

Your Health Is Not for Sale

JIM: I got involved with health and safety mainly because I saw it as something of real concern to workers. All my experience suggests that health and safety issues reflect a much deeper problem: the complete lack of democracy in the workplace. The fact that we accept at work what we would never accept in civil society is the real basis for workers being at risk.

Almost any worker will agree with that statement. If you say, "Isn't the reason that you're at risk of getting injured and diseased in the workplace that you have no control over the work environment, that no one ever asks you what chemicals or substances should be used, whether money should be put into ventilation, shall we use this solvent rather than that one?" I can't remember a worker not agreeing with that proposition.

That's the very basis of capitalist society. Workers' own experience of health and safety shows them what Margaret was saying, how we are lulled into believing that we have a stake in society when in fact, we don't have it.

For me, health and safety has always been one of the most radicalizing, politicizing issues, not only because it deals with real social relations, but it also is connected with the things that are most important, like your health. The radical slogan used here twenty years ago was, "Your health is not for sale." In a capitalist society everything is for sale. If our health is not for sale, then it is something almost by definition at variance with the status quo.

We've never given up on that. Everything we've done has been to strengthen workers' ability to make this fight and to challenge this relationship. We've tried to empower workers. We've seen that it's their struggle. And there are no guardian angels, no special group that's shown up with a wand to make all of this go away. From the minute that you're born into the working class until your last breath, the one thing you know is that anything you get you're going to have to fight for.

Those workers are not going to have some paternal government inspector or goodwill doctor or concerned employer to protect them. If they're not active, if they're not doing something to make their own working conditions secure, then there is nobody else. We are here to help but we are not the "experts." We don't work in the plastics plant, or on the construction site, and we don't know what they know. What they may not know, where they may need help from us, is how can they build on their own knowledge, how can they get things cooking, how can they get some attention, how can they get support, how can they get some information.

That's why I think, when the clinic was being threatened two years ago, this community reacted. People occupied the Ministry of Labour. Thousands of faxes from Ford, General Motors, and Chrysler fax machines were going into the Ministry of Labour, from workers on the line, demanding that the clinic be kept open. The city council unanimously supported us. The Windsor *Star* wrote a lead editorial supporting us. The Catholic Bishop supported us. But the thing that was decisive was that thousands of workers, knowing what they were facing in the workplace, did not want this resource shut down. They knew that it was an attack on them.

MARGARET: When this whole thing started after 1979–80, I think we were envisioning a coalition of different unions, and that we would have a group that was cohesive and active, and would grow and grow and grow. It hasn't turned out to be exactly what we pictured. The health and safety reps have come and gone, as their issues have come up and been resolved. We're here when they need us.

But when we get in a crisis, and we need help, all of a sudden there are thousands of people. That's when you see the impact that you've made on the community.

IV
IN OUR HANDS
IS PLACED A POWER

Rich Feldman

Virginia Yu

Martin Glaberman

"Workers have to deal with their own reality and that transforms them"

During Marty Glaberman's twenty years as an automobile worker in Detroit, he was associated with the West Indian Marxist intellectual, C. L. R. James. The group around James developed a sweeping critique of conventional trade unions. In a pamphlet entitled Punching Out, *published in 1952, Marty argued that in a workplace where there is a collective bargaining agreement with a no-strike clause, the union representative—whether officer, full-time committeeman, or even shop steward—tends to become a cop for the boss.*

In the late 1960s, Marty Glaberman conducted a class on Marxism for the executive committee of the Detroit-based League of Revolutionary Black Workers. He believes that workers will develop new organizational forms through which to express their militant solidarity and their ability to run the economy themselves. He finds examples in the Russian soviets of 1905 and 1917, the workers' councils in Hungary in 1956, and the occupation of factories by ten million French workers in 1968.

Since his retirement from industrial work Marty Glaberman has taught at Wayne State University. He has written a book on the wildcat strike movement in the automobile industry during World War II, *and edited* Marxism for Our Times: C. L. R. James on Revolutionary Organization *(Jackson: University of Mississippi Press, 1999). He has also co-authored, with Seymour Faber,* Working for Wages: The Roots of Insurgency *(available from Bewick Editions, P.O. Box 14140, Detroit MI 48214).*

This account is based on an interview in November 1997; a talk at a conference on "workers' self-activity" in Youngstown, Ohio, in June 1997; and an unpublished oral history.

C. L. R. James

I belonged to a group around C. L. R. James. James pioneered the idea of working-class self-activity. He rejected the concept of a vanguard party and the imposition of a party line on any mass movement.

Together with many others in the group, I moved to Detroit in the early 1940s. But moving to Detroit didn't tell us what our relation to the working class should be. Without the working class, you can't do anything. Whether the working class does it, or you do it as their leaders, was ambiguous.

Bunches of middle-class kids went into factories. What did they see? They saw dumb workers. I think it was James who gave us eyes to see different things. We believed in the revolutionary capacity of the working class even though nothing was visible.

In 1956 in Hungary we were absolutely confirmed. You had a totalitarian dictatorship for ten years and then the thing blew. The whole working class, without any prior organization whatsoever, made a revolution. The same thing was true in France in 1968. Whatever organizations of the working class existed were opposed to what the workers were doing. The Socialist Party, the Communist Party, the trade unions, were all saying, "Keep this a traditional strike. Walk back and forth in front of the plant." And ten million French workers occupied their factories.

The Steward's Dilemma

When I moved to Detroit, I shared the common view of radicals working in industry that we should try to become union representatives. That was why we were here, right? To become big shots in the union. So you had to go to union meetings, you had to run for union office when you got the chance.

My colleagues and I came to question these notions. I had some personal experiences.

I was a committeeman at Fruehauf in 1946. It was a relatively small plant so you didn't get off work full-time. What you got was all the time you needed for a grievance, but you had to indicate that you were working on a grievance, either researching or negotiating. I would go talk to the superintendent, and then, when we were done, he would say, "Well, you know, stay here." And he would go off to do his managing. It was clearly a bribe. I didn't have to go back to work. I could sit in this comfortable office. But I was goddamned if I was going to do that, and have everybody looking at me. So I just went back to work.

In 1953 I was hired in the Detroit Transmission Division of General Motors. I did a very simple operation on an engine lathe. The last day of my probationary period was a Saturday in the summer. I often quit before lunch and went to the lunch room maybe five minutes early. On this day, I was called in by the foreman to be told that I was fired. I asked for my committeeman (whom I had never seen in 89 days of work) and then became witness to a remarkable exchange. I tried to tell the committeeman my side of the story, but he didn't want to hear it and simply assumed that all of the foreman's charges were valid. He and the foreman went off into the plant and I was left sitting in air-conditioned comfort, wondering what my fate was to be. They were gone an hour. Then they came back, and the committeeman informed me that if I promised not to violate the rules any more, the foreman would not fire me.

What most impressed me about this experience was the fundamental argument used by the committeeman to win my case. He said, "We (that is, plant management and the union) had a meeting a few months ago, and we agreed we couldn't run the plant without each other. What's the idea of firing this guy and then I got to come in and defend him? What you should have done, if you see him going wrong, is call me in and I put my arm around him and say, 'Hey, buddy, we don't work like that here.' I straighten him out, and you don't have a problem, and I don't have a problem."

This incident gave me some insight into my own experience as a steward and a committeeman. Suppose I entered the toilet and found a worker asleep. I could ignore him, or I could tap him on the shoulder and tell him that if he were caught there was no way I could protect his job. How was this fundamentally different from the role of a conservative union representative? I am enforcing the contract and enforcing the company rules.

Johnny Zupan, UAW Committeeman

My experience with Johnny Zupan was important in shaping my views. I had a lot of respect for the guy. In fact I recruited him to the movement, and spoke at his funeral.

Zupan had come to Detroit from a town in Pennsylvania, where he worked at a zinc smelter. He had got his training and education from the chairman of his local. It was a relatively small international union and the chairman was an old Spanish anarchist. He would do things like follow the industry press. And if at any point the price of zinc went up, say, a penny a pound, the chairman would be knocking on management's door the next day asking for a comparable wage increase. He also began to organize people in the local, including Johnny, to run for political office in the town.

I think Johnny left Pennsylvania because he wanted to get into a larger milieu. He came to Detroit during the war, got a job at Ford's Willow Run plant, and very quickly became a steward and a committeeman. When

Willow Run shut down at the end of the war, he was transferred to Ford Highland Park, where, again, he was active in the union and became a committeeman.

Stewards represented relatively small groups of workers, worked alongside them, and tended to be responsive to their needs. The steward represented fifty to a hundred workers whereas the committeeman represented several hundred.

The separation between worker and union official, which Zupan experienced almost from the start of his working life, but never understood, was intensified at Ford. Ford was the last of the Big Three in auto to recognize the union. When the settlement was announced it was claimed as the biggest victory of all. Ford gave the union (not the workers) all sorts of concessions to establish the union bureaucracy as a special caste in the plant. Ford was the first to establish the full-time committeeman.

The committeemen at Ford don't work. They're full time on union business. Each committeeman represents between 200 and 500 workers. The committeeman's only work is to service and administer the differences between the company's demands and the workers' resistance. Aside from that, they do nothing but sit in the committee room and have long discussions on the "backwardness" of the workers. Every time a worker goes in there, that's the atmosphere he finds. The committeeman's job is talk. Many workers refer to them as lawyers.

An ordinary lawyer will try to do the best for his client under the law. That is not the case with the committeeman. He is more a cop than a lawyer. He enforces the law. Workers have often said that what they want to know from the committeeman is what they *can* do, not what they *can't* do. But what they get is a running lecture on what the contract doesn't allow. The committeeman is the key to enforcing the contract and maintaining discipline in the plants.

Committeemen can and do leave the plant during working hours, with the company guards looking the other way. They also get the top overtime that any worker in their district gets, because a union representative has to be present if just one worker is working. Full-time status for the union committeeman, which began as a means of freeing the union representative from the pressures of management, became a means of freeing the representative from the pressure of the workers.

In the case of Johnny Zupan, there was no self–aggrandizement. There was none of this business of, "I've got to get off this machine so I'm going to run for office." Zupan was militant. He was willing to take on the establishment, willing to take on the company. It was not a question of good or bad about Johnny Zupan, but that, if you become a committeeman you have an objective role, and no matter who you are, you are an alternative bureaucrat. There's a certain objective reality to enforcing the contract that separates union officials from the rank and file. The role creates the person and how you have to function.

Leading from Below

Our group made no formal decision about whether or not to run for full-time union office. I suspect the feeling would have been, there was no problem about running for union office if you were in that kind of situation, but that wasn't your object, and if you didn't run for office it didn't matter. Nobody said, "You've been there a year, how come you're not running for steward?"

I remember that we had some people in Morgantown, West Virginia. There was a big issue nationally, and John L. Lewis simply said, "We have to accept it." What this guy of ours did was to start a discussion which led to sending people to neighboring mines, and ended up in a national wild-cat. We felt proud that we could play a role in getting a massive undertaking like that under way. Our concept was not that we weren't going to be activists or we weren't going to be leaders, but it didn't have to be formal leadership.

I had an experience at Buick. There was a packed union meeting (it must have been contract time). I'm a minor figure in the opposition caucus. The president of the local, who was chairing the meeting, made a ruling from the chair. If he had his way, there was no way that opposition to the contract could be expressed. I turned to a classic union goon who was my buddy, and one of the leaders of our caucus, and said, "Look, you gotta appeal that." He didn't see why, and he let it go.

I'm sitting there, and I finally decide, "To hell with it. I'm going to do it." I appealed the ruling of the chair. The president had a couple of minutes to explain his point of view. I got up and explained my point of view. And by God, the chair gets defeated!

This kind of experience makes you feel that you are invaluable to the working class, that the workers wouldn't have done this by themselves. You have an independent power. You feel that without you, stuff wasn't likely to happen, or didn't always happen. That can be corrupting. Wow! Next thing I know I can be running for president of the goddamned local, because I beat the president in a vote of confidence on the union floor. You have to have a sense that holds you back.

There are always these narrow lines you have to walk. How do you get elected by saying, "If I get elected nothing too much is going to change"? Can you tell the voters, "I'll give you honest representation. But I'm not going to make your work pleasant. I'm not going to be able to change the contract"? That's hard to do.

The League of Revolutionary Black Workers

My first contact with the League of Revolutionary Black Workers was through George Rawick. He was teaching at Monteith College of Wayne State University in the late 1960s. Johnny Watson and perhaps one or two other leaders of the League took classes with him. This was before DRUM (Dodge Revolutionary Union Movement) was organized.[1] Through Rawick I met these League people, and eventually I taught a class on Marxism that included the entire executive committee of the League. There were about half a dozen people in it, all black. This was 1968 or 1969.

The members of DRUM and other groups founded by the League were alternative unionists, although they also extended their reach into the community. Their strength was that they were not a *loyal* opposition, committed to obeying contracts and union constitutions. For the most part they did not run for office to replace the bureaucrats. They called strikes in their own name. The League's biggest successes were at Dodge Main. A decade earlier, because of the introduction of automation, there had been a wave of strikes at Dodge Main. In fact there was a joke in Hamtramck, where the plant was located, that an optimist is a Dodge worker who brings his lunch box to work. Day after day, some department would wildcat, and by the middle of the day the plant was shut down.

A little-known fact is that the first strike the League was involved in at Dodge Main was started by white women. The women were pissed off and stood at the gate to keep people out. These black dudes came by and said, "Yeah, that's cool," and they joined them and shut the plant down.

The League's attack on whites was not directed at their fellow workers. It had to do with the fact that Hamtramck is overwhelmingly Polish, and originally, the personnel in Dodge Main was overwhelmingly Polish.

The Ford Rouge in Dearborn, Dodge Main, and Buick in Flint were the three plants with foundries and heat treat. This meant that they always had a certain core of black workers, because blacks were hired (as in steel) to do the hardest, dirtiest, and most unhealthy jobs. By the late 1960s, there was probably a black majority at Dodge Main. But the executive board of the local union was still overwhelmingly Polish.

It didn't affect in-plant jobs like committeeman, because retirees couldn't vote for committeemen. But retirees could vote for president of the local. The union would send buses to bring them to the polls and outvote the people working in the plant.

---

1. The League included organizations in specific plants, such as DRUM (Dodge Revolutionary Union Movement) in Dodge Main, and ELRUM (Eldon Avenue Revolutionary Union Movement) in the Chrysler Eldon Avenue plant.

DRUM ran against the UAW-backed administration at Dodge Main and lost. However, they forced the national union to take stock. The UAW wasn't going to be able to keep people in check, and stop wildcat strikes, and maintain a Polish leadership in a plant with a black majority. Within a year there was a black president of that local, but he was an administration president. They made no concessions whatever to the League.

Dodge Main was one of the multi-storied plants from the early 1900s that simply didn't work any more with automated technology. Eventually the outdated plants disappeared. I have a picture of the old Dodge Main with the caption, "Remember the Main." There's a huge square block just east of Chrysler Jefferson which is basically a parking lot. That was Hudson Motors. On Grand Boulevard, on the East Side, you come across a plant that's on both sides of the street with a walkway between. That was Packard.

In 1981 or thereabouts I went to Japan and spoke to dissident unionists in Osaka. This was when the talk was that the Japanese were wiping out the American automobile industry. I said that the problem was not Japanese competition. Packard disappeared, Hudson disappeared, Studebaker disappeared, long before there were Japanese imports. The problem was that these companies didn't have enough capital to participate in the next wave of technological change. They went down the drain.

One of the most intriguing things the League did was to take over the Wayne State University newspaper. The year before, some hippie—I think his name was Johnson—became editor of the paper and changed its name from *The Collegian* or some such traditional title to *The South End*. The "South End" meant the south end of Wayne State, which was the Cass corridor, working-class, the place where new immigrants to the city came from the South. The following year Johnny Watson became editor for two years. Johnny went to one class, which made him technically a student while working in a plant.

What they did was to print about 20,000 copies. They'd give out a thousand on campus and give the rest out at plants, and use it as an organizing tool. It was fun. I remember a masthead, "One Class-Conscious Worker Is Worth A Thousand Students." Finally the administration cracked down. Ever since, the editorial board has been restricted in what it could do, and who could be picked was restricted as well. It became a lousy paper.

The League ended in a peculiar way. They had a national convention which was no longer just auto workers. There was a demand for reparations from white churches. After that, the leadership scattered. Johnny Watson, for example, went underground. By the middle 1970s the thing was falling apart.

Workers' Self-Activity

What forms are available to the working class? The union movement is not a force for revolutionary change. I do not think it can be transformed. Mostly workers boycott and ignore unions: they do not go to meetings, they do not vote in union elections. Occasionally they will vote a contract down. They will occasionally, but rarely, participate in opposition caucuses. Whether the workers become revolutionary or not does not depend on what the union leadership does.

This means that the course of future developments in the workplace has to be sought outside the unions. Caucuses and factions will still be built and, here and there, will have temporary and minor successes. But the explosions that are still to come are likely to have the appearance of new revolutionary forms, organizations that are not simply organs of struggle but organs of control of production.

My understanding of Marxism is that it is based on the reality of the working class. Practical tactics, whether we like it or not, have to come from that.

If I work in a GM brake plant in Dayton, Ohio I have a certain amount of power, and therefore a certain amount of militancy. I go out on strike, and within two or three weeks I have two-thirds of General Motors shut down. But if I work in a plant making nuts and bolts, and there are ten other plants making nuts and bolts, I'm not going to be very militant. I could shut the place down, and stay out forever, and starve to death. This little company I work for is not going to make any concessions because if they did, they could not compete.

We have to respect that. Some people say, "Oh, these workers are backward." They're not backward: they understand what's going on in the world. The point is, theory is important but it can't be imposed on workers or on particular situations.

I think self-activity is the response of working people to the nature of their lives and work. Sometimes it's good, sometimes it's bad, sometimes it's quiet. Part of the reality is that we're going through a considerable technological revolution, which means that experiences, even jobs, that people depended on and know about, begin to disappear. To expect workers to say, "Yesterday, they automated my factory; today, I know exactly what to do about it," is Utopian. It takes a while. It takes a generation. Workers will learn.

And the one thing that I think is an absolute given: workers will resist, because work sucks. Until someone can tell me that work has become real nice under capitalism, whether in the United States or anywhere else, I say that is the fundamental basis of our theory and our practice. Work sucks, and sooner or later workers are going to resist it in whatever way they can.

One of the things George Rawick said is, "Unions don't organize workers. Workers organize unions."[2] Workers' self-activity does create organizations, does create unions and other institutions, which may become bureaucratized and turn against the worker. Unions are not a secret plot designed to fool the workers. Workers organize them and then they get out of control.

Marx believed that the conditions of life and work of the proletariat would force the working class to behave in ways that would ultimately transform society. In other words, what Marx said was: We're not talking about going door-to-door and making workers into ideal socialists. You've got to take workers as they are, with all their contradictions, with all their nonsense. But the fact that society forces them to struggle begins to transform the working class. If white workers realize they can't organize steel unless they organize black workers, that doesn't mean they're not racist. It means that they have to deal with their own reality, and that transforms them. Who were the workers who made the Russian Revolution? Sexists, nationalists, half of them illiterate. Who were the workers in Polish Solidarity? Anti-Semitic, whatever. That kind of struggle begins to transform people.

2. What Rawick wrote was: "The unions did not organize the strikes; the working class in the strikes and through the strikes organized the unions." George Rawick, "Working Class Self-Activity," *Radical America*, v. 3, no. 2 (Mar.–Apr. 1969), reprinted in *Workers' Struggles, Past and Present: A "Radical America" Reader*, ed. James Green (Philadelphia: Temple University Press, 1983), p. 145.

Andrea Carney

"I declined to join the staff"

Andrea Carney has for many years been a steward at Kaiser Permanente in Los Angeles for Local 399, Service Employees International Union (SEIU). Local 399 carried on the celebrated "Justice for Janitors" organizing campaign in the late 1980s.

Andrea tells how the newly-organized janitors, many of them recent immigrants from Central America, joined with Anglo health care workers like herself to form a Multiracial Alliance. In June 1995, the Alliance elected a new Local 399 executive board. Just before he became head of the AFL-CIO, SEIU President John Sweeney imposed a trusteeship. The trustee appointed by Sweeney removed Andrea and others from the offices to which they had been elected. Andrea concludes her account with a letter in which she refused a full-time staff job offered by the appointed trustee.

This account is drawn from two narratives of events at Local 399 that appeared in the rank-and-file newsletter Impact, *and from an interview with Andrea Carney on June 5 and 7, 1998. Andrea's husband David Hughes was also present, and is the "David" referred to in what follows.*

I was born right before World War II broke out, in 1941. The war had an impact on me as a small child. My dad was drafted. From all the talk I heard, I knew something was very wrong.

My father was a landscape gardener. My mother was a housewife until the time I was fifteen, when she went to work on the assembly line in a toy factory. She stayed in that job for a number of years until she went to work for an answering service. I have two sisters.

My parents were pretty apolitical. But my grandfather on my mother's side was not. He lived with us for a period of time in the early 1940s, when he became chemically imbalanced and psychotic from a drug. Eventually he went to a state hospital where we would see him periodically. But he wasn't sick at all. He just didn't fit in, like a lot of people in the 1940s who kind of went against the grain. He finally escaped, and from time to time came back to stay with us.

It was my grandfather who interested me in the injustice that was going on in our country and in the world. He would bring things up, such as what was happening in the South. I paid attention to him. The other family members unfortunately did not.

I never had a teacher who motivated me except in fifth grade. He was a substitute teacher. I'm surprised he lasted as long as he did because it was the McCarthy period. He gave us ideas. He told us there was a fuel for cars that was made from animal waste, and there was a conspiracy by the auto and oil industries to buy up patents for technologies by which they felt threatened.

I was impressed with this guy. He would sit on top of a little desk and tell us all kinds of things. That's how I learned about "buyer beware" and "laissez faire." One time he talked to us about who the Russian people really were. At school we were told that now the Russians had the atom bomb, they were going to come and bomb us any day. We went through air raid drills. They would ring the fire bell, and we got under our desks. It went on through the 1950s.

But he told us that the people in the Soviet Union were working moms and dads, with kids, people just like you and me and everybody else. There was no difference between them and us. They had the same desires, they went about their business just as we did. He wasn't there the next year.

I got very interested in the Rosenberg case. When they were executed I was the same age as their oldest son. I was convinced by all the propaganda that they had probably given some secret away, but I felt that that is not something for which you should be killed. These were somebody's parents. Even though I had grown to be very patriotic following the war, I never again had any faith in our government.

I don't remember any adult who felt the way I did. I don't remember discussing the Rosenberg case even with my grandfather, as he was probably out of my life in that period. It was just what I was reading in the newspapers and seeing on TV. There were thousands of people demonstrating to save the Rosenbergs, not only in this country but everywhere else.

I was rather shy as a child. When I got to junior high I became a little more outspoken. I became a radical, although I didn't know I was. My mother was upset that I was so outspoken and had opinions. She wanted to know why I couldn't be more like my sisters. I felt alone but I was not a loner. I ran with a lot of friends at school, and when I went to work it was the same. It's always been that way.

After I got most of the way through high school I sought out older women to talk to. I wanted to hear their experiences, I wanted to know what they'd been through. I wanted to know right away. And I didn't want to go to school. I wanted to get out and work. So I quit school in my senior year of high school and went to work as a riveter in San Fernando.

Working

At that time, in the late 1950s, it was easy to get a job. A lot of industry was booming, especially in electronics.

I stayed at my first job only a few months. The guy wouldn't give me a dime raise, so I said, "Forget you. I'm out of here." I walked off the job, went across the street and got a job as a floor girl in a sewing factory.

There I observed women, most of whom were Latina, being abused by piece work. A floor person made less money than the women on the machines but it was her job to distribute the bundles of material. I realized what was going on, and had to run around and make sure everybody got her fair share. Some of the workers tried to pay me to give them the big bundles of material. I said, "No. *Everybody* gets a big bundle and everybody gets a small bundle."

I stayed there for a year. Unfortunately, I didn't speak Spanish. I grew up in Pacoima and I should have learned Spanish, but I didn't. However, the women came to respect me.

Then I went into electronics. I met some wonderful people who taught me a lot. I learned how to wind transformers, to put them together from scratch. I learned how to follow a diagram. It was sporadic. We were in and out of work.

I left that job and found work in another big plant. There I stayed for two years, testing diodes. Diodes end up in little circuit boards that are used in aircraft and electronics. It was a mixed group of white and Asian workers. That was a new experience for me.

One day I was sitting out in the yard, eating my lunch by myself. A group of African American women came by and said, "Is this place hiring?" I said, "Yes, they are. They have been running ads." They wanted to know where the personnel office was. I told them. They were back in less than five minutes. They said, "They're not hiring."

During the next few days I heard my supervisor ask one of the Korean workers if she had any friends who wanted to work there. I went to another Korean worker, and I asked her to go back to her community, and get the Korean newspaper, and see if the company was running an ad. She came back and said, "Yes."

I wrote to the NAACP and told them exactly what had happened. As a result, the company hired one very light-skinned African American woman. It was hard to tell that she was African American. And they slapped up posters all over the place saying, "We are an equal opportunity employer."

About the same time, I heard that two women in another part of the plant were trying to organize a union. One of my co-workers was an older woman with a couple of children. I went to her and said, "Why don't we check this out?" She said, "Yeah, we should." So we went to a union meeting. We sat and listened to the concerns of other workers, and talked about what we felt. The next week the two women were fired. And everybody got quiet again.

Hospital Work

I decided that I should try another field. I went to work in St. Joseph hospital in Burbank as a nurse's aide. That was a real eye-opener. In a hospital you have to work as a team. If you don't, the work doesn't get done and patients will suffer. The camaraderie with the other nurses was like a community.

I met a woman who became a very close friend. She helped me and I helped her. Ardath had taken the job in her fifties after not working most of her adult life. She had only been working there a few months when I was hired. She talked to her patients, she fussed over them, and the patients really loved her. Management had the attitude, "Ardath can't finish her work. She spends too much time with certain patients."

I said to myself, "She's going to make it, and I'm going to help her." I would say to her near the end of the shift, "I'll help you." I would finish my patients, and then make sure that her patients were completed by the time we were supposed to fill out reports.

I burnt out after a year and a half at St. Joseph hospital. I worked on the medical floor. People came in to die, so I saw a lot of death. I got very close to some patients who died. Many of them were young. Finally I felt, I can't do this any more.

Several years later, I found work at Kaiser Permanente. I was on the verge of taking it when I was offered a job by AFSCME. I was in a radical women's therapy group at the time, and one of the women who came to the group had a high-ranking position in AFSCME. She told me that I would be a great organizer. I turned down the AFSCME job. I told her that I didn't think I had the experience to be an organizer.

Of course, in another way I had been organizing all my life. From junior high on, I noticed that I could motivate people to do things with me if they were good things. And there have been times over the years when I have thought, I could be a lot further along in the labor movement if I had taken that job with AFSCME. Then I realize that I am so glad I didn't do it, because I learned so much more in twenty years at Kaiser by doing it on my own, by being rank and file.

I went to work at Kaiser in 1978. By 1981 or 1982 I was saying, something really is wrong with this union, and maybe I ought to step in and figure out what we can do. I'd call a business agent and he wouldn't call me back, or, rather than help, he'd tell me, "I'll make you a steward." I'd say, "I don't want to be a steward." But things kept getting worse, so I finally called him and said I would be a steward.

What I Learned as a Steward

In one department where I worked, there was a lot of racial discrimination.[1] The Latinas were harassed by supervision. I went to the Latinas and said, "Do you realize that the only people being written up are Latina, that the only people who are fired are Latina?" I said, "We need to do something about this. That's why I became a steward. We need to stop it." Three of us filed a class action grievance on racial discrimination: one African American, one Latina, and myself.

Then I began to be severely harassed. I was written up regularly for lateness when other people who came in as much as forty-five minutes late were not being written up. I tried to get the officials down at the union hall to deal with this. We met with the senior business agent and the vice president. They told me, "You just have to be on time."

I concluded that my friends and I were going to be terminated if we stayed in that department. We looked for any position that was open. We took positions in a brand new department called the "float pool."

We floated to every department in the medical center, and I filed grievances in them all! I uncovered all kinds of issues that would never have been brought to light had the people only grumbled to each other. They would say to each other, "This isn't fair!" And I talked with them and said, "This isn't fair! You need to be paid more for what you're doing." I filed requests for reclassification, and we won a lot of them.

Clinic assistants had been doing ear washes, they had been removing sutures, they had been doing catheterization. Finally we were told that, under state law, clinic assistants could not perform many of the duties they had been doing. Kaiser gave us memos saying that the assistants would be paid retroactively for two years' work but henceforth they could not do it.

---

1. Local 399 was made up of approximately 27,000 members broken down, roughly, as follows: 14,000 health care workers, 8000 janitors, and 5000 workers in allied industries. As of the summer of 1995, 48 percent of Local 399 members were Latino, followed by African Americans (20 percent), Caucasians (20 percent), and Asians and Asian Pacific Americans (10 percent).

Well, guess what? Right now I have filed a grievance and Labor Board charges against Kaiser for asking clinic assistants to do the very things that, during the 1980s, they told us we could not do.

In the early 1990s we formed a Solidarity Committee. Thirty or forty of us met at a restaurant. The issue was Kaiser's practice of hiring hundreds of on-calls. They had to be on call 24 hours, seven days a week, and received no medical benefits.

We started a campaign. We picketed the hospital. We made signs and walked up and down before work, after work, and during lunch. The hospital took pictures of us. The union leadership said that the union was not supposed to do informational picketing without giving the hospital ten days' notice. So we said, "We'll do it on our own."

I called the Labor Board to find out if we could be fired for picketing. I said, "We are exercising our right to free speech during our off hours. Doesn't that supersede anything in the contract?" They couldn't give me a clear answer. We did it anyway. And we weren't fired.

Local 399 removed two stewards without explanation. There was a stormy union meeting. A third steward said, "Give me an explanation as to why these two were fired or I will consider resigning." President Jim Zellers said, "There was Communist rhetoric in their leaflets." The NLRB held that the stewards could be legally removed because they were appointed, not elected.

One time in 1993 six parking lot attendants at Los Angeles Medical Center were fired for allegedly stealing money from parking lot receipts. The supervisor's cousin had a non-union parking company, and had the supervisor been able to get rid of the unionized attendants, Kaiser would have been free to subcontract with his cousin's company.

We went down to the union hall and said, "We want to do a demonstration for these men and women at their Step II hearing." The business agent agreed. (I think he thought that I would be the only one who showed up.) The night before the hearing about ten of us got together and made picket signs. In the morning we showed up at the hospital. The regional personnel director came down and told us it was against the law, because the union officials hadn't given a ten-day notice. I said, "We're all staying." Then the senior business agent was sent down. I said, "I have taken the day off, and I'm not leaving here till that grievance is done." He said, "Well, at least take 399 off the picket signs." So we agreed to cross off 399, and we stayed.

One third of the workers at the Los Angeles Medical Center were undocumented. There was a woman from the Philippines whom I will call Lupita (not her real name). Her husband was a resident alien, and she had a baby.

One day Lupita was called to the personnel office and did not come back. I resolved not to go home until I found her. When I went to her house, her husband had to bring her out of hiding and I had to drag out of her what was wrong. She was suspended for undocumentation.

The union business agent referred her to a management attorney! The attorney told her to resign. I appealed to President Zellers who referred me to a second business agent, who recommended another attorney. That lawyer said the company had acted unlawfully and Lupita should file a grievance. The attorney also told me that I could not fight the employee's battle for her. I told the attorney I wanted to quit Kaiser. She said to me, "If you do, someone will take your place who doesn't give a damn."

I left the attorney's office and drove toward Lupita's apartment. On the way I was rear–ended. When I got to her place I was physically shaken. I told Lupita what the second attorney had said. I lay down on the floor, saying, "I'll support you whatever you decide." Lupita said, "I'll file."

The Multiracial Alliance

It was very difficult for health care workers in Local 399 to meet with janitors. Janitors worked the night shift. If they came to general membership meetings, it was at two in the afternoon. Most of the health care workers worked the day shift.

We repeatedly asked the union leadership to inform us of any activities they were conducting with the janitors, and to give us a chance to be involved. The union was waging the "Justice for Janitors" campaign. We wanted to be at any demonstrations if we could get time off from work. If we knew in advance we could take the day off to go and help.

The leadership would not let us know. They would not give us the janitors' fliers. They would not let us participate. It was very difficult to get to know any of the people who worked in the union's other division.

Executive board members had been appointed throughout the union's existence. They were always staff members. They were insiders beholden to the local union president. In 1991 there were some open seats on the executive board and I said to my friends, "Let's go down there and ask Zellers to appoint us." At that meeting, he denied that there were any openings, but over the next six months he appointed three janitors and three health care workers, one of them from Kaiser.

In 1992 we decided that we should run a group of people for the local union executive board. I talked to a friend from another union who looked at our bylaws and said, "Andrea, these are the most undemocratic bylaws I've ever seen, but your power is on the executive board. Get on the executive board."

We went to a general membership meeting. I asked President Zellers to give us nomination petitions. He said there weren't any. So my husband, David, helped me design a nomination petition, and six people ran, myself among them. All of us ran for seats held by staff members.

We weren't prepared for what came next, and that was disqualification. People were disqualified if they couldn't find in the computer the name of every person who signed their petitions. One person was disqualified because she'd given her petitions to someone else, and the other member didn't know what they were, and kept them in his pocket. One after another the five persons other than myself were eliminated. I never felt so alone in my life.

I ran, and I lost. The janitors later told me the union led them to believe that I was a Communist, and that I hated Mexicans. I also learned later that the man who beat me won illegally, because the union stuffed the ballot box. On election day, there were only two of us at the polling place. One of us would campaign near the parking lot and the other watch the ballot box. Then we would trade roles. Because of this some persons were able to vote two or three times without my friend and me knowing it.

The 1995 Campaign

The successful 1995 campaign began in 1994. A group of health care workers met and called themselves "Change 95."

A group of janitors had already been meeting for two years. They were upset because they had tried to break into the union, and participate, and direct it the way they wanted to direct it, and they weren't allowed to do that. So they formed their own group called "Grupo Reformista."

I came into Change 95 in September 1994. I could see that they were talking too much to a particular staff member, director of research and chief negotiator for the contract. A woman at my first meeting, a Chilean health care worker in a wheel chair named Lizbeth, suggested that it would be a good idea to meet the janitors. She said they were going to have a conference and after that, a march. I missed the conference because I had to work that day. But I made the march. And Lizbeth made a speech that we all had to unite, and come together, and figure out how to do this as a group. The janitors came up to her afterwards and wanted to know how we could connect.

We told the janitors we were meeting on Sunday, and five of them showed up. Change 95 and the janitors worked together for a while but eventually they broke apart. I left with the janitors. I felt, These are the people that are going to move this thing.

By January 1995 I was working with the janitors. There was one other health care worker with us. She was bilingual but I am not. Sometimes the meetings were in Spanish, and there was no interpreter.

I was one of those who argued that we should run a candidate against Jim Zellers as well as running candidates against the whole executive board. The staff who were sympathetic to us had inside information from a reliable source higher up in the union that if we ran someone against Zellers, SEIU President Sweeney would put the local in trusteeship a week before the election. We weighed that, and finally decided that it was too risky to run someone for president. We wanted to get through the election. We wanted to prove that we could win. We named our slate the Multiracial Alliance.

According to Alliance literature, before 1995 the union was governed as an "old (white) boys' network." The only difference was that in this case the old boys were "liberals," "progressives," even self-described "radicals," who had fallen into practices associated with more traditional union bureaucracies. These practices included grievances that were never pursued, inadequate training for members and stewards, and an executive board that functioned only as a rubber stamp for the autocratic decisions of top officials.

The Alliance faced tremendous odds in the election. The campaign was funded by contributions from the members themselves, depended entirely on volunteer labor, and had to unite workers who spoke different languages. The Alliance organized vans to transport workers to the polls, stationed observers at every voting site to prevent electoral fraud, formed reception and education committees to provide information to the voters, conducted phone banking, and set up organizing committees at the worksites to get out the vote. There were even coordinators at each polling place equipped with cellular phones.

On June 8, 1995, the entire local union executive board was voted out of office. The 21 successful candidates of the Multiracial Alliance included 11 Latinos, 4 African Americans, and 6 Caucasians. A particular target of the Alliance was David Stillwell, executive vice president and director of the Allied Services Division. The division's membership is 90 percent Latino. Stillwell was defeated by Cesar Oliva Sanchez, a janitor from Guatemala.

On July 13, 1995, the new executive board was installed and immediately convened a meeting that passed a number of resolutions. Article XV of the Local 399 Constitution states: "The Executive Board shall meet . . . at any time at the call of a majority of the Board." Article XV also states: "The Executive Board is hereby authorized and empowered to take any and all lawful action not inconsistent with this Constitution to safeguard and protect this Local Union."

Nevertheless, four days after the executive board's initial meeting, Local 399 President Jim Zellers asked national SEIU President Sweeney to rule that the meeting of the new executive board on July 13 had been held in violation of Local 399's Constitution and Bylaws, and that its resolutions were improper.

We tried to negotiate a peaceful resolution with the international. According to the *Los Angeles Times,* a member of President Zellers' staff stated that the newly-elected executive vice president, Cesar Oliva Sanchez, "cannot speak English to conduct negotiations with cleaning company executives and lacks the experience to do the job." I heard the same sentiment expressed *several* times. A Vision Statement from the Alliance, dated July 25, 1995, stated: "as people of color, we are very sensitive to rhetoric about 'competence' and we wonder if the same rhetoric would be used if the majority of us were not Latino and African-Americans."

On August 3, 1995, a dozen Alliance supporters including Sanchez began a hunger strike in front of Local 399 headquarters. A banner said: "Respect the will of the workers! Let us govern!" I was one of the hunger strikers at the union hall. I lasted eleven days. Some of the men stuck it out until the 23rd of August. Some of them had been on hunger strike in their own countries, El Salvador, Guatemala and Honduras.

On September 14, 1995, Sweeney announced that a trusteeship would be imposed. That same day, Trustee Mike Garcia wrote a letter to the members-elect of the new executive board, stating: "Pursuant to my authority, I am hereby removing you from your elected position in Local 399, effective immediately."

In the summer of 1996 I was offered a job as a full-time business agent for Local 399. For years I had thought that I could help fix what was wrong with the union by being on staff. But I gradually came to realize that it didn't matter who got the staff positions. And the aftermath of the 1995 campaign showed me that it didn't matter who was elected. I'd seen good people tossed out by the trustees. I'd also seen the way good people changed for the worse when they ran for office.

I was afraid of changing, too. When the offer came, I felt torn and depressed. Then I got a letter about the Ed Mann Labor School and other organizations back East. It made me realize there were other people struggling, too. And I felt, I'm not alone, I don't have to work on staff to change things.

I declined to join the staff. My letter stated in part that "were I to join the staff, I figure I'd be expected to support an International team for election."[2] I also mentioned male leadership in what was largely a women's union, and that activism of any stripe was looked upon as sedition by Local 399 leadership. I recalled a recent meeting of the SEIU Western Conference Latino Caucus. Although approximately 48 percent of Local 399 members were Latino and the meeting was to be held in our own union

---

2. The full text of the letter appeared in *Impact,* Dec. 1996.

hall, the meeting was not publicized in our local. I ended the letter by saying that when I got home that day, "I broke down and wept: tears for myself and what I could look forward to on staff, and tears for my dear
union." I signed it: "Your sister, Andrea Carney, Shop Steward, East L.A.
Clinic, Kaiser Permanente."

Rich Feldman

"How do unions become concerned about the people who are outside the workplace?"

Rich Feldman works at Ford Motor Company's Michigan Truck Plant in Wayne, Michigan. During his first years in the plant, Rich found mentors in James and Grace Boggs, who emphasized community as well as workplace concerns. He began to ask such questions as, "Why doesn't the union do something for people in the community whom society has left behind?" and, "Shouldn't workers turn down overtime as long as anyone is unemployed?"

In 1988, Rich Feldman and Michael Betzold edited a collection of interviews with Feldman's fellow workers, entitled End of the Line: Autoworkers and the American Dream *(New York: Weidenfeld and Nicolson).*

In 1996 Rich Feldman ran for plant chairman, the most responsible position in local unions of the United Automobile Workers (UAW). The company and local union leadership jointly put out bulletins saying that if Rich won the election they would eliminate one of the three crews. Rich lost the election, and appealed to the UAW Public Review Board. A rerun was conducted that Rich Feldman won. He was re-elected plant chairman in 1999.

The following narrative was drawn from two sources. The first was an interview in July 1997, shortly before Feldman became plant chairman. The second was an exchange among three local union officers, including Rich, during a conference on "solidarity unionism" held at the hall of Teamsters Local 377, in Youngstown, Ohio in June 1998. The transcript of that exchange appeared in Impact, *September 1998.*

Beginning

I hired into the Ford Michigan Truck Plant in 1971. I had the dream and the commitment to bring the student movement of the 1960s, and the social relationships and the belief in the future that had become me in the student movement, into the plant.

There was a lot of rank-and-file activity going on in that period. The League of Revolutionary Black Workers was becoming the Black Workers Congress. It was struggling for the jobs in the plant that blacks had been denied, as well as talking about socialist revolution.

My roommate from college and I hired in together. There was a group of about twenty of us. Some were Vietnam veterans. We were all in our early twenties, part of the youth rebellion of the time.

I worked in the paint shop, in the prime paint booth. I painted underbodies. That was before cars and trucks were dipped into rust-proofing in the States. In Europe they already had rust-proofing systems, front wheel drive, and disc brakes, because they had to rebuild all their plants after World War II. We still used hand-held spray guns. Sometimes we wore masks, sometimes we didn't. Eventually they gave us air hoses that were pretty hard to work with. When you're twenty-three, twenty-four years old, you feel invincible.

For a number of years in the plant, our group put out a rank-and-file newsletter. We worked on issues like honest elections, and health and safety. There were paint shop walkouts about overspray and excessive heat. People would get fired and we would walk. We would have picket lines in front of Solidarity House[1] as well as the Ford Motor Company to get them rehired.

We also did community work. We put out a newsletter called *Down the River*. We did education on the war, on the Middle East, on support for the Black Panther Party.

The early 1970s was a time when in River Rouge high school, black kids would be on the left three rows of the classroom, white kids would be on the right three rows, and there would be an empty row in between. We would celebrate African liberation day and picket the military recruiters in an all-white area near the school. We showed films about Vietnam, racism, and women's liberation. In 1974 and 1975 we struggled against antibussing and had fights with the Ku Klux Klan.

I actually formed a group in the downriver communities, the first working-class suburbs south of Detroit. River Rouge was multi-racial. Wyandotte was all white. We saw ourselves as organizing particularly whites around changing America, revolutionizing America. I was doing similar stuff in the plant. Coming from New York, I'd never met folks from the

---

1. Solidarity House is the UAW national headquarters, located in Detroit.

South. I never knew folks who ate hot sauce: they put it on everything! There were Arab Americans. To me it was a whole awakening to what America was.

From the very beginning, I was totally honest with people. They said, "Why did you come to the plant?" I said, "I came here to do political organizing." I couldn't deal with the hypocrisy of radicals in the plant who were hiding newspapers, and hiding what organization they belonged to, and hiding who they were.

Whatever I believed politically I put on the table. I had no problems defending Cuba, defending the National Liberation Front in Vietnam. Part of it was honesty, and part of it was arrogance. I would have fierce arguments about the war in Vietnam with older men whose sons had been killed there. It was painful to learn that you have to see the world through the eyes of the people you're talking with, even when you're trying to give a full picture of your own politics.

I noticed that the newsletter we put out helped other people to get elected. The president of the local was Jimmy Coleman, an African American. The man running against him was white, Eastern European, and a member of the Moose Club. About twenty-five of us had a big meeting on a Saturday. We talked about how we could not support the white guy who was involved with the Moose Club, nor could we support the black guy, who was basically useless. We decided to put out a bulletin with this position on Monday. Only one other person showed up to do it with me. Everyone else was afraid to draw that line. The blacks were afraid to alienate the black guy. The whites were afraid to deal with the guy in the Moose Club.

This was the tension for people who wanted to get positions in the union. The way you got a position in the union was to be on the coattails of someone already in office.

James and Grace Boggs[2]

I heard Jimmy Boggs speak in 1974. His speech was called "Beyond Militancy." He said that it was not enough to be against what was. Militancy was not enough. You had to find the short-term goals that people could reach, which would transform them, as well as a long-term vision of what was socialist and what was revolutionary.

He posed that question at a time in my life when I was saying to myself, "If all I'm going to do is paint the underbodies of the trucks for ten,

2. James Boggs was an African American from the rural South who worked in auto. His wife, Grace Boggs, was Chinese American. The Boggs wrote many books and pamphlets, most recently Grace Boggs, *Living for Change: An Autobiography* (Minneapolis: University of Minnesota Press, 1998).

eleven, eleven and a half hours a day, and just be six months ahead of what the corrupt plant chairman is saying—we're going to do a better job, we're going to be responsible, we're going to do something about these health and safety conditions—I could become a lawyer." Being a lawyer was what people were becoming to combine socially useful work with their politics. Jimmy and Grace came along and made it possible for me to stay in the plant.

This was before OPEC [the Organization of Petroleum Exporting Countries], so things were still on the upswing for auto workers. The automobile industry was a place where people's wages were constantly increasing. What capitalism had to offer was financial rewards, and that's what people's lives were about, that's what people wanted.

At the same time, you could have discussions in the plant as profound as discussions you could have anywhere, with anyone, about how money was not enough in life.[3] Having come up in the 1960s, when the student movement was against consumerism, against the materialism of our culture, and was looking for greater meaning in life, here I was in a workplace where, despite a great radical legacy, people would pretty much sell out anything for a dollar.

I began to find and create an ideology that talked much more about contradictions in the community: how people were living in neighborhoods, how their life was being destroyed by crime. Eventually I developed an analysis about rebuilding institutions of dual power in the community. That was where capitalism was at its weakest. That was where people could come together and rebuild the nation, and actually struggle for power.

The old Marxist analysis said that as times became tougher people would become more active, get more political. We learned that in hard times people became more concerned about economic survival. They were also growing older. People were getting into second marriages, buying homes. They were less likely to walk out over a smelly, poorly-ventilated paint booth than they had been when they had just come back from Vietnam, where their commanding officers had treated them like dogs, and they weren't going to take it again.

Our plant was not dramatically hit by recession in the automobile industry until 1980, when we lost an entire shift that we did not get back until 1988. We had fewer layoffs than most of the other plants in 1974–1975. Still, the workers understood the direction in which things were going, and it made them more conservative, not more radical.

During this time UAW leader Doug Fraser was invited by the union to tour the plant. People talked about what a wonderful union leader he was. But what I remembered about Doug Fraser was how he had called out the

---

3. Rich Feldman concluded an article in the newsletter for members of UAW Local 900 with the words: "Your life is more than your work! Your work is more than your job!"

entire staff at Solidarity House to put down a wildcat at the Chrysler Mack stamping plant, with clubs, in August 1973. Fraser was against jointness but he was not a very good democrat.

Things jelled for me in connection with a guy who is in my book. He was a Vietnam veteran. It made no sense to him to talk about revolution in China or Cuba, and what socialism would be like, when he was still beating his wife and hating himself from his experience in Vietnam. I began to put out an analysis to folks like Dick that for him, being involved in a long-term revolutionary struggle meant changing as a human being. He began to see politics as a very personal transformation. I was giving the revolution some meaning to someone at work.

I no longer romanticized the consciousness of the working class, or believed that they were going to lead the revolution. I no longer had a belief in the inherent consciousness of any group of people. People had to change and to take responsibility for that change. They couldn't just talk about how rotten the system was. People had to change in the process of transforming the system.

My initial view of the central role of workplace organizing came out of a time when more workers lived in the city, and took that common experience into the plant. As the 1970s turned into the 1980s, more and more workers moved out of the city, moved out of working-class suburbs into middle-class suburbs. This was true of black as well as white workers. If you drove fifty miles to get to work at our plant you had a different experience than someone who came to work from the inner city. People experienced less and less need to rely on others. People became more independent, rather than interdependent. There developed the attitude, "Let the union take care of union stuff and we'll take care of our own lives, and try to educate our kids so they can get out of the workplace."

Bringing the Needs of the Community into the Plant

In the late 1970s, we started posing the right of people in the community to have jobs before people in the auto plants worked overtime. I remember picketing Chrysler Jefferson assembly the week before Christmas, when Chrysler was working overtime and people were on cheese lines in Detroit. Our signs said, "Give a Gift for Christmas: Stop Overtime."

The League of Revolutionary Black Workers had said, UAW means "You Ain't White." By the late 1970s UAW began to mean, "You Ain't Working." The leadership in certain plants did not stop overtime when their own members were laid off. The schism between the community, between those people who were unemployed and were no longer needed by capitalism as we entered the multinational stage of capitalism, and the workplace, got larger and larger.

In our plant we had reached the point where we were working ten hours a day, six days a week, on one shift. Overtime was mandatory. At first mandatory overtime meant you had to work as many hours as they said you had to work. Eventually, in 1983 or 1984, it was changed to a maximum ten-hour day plus twelve Saturdays a year. That changed again in my plant when they put on a third crew in 1988, and now it's unlimited overtime but only four days a week.

Usually management can get volunteers. It's at a point where people will just show up on their fifth day and say, "Please work me, boss." It's like farm workers waiting for the straw boss to come and say, "I'll take five people to work." There's no procedure and no overtime equalization and no contractual language. Whoever has the initiative and wants to work, gets to work.

I would talk about how this was not in the interest of those who were working, or in the interest of their children, who needed jobs. But once when I asked people to picket Ford world headquarters, I was the only one there.

The plant became pretty stagnant between 1980 and 1988 with no new hires coming in. Most of the time we didn't have a quorum at union meetings. We didn't have eighty people out of 5,000 or 6,000 in the local. Now we have them again. But there were years when you'd have two meetings a year because there weren't enough people. There was no union activity to participate in unless you wanted a job with the union. It was a clique of people who passed around benefits such as trips to Black Lake, the UAW educational center.

We had three or four suicides in the plant, dear friends. Others committed suicide at home. Times were scary, there was tremendous fear of the future. Even those who were laid off in 1980 responded, if they had the chance they'd work the overtime too.

The plant is located about twenty miles outside Detroit in a white suburban area. But because of federal law it has to have a certain balance between blacks and whites. The reason given for not having a lottery system for new hires is that you can't insure that the work force is racially and sexually balanced. Bob King, the UAW regional director, insisted that the company use more than one unemployment office to recruit new hires, so that you'd have a city-wide, metropolitan referral system. But if you are part of the union structure you get as many referrals as you want. A health and safety rep may have ten or fifteen people from his church. A guy with thirty years on the line is still waiting for a chance to refer someone.

In the 1980s I tried to bring people to anti-drug marches in the community, but the UAW didn't want to get involved. They should have been marching against crack houses in Detroit. They should have been marching against overtime. They wouldn't come out to help us with people who were on cheese lines. To them, these people were just human waste.

The union got some social workers to come into the plant and run the employee assistance programs but nothing about the community. Everything was about what the community can give to the unions. The union might try to get some legislation passed, but basically, the union didn't care about people who had become excess. Even members reacted, I'm glad it's not me.

We had the example of building the Poletown plant in Detroit. That was a symbolic moment. The company *and* the union supported the destruction of the Poletown community to build a new General Motors plant and tear down two older plants on the southwest side. Fifteen hundred houses, two to three hundred businesses were being destroyed. The community was trying to save the neighborhoods, save the small businesses.

The people I was working with politically tried to get union and community folks to stop the bulldozing. The union took the position that the only thing that mattered was holding on to existing jobs. The union was concerned only with what's left of their Big Three plantation. The union was for jobs no matter what the cost to anybody else. Every concession was worth it. Every tax abatement was worth it, no matter whom it affected.

The membership was lost. With a global market, the United States makes 30 percent of the world's cars, rather than 85 percent as in the past. I used to talk with folks about an alternative economy: not just about saving the auto industry as it is, but about electric cars, mass transportation, or even turning all the parking lots around the plant into greenhouses. It was a way of talking about what a subsistence economy could mean. We did not envision a reindustrialization of Detroit. We were looking for economies of scale, for factories to rebuild local communities, for whatever would be necessary to starting afresh. We felt Detroit was like a Third World country. The only thing connecting it to the mother country was electrical and water lines.

Recently what has been pushed is casino gambling and sports stadiums. The UAW supports casinos. Casino gambling didn't pass in Detroit until Windsor, Canada got it. When people in Detroit saw the money leaving, they changed their minds.

I ask myself: how can the local union members, and as a local union leader, how can I link up with the community and the people who aren't in the union? How do we relate to the poorest in the community and become an interracial union?

When unions go on strike they want the community to support them, but the unions don't do anything to support the community. In Detroit, we've had scabbing going on for at least twenty years in a lot of small plants. It made perfect sense that people would scab on the unions. The unions hadn't done anything for them except to work overtime so they didn't have jobs. The unions didn't care about people on welfare. The unions didn't care about people on dope.

So my question changed from, "What's the role of unions?" to, "What's the role of cities?" And then, "What's the relationship of the union to rebuilding cities?" I believe the community as a social force and the rebuilding of cities is the center around which every question needs to be asked. How do unions become concerned about the people who are outside the workplace? I don't see the unions as they exist, or even the so-called union reform movement, doing much of that.

Business as Usual

After I wrote the book, I thought about leaving the plant. I wanted to teach in a high school. But to teach would have meant a 30 percent cut in pay. Instead of making $32,000, I would have started out at $21,000 or $22,000. We had just had our second kid. That took care of that issue.

I had been an alternate committee person when I first hired in. In 1990, when I knew I was going to be there for the next ten years, I felt that I would rather be doing union work as a grievance person than working on the line. I went into the job with the simple goal that I would not cause the people I represent to become more cynical about the union, that I would at least make my word dependable. I didn't have any belief that I was going to change anything dramatically.

Our plant has hired 2600 people since 1988. The truck business has taken over the automobile industry.[4] We were down to 1200, we're now up to 3800. In 1996 the company added a third shift. Our plant was chosen because we are close to a lot of other Ford plants, so if workers have to be transferred under the job security agreement with the union, it won't cost the company much money. Also, having a hub near other plants helps to make possible "just in time" inventory.

Once the plant began to hire new people, I began to be energized again. There was new life, new people to talk with. Most grievances have to do with overtime, supervisors doing hourly work, skilled trades contracting out. In the scope of life, so what? It matters for the individual who wants a fair shake. But unless you can pose the question as an issue of fairness and rights, it's really just people wanting a bigger piece of the pie for themselves. It's not really a collective concern.

Early in the 1970s we won a sex discrimination grievance through pressure from the newsletter. There were very few women in the plant. They didn't come in until 1974 or 1975. A woman won $3,000 or $4,000. The first thing she did was buy a new car. It was a symbol of the fact that even

4. In 1998, according to the *New York Times*, Feb. 14, 1999, the Michigan Truck Plant accounted for one-third of the profit made in Ford's 53 assembly plants worldwide. Financial analysts, according to the *Times*, estimated that Ford earned a profit of about $12,000 on each Expedition and $15,000 on each Navigator.

fighting discrimination is not so that the individual can do something for the social good, it is so that the individual can benefit.

The same thing is true now. Discrimination grievances help individuals to get ahead. They deserve it, no question about it. But that's different from opening up the skilled trades to African Americans, where they were fighting not just for themselves. They were fighting for themselves *and* their entire history.

Similarly, an overtime grievance is so that the grievant can get his share, not so that everyone can share equally. That's what unionism has become, unfortunately. It's become individuals getting their piece of the pie rather than the organization standing for the betterment of the whole.

During the 1980s there came to be more *appointed* local union officials than elected ones. There are standards representatives, health and safety representatives, benefits representatives, education representatives, employee assistance representatives, and representatives for the newsletter. These people are paid $50–60,000 a year by the company. Those jobs had to come from somewhere. They came from people who were busting their butts with 95 percent workloads in the plant. It's cheaper for the company to have all these policemen for the contract.

When I first hired in you would work 80 to 85 percent of each minute performing an operation. That was acceptable. Anything more than that was considered speed-up. Now, they're up to 95 to 97 percent of each minute. That's considered acceptable.

Also we now have a two-tier wage system. A new employee comes in at 70 percent of the regular wage rate. It takes three years to get up to fully-paid wages.

I'm striving for this younger generation that's coming into the plant to understand the legacy of unions. They will define what the union is to become.

When unions were getting recognition, that was a symbol of pride and dignity for working people. From that flowed policies: security, fairness in overtime, fairness in promotion, a layoff procedure, fighting discrimination. You have the end of the union movement, in my view, by the mid-50s. Unions are nothing more than institutions to police the contract. They are no longer the center of workers' beliefs and views.

My role is not as revolutionary as the concept I began with in 1971. I remember consciously deciding to stop talking about Cuba. That was the price of deciding to run for union office. But that's where it's at for me.

Coalition of University Employees (CUE)

"Other than having a baby, it's the most optimistic thing you can do"

In the following account, organizers for the Coalition of University Employees (CUE) tell how they built from the bottom up a horizontal network of university clerical workers in which whoever did the work had a voice.

Nearly 19,000 clerical employees at ten locations of the University of California (UC) voted in November 1997 to decertify the American Federation of State County and Municipal Employees (AFSCME) and to be represented by CUE. In the election, CUE received 62 percent of the votes, AFSCME (the old union) got 21 percent, and 16 percent opted for "no representation."

We first met with CUE organizers in December 1995, just after the organization came into being. This follow-up conversation took place in August 1998 in Berkeley.

At the time of this interview, the agency shop for employees at public universities—that is, the requirement that members of the bargaining unit pay an agency fee to the union whether or not they join it—had not yet been enacted in California. The agency shop became law in 1999.

Why CUE?

JUDY SHATTUCK: I was active in the old union from the beginning. AFSCME chartered our local in 1967. We were a non-exclusive representative. We did not have dues checkoff. We had no formal relationship with the University except that, by law, UC was required to "listen" to us. We never negotiated a contract.

In spite of this primitive legal situation, or because of it, we had a good time building the union. We were a rank-and-file run, gadfly organization. It was totally member-driven. We collected our own dues. We were troublemakers. We used to have sit-ins, demonstrations, rallies, agit-prop theater, petition drives, and sick-outs. Most of our members honored an eleven-week strike initiated by the building trades unions at UC. And there were lots of payoffs for that activity.

Then the Regents, seeing there might be legislation, voluntarily agreed to dues checkoff. They said they would revoke it if we did not act properly. And they did revoke it once. The issue was that the women who cleaned the dorms, mostly African American, were doing the same work as service workers who cleaned the classrooms and were mostly men. The women were paid about a third less. We got involved in a campaign for wage parity. It was more than a union issue. We got tremendous support from students, faculty, other unions, and off-campus community groups. In the end we negotiated a mini-contract for these workers, which got them almost to parity. Somewhere in all of this we broke some UC rule and lost dues checkoff briefly.

MARGY WILKINSON: Another issue had to do with the six-month probation period. A woman was let go literally fifteen minutes before her probation would have ended. A couple of weeks later we had 700 people picketing.

Those were the kinds of things we did. Many of us had come into the union movement out of the civil rights movement, and out of the university struggles of the early 1960s. We brought those tactics and notions with us.

JUDY SHATTUCK: Meanwhile AFSCME ignored us. They didn't care what we did. They were happy to take the little bit of money we sent them every month. They didn't like it too much when we showed up at conventions. We got into a lot of trouble for showing up at the convention in May 1970, the week of the invasion of Cambodia and Kent State.

When we got dues checkoff, the national union became interested. AFSCME sent out some guys who set up an office in Oakland.

MARGY WILKINSON: The national union was interested in organizing the entire non-academic staff of the University, which was something like 35,000 people. They were looking at big bucks.

JUDY SHATTUCK: There had been a law passed earlier that gave collective bargaining to public school employees, and then to employees of the State of California. People who worked in higher education were the last. That legislation went into effect on January 1, 1980.

MARGY WILKINSON: On that day, in the freezing cold, we started collecting signatures on cards for a union election at the Lawrence Berkeley

Lab. Because we were going for the whole non-academic staff of the University, we needed to collect more than 10,000 signatures.

Then there was a two and a half year period of unit determination. The national union made every effort to keep rank-and-file activists completely out of it. They handled it completely. It was a matter for lawyers, for experts. They didn't want us to touch it. One of my favorite memories is when a union sister and I walked into the room where the unit determination hearings were going on. We found out where it was because the woman who reserved the room was a friend of ours. She told us. The union wouldn't tell us. When we walked in, the AFSCME guy just about dropped dead.

JUDY SHATTUCK: AFSCME was chosen as bargaining unit representative in an election, under the new law, in 1983.[1]

After the 1983 election, with roughly 30,000 employees about to be represented by AFSCME, what did AFSCME do? They immediately engaged us in an internal battle about splitting up the locals along what were, in effect, lines of sex and race and occupation. Their original proposal involved sixty different locals in the University system—one on each campus for each unit.

I don't believe this was simply because they think that way. It was also a political decision. There were Communists, there were socialists, there were lesbians, there were all kinds of people whom AFSCME didn't view as equals and who they wanted to exclude from any significant role in union leadership. National staff did Red-baiting around contract votes.

The whole spirit of the program shifted. 1983 until 1995 was a period of gradual disillusionment. We had had a real-life experience of members controlling their own union to compare with the AFSCME experience, which was a union driven by staff. These staff seemed, as individuals, to have contempt for clerical workers. That took a toll.

CRAIG ALDERSON: I was president of the local for a couple of years, and like several other people here, held statewide positions in AFSCME.

In my view the dues was an organizing issue, but the bigger problem was one of philosophy, of principle, of instinct. The rank and file in the local union was opposed to the national union structure. It expressed itself in various ways.

AFSCME broke down the unity for which a lot of people on the grass-

---

1. "Nearly 30,000 UC clerical, service and patient care technical employees have voted for AFSCME representation. Another 5,000 librarians, nurses, skilled craft workers and printing trades workers voted for representation by other unions, with only one unit (systemwide patient care professionals) voting for no representation. . . . Overall, UC employees voted for representation by a 60 percent margin, ranging from over 90 percent in the printing trades unit to 76 percent in the service unit and 53 percent in the clerical unit." AFSCME 1695 *Union News*, vol. 17, no. 5 (July 1983).

roots level had been fighting. The bargaining units on many campuses had operated in a joint fashion for years, but as Judy said, one of the first things AFSCME did after the 1983 election was to divide the workforce into separate locals. Clerical employees were the largest bloc of workers at the University. There were some other bargaining units, such as 5–6,000 service employees and employees at the teaching hospitals. The service unit, which tended to be male and blue collar, and had more people of color, was split off from the clerical unit.

Another example was that at first we had contracts in the different bargaining units with the same termination date. AFSCME eventually got away from that. They undermined attempts at solidarity. I think this was because AFSCME looked at things from an administrative point of view. As they told us countless times, AFSCME was the biggest union in the AFL-CIO.

Also, the union put out literature that looked like shit, that was full of misspellings. Clericals type memos. They revise memos. They do this and that to make memos look professional. The union's literature was really embarrassing.

The union never communicated with people. Sometimes people didn't know the union even existed. And when it did communicate with them, it tended to treat them as though they were stupid.

We lost several excellent moments to organize, including the pay cut in 1993.

ELINOR LEVINE: Membership was well over 10 percent of the unit at the time of the 1983 election. By 1995 it was about 5 percent. People were saying, "This is really critical," "The situation is really bad," "AFSCME has to do something about membership in the clerical unit, or else this unit is just going to disappear."

The people who ended up starting CUE began as reformers inside AFSCME. There were moves toward reform. At that time a lot of people were paying $22 dues per month, of which $6 went to the national, $13.50 or $14 went to the District Council, and $1.46 remained at the local level. AFSCME was asked to let us keep our dues money.[2]

We obtained the names and mailing labels of all AFSCME members in the State, and sent out a postcard, saying, "Are you satisfied with AFSCME? Dissatisfied?" There was a space to say, "I think the situation is serious. Please call me about what I can do." We got a fair number of responses. Nobody said they were happy. It was a combination of slipping membership and almost total neglect.

2. According to Susan Stanton, "New Clerical Union Ousts AFSCME at University of California," *Labor Notes* (Dec. 1997), "an arrangement to let us keep our dues for a three-year period to give us added resources to organize—an accommodation AFSCME had made to other locals—was rejected."

I remember I went to a national AFSCME convention, and at lunch I was seated next to the national director of organizing, Paul Booth. I said, "Things are really terrible. You better do something quick about the clerical unit, because at the rate it's going it will just fade away." He said, "Oh, you know, we have our priorities. Service is our priority right now. And of course, hospitals are really important. We'll get to the clericals." Years after they had won the election, they were still saying they would get to the clericals, if we were just patient.

All our attempts to get a response from AFSCME were unanswered. We sent them the results of the postcard survey. We sent letters pleading with them to talk to us. Answer came there none.

After that there was a pretty long period of anguish. Should we leave AFSCME? Should we stay? What should we do? Oh my God! Susan Stanton used to say, "If we leave, we may fail. If we stay, we know we'll fail."

MARGY WILKINSON: On the Berkeley campus, we had a membership meeting in September 1995, and actually had a vote. It was one of the biggest membership meetings we had had in years. The members voted overwhelmingly to leave AFSCME, to renounce our membership and send everything that was AFSCME's back to them.

It was very exciting. It was incredibly liberating. We had been in the situation of working for a terribly nasty employer. Our principal objection was to the employer. But we were also constantly in battle with our union: over resources, over how the union should present itself, over what role the paid staff should play. The staff flagrantly intervened in local union politics. There were elections that were hijacked by the staff. It was so much easier when all we had to do was build the union and fight the employer. It was like, Wow! This is fun!

TOM BOOT: I was hired in 1984. I had no previous union experience. It readily became apparent to me that the union was rank-and-file activists up and down the State. When we did things that the international didn't like, that's when they would step in and you saw them when you had never seen them before.

ELINOR LEVINE: The people who were active in the local on the Berkeley campus, and angry at AFSCME, ended up starting CUE. When we said, "Come to a meeting so we can vote on whether or not we want to stay in AFSCME," they came because they trusted us. When we said, "We think we ought to leave AFSCME," they didn't say, "Are you crazy?" They said, "Gee, what a good idea."

The average clerical didn't know the union existed, or never heard from it. We ran into people when we were gathering signatures for this election who had worked at the University for many years and didn't know they were represented by a union. They were so excited that here was a union person, standing in front of them. They had never seen anybody from the union before. And then to have it be somebody who was a clerical, just like them!

CLAUDETTE BEGIN: I learned from Margy about the likelihood of a new independent union being formed at UC. Organizing an effective union for clericals had a particular, personal appeal for me. I've done clerical work most of my life. After I left college, that was all that women were hired to do. No matter what your education or interest, they asked, "Can you type?" Now, twenty-five years later, I was looking for a job where I could do some organizing at work.

I had previously looked at the University, but the wages were comparatively low, and I was dissuaded. But on the other hand, I had run into problems organizing rank-and-file stuff in places where there was no union and no protection against reprisals.

So when Margy told me that they were organizing a union that was really going to be a union, that was very exciting. All the better that the organizing would be primarily amongst women, bringing in my feminist activist side too.

Campaign to Decertify

MARGY WILKINSON: The first thing we had to do was to collect cards from 30 percent of the work force. We only had twelve months in which to do that. That was the framework, the goal. Through our days in AFSCME we had contacts. We had the postcards that we had gotten from people. We did it by doing it.

ELINOR LEVINE: The membership list came from a clerical who worked at the AFSCME office. They were moving. We asked for the list. Somehow, we got it.

CRAIG ALDERSON: We were helped in this effort by the University. In 1995 the University cooked up a new fad called the Human Resources Management Initiative (HRMI). Basically it was the iron heel approach to labor relations that had already been sweeping the private sector: things like doing away with cost-of-living increases, putting everybody on "merit pay," generally making people's lives miserable. This was causing a lot of consternation on different campuses. One of the issues when we left AFSCME for CUE was AFSCME's non-response.

It was just a lot of hard work. We went to the Davis campus, for instance, where we had workshops on HRMI, workshops on re-classifications, workshops on dealing with difficult supervisors. We did this at different campuses. We would put out advertisements to come to a workshop. That's how we started identifying activists and slowly recruiting.

JUDY SHATTUCK: During the campaign we did not represent people in grievances. On most campuses they didn't know there was a union. There wasn't the idea that if you had a problem, you called the union.

ELINOR LEVINE: We made a conscious decision to have a moratorium on handling grievances. The same people who were doing the card drive were the people who had been handling grievances before. We decided that, during this period, we couldn't do both. We were going to explain it to people and hope that nobody got totally shafted.

MARGY WILKINSON: We said, "We're happy to give you advice but we can't represent you because we have this big, important thing to do, and we're spending all our time and energy doing that." People said, "OK." I can't remember any case of someone being angry because we weren't handling their grievance.

ELINOR LEVINE: I was involved in a lot of grievances that were being handled by a dreadful woman who worked for AFSCME Council 10 and kept screwing up grievances. Her grievants would call me and say, "Now she's done this. What should I do?" I'd tell them what to do. I kept a list of names and phone numbers of lawyers who did duty of fair representation law suits. I would say, "Call this lawyer." I wasn't representing people but I was telling them how to protect themselves. I know of two persons, one of whom was fired by the University, and the other one demoted. They both had really good cases. The AFSCME staff person just dropped their grievances.

JUDY SHATTUCK: We were afraid that there would be a spillover, that people's hate for AFSCME would be a hate for unions. Had we waited five minutes too late?

It was not so. Even now you talk to activists and ask them, what made you decide? They say, "A nice person walked into my office and said, here, we're building a union." There was a lot of generosity and willingness in people's hearts.

ELINOR LEVINE: I think 1993 was a turning point. Up to about 1990 the University was a pretty good place to work. We got annual wage increases of 3, 4, 5 percent. In the 1990s there was speed-up. People were being laid off and not replaced. Everybody was doing more work, and it began to seem that wages were not keeping up with private industry. Then they started nibbling away at our benefits. We used to have 100 percent health care. There started to be co-payments.

One component of the HRMI was incentive awards: one-time bonuses, with absolutely no standard criteria for how they were given out. They were taxed at different rates on different campuses. The incentive awards made people really mad. To this day you could get a hot conversation going in any group of clericals by starting to talk about incentive awards.

CRAIG ALDERSON: Many people felt there was a sea change in University policy. It used to be a fairly comfortable environment. People began to feel more stressed out, more expendable. It was different on different campuses. HRMI was a big issue at Davis. It was not as important in San Francisco. But it was big at Santa Barbara, and a few of us went down there and spent a week.

Santa Barbara is not known for its organizing experience or its activism. Fifty people showed up at a meeting, out of only six or seven hundred on that campus. In this meeting someone stood up and said, "I voted against the union in 1983. Now I think we need it. Now I'm pro-union."

ELINOR LEVINE: People seemed starved for information. They wanted to know what was going on. We sent out e-mails and newsletters. Between the time we left AFSCME and founded CUE, and the election two years later, we had seven newsletters. These were newsletters that were written and laid out by other clerical employees. They had a good look to them. People would tell us, "They look so professional."

JUDY SHATTUCK: But they didn't look like Honda ads. A lot of unions do that.

ELINOR LEVINE: There were lots of pictures of clericals. The last piece of literature before the election was a flier that said, "We're voting for CUE. We hope you will, too." It was like an accordion of all these faces, with each person's job title underneath the picture, and a little quote about why he or she was voting for the union.

JUDY SHATTUCK: There were two or three campuses where before 1983 we had successes built on what we did. We learned how to take minutes, how to open a bank account, how to represent the woman next to us, how to go against the Regents' lawyers in an arbitration and win. This made it possible for us to see the national union in a very different way than on the campuses where people only got into the union once the national union came in.

On those campuses, the union was a man who took people out to dinner and told them how to vote and what to do. They did not have *confidence* because they hadn't had the experience of running things themselves. It translated directly into people's politics, and whether they felt they could trust themselves.

CRAIG ALDERSON: The University is in the habit of designing the universe: it sets out the rules, and of course they're the best rules, and they expect people to obey them. At Berkeley and LA and campuses where people had been organizing on their own, people had the experience, the knowledge, the culture to say, "No, the rules can be different, and we're going to fight for them. We don't necessarily have to recognize your rules."

TOM BOOT: Along with the HRMI, affirmative action came under attack. We came out on behalf of affirmative action for students, staff, and faculty. We made up T shirts that said, "I work for U of C and I support affirmative action." It showed that this union-in-formation was not afraid of a controversial issue.

ELINOR LEVINE: When we began on the Berkeley campus, we happened to have a list of all the clericals who had signed a petition to the Regents about affirmative action. We decided that those people as a group would be friendly to us. And they were. We started our signature campaign on the day of a big affirmative action rally. We set up our table and wore our T shirts.

MARGY WILKINSON: CUE people spoke at many rallies in support of affirmative action. Right now we are putting together a platform stating our position as we go into collective bargaining, and one of the demands is affirmative action. There was a lot of concern in CUE's statewide leadership that this would be a divisive issue. A woman who works in my building explained it so clearly. She said, "It's a lot fairer than the supervisor hiring her best friend's best friend." There is general support of fairness and fair play.

CLAUDETTE BEGIN: CUE was rebuilding the union. A lot of people took weeks of vacation time and travelled all across the State. You'd call people and ask for a place to stay when you got to whatever campus it was. There was a lot of devotion. We'd get up really early and catch people before they went to work.

ELINOR LEVINE: CUE had no full-time staff. To this day, we still don't. We hired part-time students. After being in an organization where the staff would do things and not bother to tell anybody, the whole signature-gathering campaign was run by clerical employees who told the "staff people" what they should do.

CRAIG ALDERSON: I don't believe we could have done what we did without e-mail. We've had a web page. It was a mark of legitimacy. You could see people's eyes start sparkling: "Oh, you've got your own web page! I'm going to go look at it."

During the campaign, people spent hours looking up names in on-line directories, getting e-mail addresses, compiling the list, figuring out how to make the list work. We have something like 10,000 people now. On a moment's notice—well, maybe a couple of moments—we can send out information and get responses. It's a very two-way thing.

We kept track of who had signed cards, what their sympathies were, where they were located. It was a huge effort. I probably wouldn't be too far wrong in saying that this was one of the first union elections in the country that relied so heavily on e-mail. We got no coverage about that in AFL-CIO publications.

ELINOR LEVINE: I'm sure we were the first union to send out authorization cards on e-mail. In the end the University and AFSCME began to send out their messages on e-mail. But our lists were better than theirs. Today we are sending out membership forms in the same way.

CRAIG ALDERSON: And we have electronic transfer of dues. It's totally separate from the University and the University has no idea how many people pay dues. It didn't bring in much money, but it was a steady income.

MARGY WILKINSON: We have a flexible dues structure. We allow people to tell us what their dues will be. The recommended amount is $15 a month for full-time workers and $7.50 for part-time. But we say to people, "You tell us. You pay what you want to pay." When you first tell people they can't believe it. Often they will explain that at the moment they can only pay $5 or $10, but as soon as they can they'll pay $15. It works. I think it's really one of our strengths.

CLAUDETTE BEGIN: People think that a union is like a lawyer. Through the union they have a little insurance plan. The union is required to represent them. They don't do anything themselves, they just sit there and observe. That's what we have to counter. We approach people and say, "It's much more important to us for you to be a member, to be involved, to vote on things, than the amount of money you give us."

CRAIG ALDERSON: It demolished the argument that people couldn't join the union because they couldn't afford to pay. We said, "Look, we're interested in your participation and your energy."
We were not the first group at the University to leave AFSCME and organize its own union. They called themselves the University Professional and Technical Employees, and eventually affiliated with the Communications Workers of America.
We were looking to them for tips on techniques. Their authorization card had name, address, telephone number, the whole thing. That's what we started with. We used them for seven, eight, nine months. At some point Susan Stanton, our master tactician, said, "Let's do petitions." That was the breakthrough. The petition had a statement at the top, "I want you to represent me...." It asked for name, department, and job title. That was all we needed according to State law.
We've all signed petitions at shopping malls. People knew what it was.

And it gave them confidence to see the names of all the others who had signed. They signed it like crazy. In three months we gathered more signatures than in the previous six or eight months.

CLAUDETTE BEGIN: Three months before the March 1997 deadline we had less than half the signatures we needed. And then it started to pick up, and at the end they were just rolling in. We went by public transit to the office where the signatures would be counted. We turned in signatures in ten brown shopping bags. They stopped counting at 45 percent.

Election of CUE

MARGY WILKINSON: Workers got their ballots in the mail and had a month to mail them back in.

CLAUDETTE BEGIN: AFSCME sort of came to life. They sent out a flier with some truths and some half truths. We did some statewide calling. We got into interesting conversations on the phone. The biggest question was, "How are you going to do any better than AFSCME?" They had given up on AFSCME. But was there a future after AFSCME? AFSCME presented itself as a big national union with resources. We responded, they have resources but they don't share them.

ELINOR LEVINE: We got a lot of help from other AFL-CIO unions that let us use their offices around the State to make our get-out-the-vote calls. We would go in there both in the day and at night. People were pretty responsive when we called them at work.

JUDY SHATTUCK: There were also some independent unions that were happy to help us. A union representing school employees paid one or two big printing bills for us. Local One, which represents workers in Contra Costa County community colleges, sent people to help us in San Francisco. That was wonderful, because even though they were not UC clericals, they knew what we were talking about. These were not staff people, they were shop stewards and people who had been on the bargaining team.

TOM BOOT: We took all the petitions that had been signed, and we designated the people who had signed as priority people to re-contact to vote for us.

ELINOR LEVINE: The University's approach was, "You've tried union representation and you don't like it, so you don't want to do that again." I expected that to be more effective. I think everybody was surprised at the way the vote turned out.

JUDY SHATTUCK: On the eve of the election we had a betting pool about the results. Only one person came close, and he was an outsider. Everybody thought it was going to be a squeaker.

ELINOR LEVINE: There was a week just before the vote count that was a strange limbo period. We couldn't do any more calling, because the ballots already had to be in. The vote count hadn't happened yet. You couldn't do anything, all you could do was wait and worry.

The ballot count was in Sacramento. People came over from Davis, and a bunch of people drove up from LA. There was a mountain of ballots. Extra people had been hired to count them. They sorted the ballots into three different stacks [for CUE, AFSCME, and no union]. There was one really tall stack. We were all guessing. Then they announced, "There will be three counters for CUE, two for AFSCME, and one for no union."

They told us the total number of ballots. Our math wizards figured out what we would need to win. So when they got to the 50 percent point, everybody started to go, "Yippee!," but we couldn't cheer yet, because they were still counting.

CRAIG ALDERSON: I think most of us were fairly certain that AFSCME was going to lose, but we didn't know by how much. And I certainly thought there would have to be a runoff. Our analysis was that people were not anti-union, they were anti-AFSCME, but this hypothesis had not been tested. That was what the election was all about.

ELINOR LEVINE: There were almost 4,000 ballots counted. We used every phone in that office to call all over the State. We sent out an e-mail saying, "We all won." It was a party waiting to happen.

What Next?

TOM BOOT: For about three months after the November 1997 election, membership just skyrocketed. Every time we sent out something that required a response from people, membership would rise again. They saw that we were asking them for something. They wanted to participate.

JUDY SHATTUCK: We mentioned before that the whole jurisdiction was asked to react to proposed bargaining demands. There was another question as to whether or not we wanted to accept the AFSCME contract on an interim basis until we bargained a new contract. The message went to the whole jurisdiction with a vote just by members. The University was trying very hard to get us to accept the old contract, but just recently it was decided not to roll it over.

The no-strike clause is not in effect, nor is the arbitration procedure.

The management prerogatives clause is no longer operative. But under State law the University must continue the old contract's "terms and conditions."

We have also asked our members their opinion of a draft constitution.[3]

CRAIG ALDERSON: We began as an organizing project, a nucleus of concerned activists on different campuses. We tried to bring in as many concerned and active people as we could, and to drape that with a minimal structure. We had a one- or two-page constitution during the long organizing period. In the not too distant future we'll probably see locals develop their own constitutions.

ELINOR LEVINE: Us trying to build this new union is such a positive thing. It's so starry-eyed and hopeful. Other than having a baby, it's just about the most optimistic thing that you can do.

3. Minutes of a statewide meeting of CUE activists on November 15, 1997, also included the following: "There is no pat answer to building locals. Each local is different. . . . Given each specific situation, the question must be asked: what internal local structure will involve the most people? The ideal: aim towards one person representative in each building, or at least in each department and work from that level to actively recruit each clerical. Each building or each building cluster, or each department can then become a viable force."

The Chinese Staff and
Workers' Association

"I felt that I couldn't stand
on the sideline any more"

The Chinese Staff and Workers' Association (CSWA) grew out of struggles by restaurant and garment workers on New York City's Lower East Side at the end of the 1970s. The concept is that where an employer offers a product or service to the ultimate consumer (as does a restaurant) the employer may be more vulnerable to a neighborhood picket line than to the grievance and arbitration procedure.

Unlike many labor organizations, CSWA fights sweatshop conditions in the United States. Some of its members work in unionized garment factories where workers are paid less than the minimum wage and where an eight-hour day is considered part-time work. CSWA's aim is not simply to fight for economic gain—although it has won improvements for many workers—but to mobilize workers to fight for control over their time and their lives as a human right.

In addition to workplace struggles, CSWA has led the fight against the displacement of Chinatown residents by luxury condominiums and resisted the spread of casino gambling in Chinatown.

The following group interview was arranged by Jeannette Gabriel, and conducted at the CSWA office in September 1998. Trinh Duong translated for some of the participants, as well as contributing her own story.

JIM ONG: I worked as a restaurant waiter for 30 years, retiring in 1992. I still care about the labor movement in New York City, so I still come to the Association. I feel deeply about the sweatshop conditions in New York. In my judgment, these conditions are more serious than on the Chinese mainland.

Many Chinese immigrant workers are not in the economic mainstream.

Most are in the restaurant and garment industries, or in low-income service industry. In our experience, whatever we complain about they have
excuses, and we don't have the power or the money to make them change.
If we push very hard they give us something. People come from Washington, but they don't have the will or determination to resolve the sweatshop
problem in the United States. It's a joke!

We have discovered that labor law cannot change sweatshop conditions. If we want to do something effective, it must be by our own action,
our own efforts, like a demonstration. That can make something happen.

In 1978 I tried to organize my friends who were working in the same
restaurant. When I reached the age of fifty, the boss began to complain.
The boss said, "You're too old." I was the head waiter and all my friends
respected me very much. They said, "That's not fair. Your work is so good.
We have to do something!"

I tried joining a trade union. But I discovered right after I joined, the
union did not offer real protection. So six of us set up a picket line. The
boss was really frightened. After three hours, the restaurant was closed
down.

We found that we could form an association, and talk to the boss ourselves. We could protect our own rights as workers. On the opening day
for our Association, about two hundred people came.

WING LAM: In 1978 I was working in the garment industry. I worked
in a union shop in Long Island City. It had been organized by the International Ladies Garment Workers Union (ILGWU). It was one of the
ILGWU's biggest shops. There were 400 people, most of them Dominican.
A couple were Puerto Rican. I was the only Chinese.

I worked as a shipping clerk. My partner was a Puerto Rican. He spoke
English, and I spoke a little broken Spanish. I also read some English. I
found out that for the past ten years the workers had been paid 50 cents
less than the wage in the contract. We were being paid $2.75 an hour. We
should have gotten about $3.25.[1]

One hundred of us marched down to the union from the shop. We went
to the Garment Center and raised hell with the union. At the time our local union had about 3000 members. Whoever controlled our shop was going to run the local.

In that union they didn't have "union representatives." They called them

1. A leaflet entitled "Welcome to the U.S.A. The United Sweatshops of America," by the
National Mobilization Against Sweatshops (NMASS), states: "80–90 percent of the garment
sweatshops in New York's Chinatown are unionized and conditions are deteriorating. . . .
Union workers are making $1–3 an hour, working 10–16 hours a day." See also Peter
Kwong, *Forbidden Workers: Illegal Chinese Immigrants and American Labor* (New York:
The New Press, 1997), Chapter 8, which states that union members in sweatshops in the
United States often work long hours without overtime pay.

"business agents." The highest position in the local, the president, was called the "manager." These people were paid by the union.

The manager of our local was the union representative from our shop. He was no stranger. That's why everybody was being underpaid.

So when we marched down there, the union manager said, "Oh, really? We've got to do something about it. Tomorrow, you know what? I'll go there first thing in the morning." People reacted that the union sounded OK.

Next day, the union manager came and talked to the boss. After he talked to the boss, the union manager said as he was leaving, "Everything is taken care of. You guys keep working. Everything is going to be fine." At the end of the day all the leaders of the protest got pink slips. There were about eight of us. We were the most outspoken. Both my partner and I got laid off.

So of course we went to the union. "What the hell are you doing? You went there, we got laid off." "Really? That's bad! We've got to do something about it. We've got to go to arbitration."

I said, "Why arbitration? Why don't we picket or strike?"

"Well, we can't strike, you know. Trust us. We're really able to help you."

They had been able to identify all the leaders. We weren't experienced. We didn't designate a leader to stay underground. All the leaders were spotted right away. Obviously the workers got scared.

We tried to talk to civil rights organizations in the Chinese and Latino communities. They didn't see workers' issues as that important. They were looking at race, nationality, that kind of thing.

All we could do was to wait for the arbitration. A few days before the hearing, I asked to talk to the union lawyer. The union president finally gave me the phone number. So I called the lawyer. I said, "I want to sit down and talk to you about what happened." He said, "No, there's no need to do that. Your union leader already told me what happened." I said, "You've got to hear from me. I have more detail. I know what's going on." He said, "I'm the lawyer for the union, not the lawyer for you." I said, "But look. I got fired, not the union leader. You've got to talk to me." He refused. I knew then that something really funny was going on.

During the arbitration, all this lawyer knew to do was pound the table. He looked mean. He looked as if he was fighting for us. But he hadn't prepared anything. He didn't even bring witnesses. We brought all the witnesses. He said, "We don't need them. It's a very clearcut case." This was my first experience of the grievance-arbitration procedure. I saw how the union worked.

We lost the arbitration. The boss said I instigated a slowdown. Some foreman testified that I told people to take it easy. What I told them was,

"Don't worry. Take it easy." He said that "take it easy" meant to slow down.

However, the boss admitted that one of the reasons he fired me was because we demanded a union wage. Some people suggested that I should go to the National Labor Relations Board. Later on we did this, and we were able to turn the arbitration decision around.

After I won before the NLRB, the lawyer for the boss said, "We don't want this guy to go back. We'll pay him. If you defy us, we'll never stop fighting you. We can drag this out for six or seven years. You had better settle or you'll never get anything." My lawyer told me, "Yeah. They could do that."

People were having hard times. There were not that many jobs. During the whole process, many of our coworkers had left. If we had gone back it would have been a different work force, anyway. So we said, OK.

When we charged the boss we also charged the union. The union told us that if we would drop our charge against the union, they would give us valuable information. My lawyer was pretty pro-union. So she convinced me to drop the union from the suit.

Working for the Union

At that time I was just working for money. The union was curious how I had been able to organize all the Spanish work force, although I did not speak Spanish. They asked me to work for them. They offered much more than I received in the shop. In the shop I had made about $125 a week. I was offered $200 a week by the union. To me, it was a pretty good job.

I was a paid picketer for the union. Wherever there was trouble, I went. If you needed a picketer, I was there. I worked around the clock. Sometimes I worked at night, watching the gate, to make sure that the boss didn't ship something out. I wasn't paid to organize, I was paid to picket. The union told me to make sure I didn't talk to the workers. They were afraid I might say something wrong.

Sometimes we used our muscle. We followed people to the train station. We said, "Hey folks, don't do that." Maybe that worker never came back to work for that boss. I learned that's how the union worked. The union used fear, rather than trying to win over the worker. I found out that many unions were like that.

Later on I worked as a "colonizer." You went to the shop and looked for a job, just like any other worker. One shop I went to made perfume. I think the union sent me there to put me in Siberia. They didn't mean to unionize that shop. They sent me there to make sure I was there, away from the Garment Center.

JIM ONG: It was exile.

WING LAM: I kept asking the union when we were going to do something. They said, "Get information. Get information." Finally they told me, "Forget it." The union paid me the difference between my wage in the shop and the union salary.

Another time I worked in a Korean shop. I was a very good worker. In the two or three months that I worked there, I got five increases. The boss paid me more than the union.

The workers were either Korean or Latino. I don't speak Korean. I don't speak Spanish. But somehow, I unionized that place. First I got the Latinos. They are the easiest people to unionize. After they were all signed up, we pulled a strike. We found out where the work came from and put pressure on the manufacturer.

The boss didn't know who had done this. It was the only Korean-owned garment shop that had been unionized. I wanted to stay there because I was learning to become a presser. The boss told the union he would sign a contract if the union told him who had organized the place. One day the manager of the local came to the shop. After he left, the boss called me in. He said, "Wing! I treat you very well. I treat you like a son. I pay you good. Why did you do that?"

I said, "What are you talking about?" He said, "You're the guy." He was confused: he didn't know if the union had told the truth, or I was telling the truth. I *was* a good worker. Probably he wanted me to become a foreman. He didn't fire me.

I went back to my local and asked, "What the hell are you guys doing? You want to get me killed?" They told me, "Why don't you get out of there? We need you."

I want you to know how unions work. I colonized in a shop where the boss was Italian. I worked as a grader. They had been in the industry 30 or 40 years. The shop had never been unionized.

When I went there, I was supposed to unionize the whole shop, and then pull a strike. After I had been there about five months, we had privately signed up most of the workers. We were ready to strike. But before we could do it, we had to tell the union, "We're ready. Do it."

My boss in the union said, "Wait. I've got to make a phone call. Call me back tomorrow." I called him and he said, "Get out immediately. We're not going to strike." I said, "What?" I went to a friend in the union who said, "We did not get permission to do it." That particular shop was protected by the Mafia. No one could touch it. My boss in the union had somehow sent me into the wrong shop.

So this was how at least the Garment Workers union worked. It had a very militant history. But this was 1978. One time we asked the Amalgamated to help us form a union of organizers. Before long most of the black organizers were gone, and only the white guys stayed.

In my heart I decided that what we needed was a workers' organization, not just a union to sell our labor.

Starting the Association

The association was to be not just for garment workers, or restaurant workers, but for all workers. The original idea was for the association to be a bridge between the unions and the community. Many workers were frustrated when the union sold them out. At that time we wanted to be a bridge, to make the unions look better. But we wished also to be a watchdog against the unions. That meant that if a union didn't do its thing, we'd kick their butts.

We helped several shops to unionize. Every one got sold out by the restaurant workers' union. The bosses learned faster than the workers. They learned how to buy the union off. For some unions the whole idea is money. So we began to think, everyone that we send into the union gets trapped. It's as if we were sending people to suicide.

In Chinatown at that time, most garment shops were unionized but very few restaurants. Silver Palace was the first. At the Silver Palace restaurant, the boss fired all the workers. We were able to rally the community behind them. Everybody went back. After they went back, we tried to decide whether to join the AFL-CIO or what? We decided that up to then we had sent several shops to suicide. We had better do something else.

We utilized the energy of the Silver Palace campaign to form a union that was independent from the AFL-CIO. We knew nothing about independent unions. But also, we didn't want the Chinese Staff and Workers' Association to be a union. We wanted to be separate. We had seen the limits of the unions. Each time we sent a worker to the union, and they got a contract, the worker would sit back and wait for the contract to expire. The workers thought they had the American Dream, now they had protection.

Many workers, both in union and non-union shops, joined the CSWA. We decided we needed to deal with community issues as well as workplace issues. We wanted the worker to have more say in the community. In the Silver Palace case, CSWA got not only worker support but also small business support against the wrongdoing of Silver Palace. We were able to get community support from the beginning because we asked people to fight against the practice of management taking workers' tips. This practice hurts all workers in the industry.

The Association was the first grassroots movement of the Chinese worker in this country. Even in San Francisco, everything was from outside. This was a labor movement from inside.

YEE TOM: I worked in a restaurant all my life. When I began, we worked ten to twelve hours a day, six days a week. We never had a vacation.

We tried to form a union. The union lost the election, and I got fired. The boss used the excuse that the subways were shut down because of a subway strike, and I couldn't get to work. The union's attitude was, "Why spend money on this guy?"

JIM ONG: Tom came to the Association about this. It was very unfair. We sent a delegation of five persons. One of them was me. The name of the restaurant was Ho Ho. It was a little fancy place, about ten blocks from Radio City. We went there and told the boss, "We are from the Association." I said, "If you don't take Tommy back by tomorrow, I will be picketing in front of your restaurant."

YEE TOM: They took me back. They paid me back pay!

JIM ONG: We did everything by ourselves. It was much, much stronger than a union. None of this, "We're going to have arbitration, next week I'll call you." It was very clear. "If you don't rehire him, I will come back tomorrow."

YEE TOM: That's very true.

WAH LEE:[2] As an immigrant to this country, my first job was at the Silver Palace restaurant. A union had been in place there for a long time. The problem was that some of the workers' representatives agreed more with the boss than with the workers. They didn't really want to be concerned with the workers' issues. Sometimes they got favors from the boss.

In 1993, when our contract ended, the employer tried to force us to sign an illegal contract. It provided that the boss could take our tips and cut all our benefits. During negotiations we saw that some of the representatives were not strong.

The boss locked us out in the middle of negotiations. We were very angry. We felt we had to take back a little bit of justice. We demanded reinstatement and a good contract.

We began to picket but it was difficult. In 1993, if you can remember, it was very hot and later very cold. That year there were twelve big snow storms. The snow piled up as high as a human being.

We didn't just picket once a day. We picketed two hours during lunch and at nighttime, during dinner, every single day. We picketed for seven months. We involved many different kinds of workers: Jewish, Latino, Japanese, Korean. We went to high schools and colleges and told people why we were picketing at the Silver Palace. Every weekend we had a large demonstration. The boycott was not only in Chinatown.

---

2. Wah Lee is an older Chinese-speaking woman. She spoke in Chinese.

There was no way out for the boss. He had to come back to the negotiating table and sit down with the workers. All the workers returned to work and we got a good contract. We went back to work March 18, 1994. A new group of organizers and leaders had emerged.

I worked there for six years and I don't think the boss ever learned my name. After we came out and fought for our rights the boss had to say, "This person knows that she has some rights, and she fought for them."

VIRGINA YU: I became active during the summer of 1995. There was a struggle at Jing Fong, at the time the largest Chinese restaurant in the Northeast. A worker was fired after he started asking questions and a campaign began in February 1995. I was in school, in the first year of my master's program in social work. When I came back from school in the summer, I was informed of the campaign. The campaign had come to a standstill because of collusion between the police, Chinese newspapers, the tongs,[3] and the Chinese Restaurant Association.

I feel I should tell you about my background. My parents came here twenty-six years ago and they have been working in the factory ever since. My father worked as a button machine operator. My mother worked as a seamstress. My grandmother worked in the factory until she retired.

When I was a young child my mother worked at home. I remember when I was five or six years old, my mom sewing and my older sister helping out. My mother would bring work home from the factory. She had to go to the factory to get the garments. She would have to bring the garments back to the factory after they were sewn. My mother still tells me today how she would drag the three of us, on the train, going up and down the staircases, with this huge cart full of sewn garments.

I myself didn't start working in the factory until I was in junior high school. It was illegal for me to be working but I had to help my father. In addition, my two sisters worked there.

I remember how I, after Chinese school, would go to the factory where my father worked. This might be on a Sunday evening. I hated going there, but I had to help out as best I could. I didn't like to do the actual machine work because at the time I was so young. Sometimes my grandmother or my sisters would work with us, if the garments had to get out the next day. When my mother finished her own work, she would come help my father. We were always there. We would not leave until nine or ten in the evening.

I remember my mom coming home late, and complaining of aches and pains in her shoulders, her back, her hands. Almost every night, after we ate I would give her a massage to ease her pain. After twenty years of work she developed an occupational disease and could not work for nine

3. A tong is an association of businessmen with connections to street gangs that enforce their policies.

months. Even today, she can only work seven or eight hours a day. The sad part is that seven or eight hours is considered part-time!

My father is still working in the factory even though my sisters and I now have jobs. I had always thought that I would go to school and make enough money so that my parents didn't need to work in the factory. But my parents are still working to make sure they earn at least the $7000 a year necessary to maintain their health insurance.

Until I found Chinese Staff, I didn't know that I could do something, that there was an organization with which I could try to change the situation of my family. Now, I realize that the only way *really* to make change is by organizing workers of all trades in the community. When I found this opportunity, I jumped in with both feet.

The worker who was fired at Jing Fong said that he was made to work over seventy hours a week, making seventy cents per hour. This was very similar to what my parents and my family had to go through, and are still going through now.

We formed a student organization. We called it Students for Workers' Rights. We wanted to organize a big rally to show that students and youth supported this campaign to enforce labor laws in our community. Then we thought, "What's a rally going to do? This has gone on for three months. We want to do more."

After many discussions, a group of us decided that on June 4—the anniversary of the Tienanmen Square massacre—we would begin a hunger strike for seven days.

The Hunger Strike

VIRGINIA YU: Five students did it. It was pretty tough out there. We were right in the street, in front of the Jing Fong restaurant. I remember the first night.

The police gave us a really hard time, especially the captain. At first they said, "Oh, you can put up something for when it rains or gets too sunny." Then they turned around and said, "No." When we tried to put something up to cover ourselves, the police drew a picture of a structure that they thought could not be built. To the police captain's surprise, construction workers actually built what the police had drawn. After all that, the police demolished it.

That was a pivotal moment for me. I saw firsthand what was going on. It was everything the Chinese Staff was talking about: the collusion between the police, the tong, and the Restaurant Association was very clear. I remember seeing gang members across the street. I knew about all this, but being there and seeing it really strengthened me.

The police station was across the street from our picket, but they wouldn't let us use the bathroom. The smell of garbage from the restaurant reeked that summer. In the late evening, garbage trucks would drag the garbage right across the area where we had set up tables to sleep. They were trying to intimidate us but we were even more determined to continue the struggle.

Since we were outdoors, right in the heart of Chinatown, every day, we were able to make an impact on the community. We were able to publicize to the community and to the city that things needed to be changed. Most people stopped to see what was going on. Some students even went into the factories to get people to sign our petitions.

Nelson, my boyfriend, wrote a letter about our campaign to an anchor for Channel 9 News. She was touched by the letter and came out to do an exposé on conditions in Chinatown. Nelson was able to discuss our campaign on TV.

We didn't get much rest. I felt I was on display in a museum. I remember waking up with cameras in my face. Every day was a new adventure since the enemy was on either side of us: to the left was the police and to the right, the restaurant. The sun finally took its toll. In the middle of the week, three of the five students had to go to the hospital because of dehydration.

My whole family didn't want me to do the hunger strike. I didn't tell my mom until the night before, because I knew that if I told her earlier, she wouldn't let me do it. In time, I was able to get my mother and my younger sister involved. My mother wanted to see why I was willing to go without eating for seven days, and if I was part of a cult.

After my mother came around, and saw what the issues were, she began to see what this organization is about. She even began to talk about workers' power and workers' rights. She is now a board member of Chinese Staff.

My mother has been involved with CSWA for three years. I am constantly amazed by the resilience with which she continues to fight for workers' rights, even though she could be blacklisted. My mother believes in justice and dignity for working people. I have gained so much strength from her determination.

National Mobilization Against Sweatshops (NMASS)

WING LAM: I think Chinese people and other sweatshop workers tend to marginalize themselves and have been marginalized by others. We unite based on color, race, sex. In a way we unite based on our differences to fight our common oppression. But such a movement does not find common ground between the people who have been exploited. If we just ask for people's support or sympathy, that won't last. Movements like that, such as consumer boycotts, have failed many times. We must find common ground.

In America, the labor movement concentrates on wages. That separates the garment worker who makes $1 an hour and the college graduate who makes $20. The college graduates believe that raising the minimum wage is no concern of theirs.

We advocate that people should have more control of their lives, their time. The labor movement should not narrow itself to the purely economic that concerns only a particular trade. We have to cut across all trades and sexes and become a class movement. Even the person that makes $20 an hour is still a slave, who has to change that. NMASS advances the right to a 40-hour work week at a living wage as a human right.

In America people are subject to a culture of compromising in which they choose the lesser of two evils. People say, "Oh, we aren't doing as well as before, but at least we're not as badly off as people in a Third World country." We think that in order to have a different kind of movement you need to have a different culture, a different perspective. We should not have to earn money just to survive. People should have a life, people should have control of their time.

The labor movement often looks at people and says, "You are higher-skilled and get paid more, while you are lower-skilled and get paid less." In our community we see that that's not true. To be able to make an entire garment takes more skill than putting a screw in a hole on an auto assembly line. You can't say that the female garment worker, who makes a whole garment, is less skilled than a man on the assembly line.

TRINH DUONG: I was born in Vietnam. I stayed in a refugee camp about two years, from four to six years old. That refugee camp taught me, you don't want to be poor, and, you don't want to be at other people's mercy. And so, for all the years that I was in the United States after I got here when I was six, what I really learned is that you just take care of yourself. You go out and try to make a lot of money. Forget anything else.

I learned to look down on a lot of people. In 1992 or 1993 I read about the Silver Palace in *The New York Times* and *The Village Voice*. I said to myself, "These people seem to have a lot of time on their hands. Why are they picketing all the time? They should just go to work." I was going to school to learn how to be a stockbroker.

In 1995, when we were eating at Jing Fong, I met some people on the picket line. It was a curiosity to me. I didn't feel that I was part of any community. I thought that the picketers would look like activists: have nose rings and so forth. Instead, they looked pretty ordinary. Some were forty years old, with little kids.

I took the flier, and went home, and about a month later I tried to find the picket line, just to see what it was like. It took me about two hours before I found the office. When I came up here, it seemed like a different world. Why were people still here at nine at night, talking, when they could go home and take care of themselves?

There was something that drew me. It was as if you got a glimpse of something that you're not allowed to see. I didn't know how to describe it, but I came back.

I was a pretty racist person. At first I said to myself, "The only reason I'm coming down to this picket line is to help these people chant in English." I really thought that. But as I was there, time after time, I changed.

One night before a picket I was here in the office. Again, I was going to give diction to the picket line. But what people were talking about was that the police said they were going to arrest everybody who went out and picketed, in the same way that we had picketed all along, for the past couple of months. The discussion was, "Is it worth it for me to be arrested?" Some people had green cards. Many of them were working in restaurants or garment factories.

At the beginning I thought, "There is no way I am going to do this, no way I am going to get in trouble." But then I saw all these people who had more reason than I to say, "No." And everybody said, "We have to go out there. This is our voice. The picket line is our voice. We have nothing else if we lose it. So we have to take it back, even if they arrest us."

That made me rethink a lot of things. It made me feel proud. These were not people you should think of as unskilled, because they work in garment factories or they are poor. For me, it taught me something about human strength and determination, and that change is possible. For a long time I had believed that you can't change anything, so you might as well join it, and be the best.

I still didn't want to be arrested. I went to the picket line. People put bags over their faces in case they got arrested. But they still walked in the picket line, and were prepared for arrest. Seeing that, I felt that I couldn't stand on the sideline any more.

INDEX